THE WRONGFUL CONVICTION METHODOLOGY

THE WRONGFUL CONVICTION METHODOLOGY

First edition. December 20, 2025.

ISBN: 979-8233695360

Written by Brian Leslie.

Table of Contents

PROLOGUE 1

CHAPTER 1 | The Cornerstone Of Justice: Law Enforcement's Vital Role 3

CHAPTER 2 | First Impressions: The Critical Nature Of Witness And Victim Statements 30

CHAPTER 3 | Breaking Points: The Psychology And Ethics Of Coercive Interrogation 52

CHAPTER 4 | Interviews Versus Interrogations: Purpose, Process, And Presumption 80

CHAPTER 5 | Theory Before Evidence: The Dangers Of Deductive Investigation 113

CHAPTER 6 | Words As Weapons: How Suggestive Questioning Alters Reality 139

CHAPTER 7 | Exploiting The Vulnerable: Interrogation Tactics And Disadvantaged Suspects 172

CHAPTER 8 | Blackout Confessions: Manufacturing Memories In Substance-Impaired Suspects 214

CHAPTER 9 | When Empathy Blinds: The Pitfalls Of Sexual Assault Investigations 253

CHAPTER 10 | Dominant Witness Theory: How Strong Personalities Shape Investigations 285

CHAPTER 11 | Under Pressure: Public Demand And Investigative Integrity 311

CHAPTER 12 | Lives In The Balance: The Real-World Impact Of Flawed Investigations 345

CHAPTER 13 | Building Better Investigators: Training And Methodological Reform 380

CHAPTER 14 | The Ethical Investigator: Moral And Legal Responsibilities 418

CHAPTER 15 | Justice Reimagined: A Path Forward 452

This Book Is Dedicated To Those Who Have Been Wrongfully Convicted

PROLOGUE

In the quiet corridors of justice, where the weight of truth is measured against the urgency of closure, a single error can ripple outward, reshaping lives, communities, and the very fabric of trust. Wrongful convictions are not anomalies—they are the product of systems designed to prioritize efficiency over accuracy, speed over scrutiny, and certainty over doubt. They are the result of unchecked biases, flawed processes, and the human tendency to cling to the first story that fits.

This book, The Wrongful Conviction Methodology, is not just an exploration of failure—it is a blueprint for reform. It examines the anatomy of error, from coercive interrogations to dominant witness influence, from the pressure of public demand to the inertia of outdated practices. It dissects the mechanisms that lead to injustice and offers a path forward, grounded in evidence, ethics, and accountability.

Through case studies, data analysis, and practical frameworks, this book challenges investigators, attorneys, policymakers, and communities to rethink the way justice is pursued. It calls for transparency in every step, for systems that prioritize truth over expedience, and for a culture that values doubt as a tool, not a weakness.

The stakes are high. Every wrongful conviction is not just a failure of the system—it is a theft of time, dignity, and trust. But the solutions are within reach. With the right tools, training, and commitment, the cycle of error can be broken, and the promise of justice restored.

This is not a book about blame. It is a book about building better investigators, better processes, and better outcomes. It is a call to action for those who believe that justice is not just a destination, but a journey—one that demands vigilance, humility, and the courage to admit when we are wrong.

Welcome to The Wrongful Conviction Methodology. Let us begin the work of reimagining justice, one step at a time.

CHAPTER 1

The Cornerstone Of Justice: Law Enforcement's Vital Role

At the edge of a quiet neighborhood, the basement of First United stands open and humming. The hall is bright with hospital-blue fluorescents; their glow turns the linoleum floor cold and shiny, highlights the chips and scuffs on a double row of folding chairs. Near the far wall, a metal-legged table sags under the weight of coffee urns, plastic-wrapped cookies, and a neat grid of safety pamphlets—Stay Alert, Know Your Neighbors, What To Do When Trouble Comes.

By six-thirty, every chair is filled. The faces in the room mirror the block outside: young parents in branded polos and weary jackets, retired teachers, business owners, caretakers, and the perennially concerned. From the corner, a pair of teenagers in matching hoodies tap at their phones, half-listening, half elsewhere. Councilmember Davis, wearing a crisp blouse and a campaign pin, sits to the left, legal pad balanced on her knees. She is one of the few not clutching a paper cup.

The hum resolves into a thrum of conversation. Each anecdote lands with a dry thud: three break-ins on Sycamore in a single month, graffiti on the playground slide, a row of garden gnomes decapitated under cover of darkness. The crowd leans forward as each speaker rises, one by one. There is a rhythm to these stories—violation, vigilance, then a note of hope or complaint.

A small woman with cropped gray hair stands first. "I'm Marisol. Lived on Pine Street since '88. They took my bicycle last spring. Cut right through the lock." She holds up a finger for emphasis, then sweeps it across the front row. "But what really burns is that no one saw anything. Not a soul. If someone had just poked their head out, maybe..."

Her voice breaks and softens. "Justice isn't just punishment—it's knowing someone's watching out for us." She nods once and sits. Several heads in the semicircle bow in agreement.

A few seats down, Jamal, a warehouse shift supervisor, raises his hand. "Look, I respect what the police do. But let's not kid ourselves. If there weren't patrols, if there weren't rules, we'd have chaos. I want to believe in the goodness of people, but sometimes you need the badge." His words hang in the air, the old argument renewed.

Councilmember Davis scribbles a note, underlines something. She looks up, addresses the room: "The city hears your concerns. We're here to listen, and we're committed to solutions that work for everyone." Her practiced tone draws a few polite claps, the applause of people who've heard the line before.

Near the back, a grocery clerk in a stained apron shares that she feels safer walking home when the squad car parks at the playground for its nightly patrol. An older man remembers when you could leave your house unlocked and not worry, "but that was a different century." There's a snort of laughter, quickly muffled.

The meeting is equal parts town hall, therapy session, and war council. Everyone wants safety, but the definition of it shifts with the speaker.

At 7:02 sharp, the facilitator stands and gestures to the small wooden lectern. "We're honored to have Dr. Helen Meyer with us tonight. She's the director of the Urban Justice Project and a professor of sociology at the university." He steps aside as Dr. Meyer approaches, sensible shoes and a tweed jacket with suede elbow patches. Her hair is coiled tight at the back of her head, and she brings her own battered legal pad.

"Thank you all for having me," she begins, surveying the semicircle. "I want to share some recent data about neighborhoods like yours—and what actually works when it comes to public safety."

A projector whirs to life, casting a PowerPoint slide onto the cinder block wall. The title: EFFECTS OF COMMUNITY POLICING, 2010–2020. Below, a pair of line graphs, one blue, one red.

"This is a ten-year survey of over seventy neighborhoods in cities your size," Dr. Meyer explains. "The blue line shows neighborhoods with robust, proactive policing—officers who walk beats, know residents, respond promptly. The red line shows neighborhoods where the force was cut or underfunded."

She taps the first graph. "Crime rates in blue-line neighborhoods fell forty percent. In the red-line neighborhoods, crime stayed the same or worsened." The next slide: two bar graphs, side by side. "Property values. The blue group saw an increase of fifteen percent; the red group, a decline of seven." She waits, lets the numbers breathe.

A hand rises in the second row. "But what about quality of life? Sometimes I feel like there's more fear, even when the stats say crime is down."

Dr. Meyer nods. "Excellent question. We surveyed for that, too." The next slide: a heat map of survey responses, neighborhoods ranked from 'Very Safe' to 'Never Safe.' "Where police engaged with the community and built trust, the perception of safety rose, even beyond what the numbers could explain. In places where people distrusted law enforcement, the fear was higher, regardless of actual risk."

Jamal leans forward, arms crossed. "So it's all about cops being out there? More cops, more safety?"

"Not just more," Dr. Meyer corrects gently. "Better. When police see themselves as guardians, not just enforcers, trust grows. People report more crime, cooperate more, and that helps everyone."

Marisol raises her hand, waits to be acknowledged. “How do we know the police are actually working for us? After the last break-in on my street, they said they’d send someone to canvas. No one came.”

Councilmember Davis interjects. “That’s not acceptable. I’ll speak to the precinct chief myself.” She makes another note, the ballpoint digging into her pad.

A few in the crowd nod, but a man near the back folds his arms and whispers to his neighbor, “Same old promises.”

Dr. Meyer senses the skepticism. “This isn’t about blind trust. The best systems have oversight, accountability, and partnerships between law enforcement and the community.” She clicks to a slide: a Venn diagram, labeled ‘Police’ and ‘Neighborhood.’ In the shaded overlap: ‘Safety.’

A voice from the teenage duo—this one reluctant, almost accidental. “What about cameras and security apps? My mom says those do more than the cops anyway.”

Meyer smiles, as if she expected the question. “Technology helps. But no app replaces a neighbor who cares, or a community that works together. Digital tools are just that—tools. Without people, nothing changes.”

A pause, the murmured assent of a room where everyone wants to believe.

Councilmember Davis stands to close. “Thank you, Dr. Meyer. I think the lesson here is that justice is a living thing—it needs both good people and good systems. We’ll keep pushing for better.”

People file out slowly, more talkative than when they arrived. Some linger at the pamphlet table, thumbing through the glossy pages before pocketing a few. Marisol and Jamal leave together, chatting in the hallway about organizing a block party, something visible to show the neighborhood is not alone. At the lectern, Dr. Meyer packs up her slides, nods at Davis, and steps into the night.

In the emptied basement, the chairs are left scattered, small islands facing the projector’s ghostly afterglow. The meeting is over, but the air still holds the residue of argument, hope, and the sense that, maybe, justice starts in rooms like these.

In the underbelly of the city’s Natural History Museum, past the blinking touchscreens and echoing clamor of the upper halls, an exhibit sits in reverent dimness. Four basalt slabs, each as tall as a man and pitted with the scars of centuries, glow under pinpricks of LED light. The slabs are carved with rows of wedge-shaped cuneiform: Hammurabi’s Code, preserved by both earth and scholars.

The most famous inscription is marked with a red arrow on the plexiglass, a small placard reading: "§196. If a man put out the eye of another man, his eye shall be put out." Visitors linger, tracing the weathered grooves with their eyes, imagining a world where justice is delivered in equal measure, pain for pain, debt for debt.

In ancient Babylon, the Code is law, and law is sacred. The king's word trickles from the heavens, pressed into stone by the hands of temple scribes. At sunrise, merchants, farmers, and laborers queue outside the palace gates, waiting to air their grievances before the magistrate. The judge sits in a canopy of palms, his black beard oiled and his gaze unwavering. He listens, then points to the tablets as if invoking divine logic.

A farmer stands accused of shorting his neighbor on barley. The evidence: two sacks, one full, one not. The judge consults the tablets, the lines memorized from childhood. "If a man cheat another in a business transaction, he shall repay tenfold." The verdict falls like a stone into a pond: simple, irrefutable, public.

To the Babylonians, the code is less a threat than a shield. It equalizes slave and master, rich and poor, at least in theory. Even as they grumble about the cost of barley or the fairness of repayment, they know the boundaries of their lives are set by something harder than whim.

A thousand miles to the west, and centuries later, the midday sun sears the stone columns of an Egyptian forum. The Nile glitters in the near distance, and the market stinks of fish, sweat, and river silt. Here, law is not hammered into stone but proclaimed from lips and recorded by nimble hands on papyrus.

A scribe stands on a dais, linen robe bleached white, voice honed by years of shouting above the noise. "By order of the royal court," he bellows, "any man who steals grain from the storehouse shall be sentenced to three seasons of labor in the fields, under watch of the overseers." He unrolls a scroll and reads a list of names, the guilty and their fate.

The crowd is thick with expectation. Fishermen cluster in salty clumps, traders shuffle their goods and glance at the guards, and the women selling bread at the edge of the square listen with faces half-covered by veils. When the scribe pronounces the sentence, a ripple moves through the assembly—no outcry, only nods and the faint sound of relief. The granaries are full this year; theft is a threat to the shared plenty.

Near the dais, a second ring of scribes sits on low stools, reeds poised above flat palettes. They copy the verdicts as quickly as they are read, scrolls unspooling in the hot breeze. These records are carried to the temples, then to the houses of record, where generations will consult them in times of dispute. The system is never perfect—bribes, favoritism, and misread names slip through like sand—but to most, the laws of the pharaoh are a bulwark against chaos.

At the close of the proceedings, the scribe steps down and disappears into the shade. The townspeople linger a few moments longer, then drift away, each comforted by the ritual assurance that justice has been done. The granaries shimmer gold in the distance, promising survival through another season. And the papyrus scrolls, filled with names and judgments, join the slow current of law and memory that binds the city to its rulers and to itself.

At the heart of fifth-century Athens, the marble columns of the agora blaze under the noon sun. Citizens cluster on the steps, cloaks slung over shoulders, chatter bouncing off the polished stone. The scent of figs and sea salt hovers above the crowd, and somewhere nearby a street musician plucks at a battered lyre. But today, the true spectacle is not music or trade—it is justice, debated and dispensed in the open air.

In the center, two wooden urns rest atop a low platform. Beside them, a stack of pebbles, smooth and white, ready for the hands of two hundred jurors. Plaintiffs and defendants, their tunics still dusty from the city streets, stand before the assembly. The audience—farmers, merchants, veterans, potters—leans in, restless, ready.

A short, broad man steps onto the platform. His voice is gravel but his words are honeyed: "Friends! Who among us has not been wronged? Who among us does not long for equity, for a city where justice belongs to every citizen?" He gestures toward the urns. "Here, today, you hold that power. Let not anger or envy sway you, but only the merits of the case."

A thin ripple of applause. Two elders in the front row murmur approval; a group of younger men, more skeptical, exchange glances.

A second orator, taller, with the air of a man used to command, addresses the assembly: "Beware the madness of the mob. Once, our fathers trusted to kings and wise men. Now, every voice is equal—so every mistake is shared." The implication is clear: democracy's gift is also its curse.

As the arguments wind on, the jurors queue up, each grasping a single pebble between thumb and forefinger. They drop them into the urns, the clack of stone on wood accumulating with a slow, relentless rhythm. When the tally is called, the verdict is close, a handful of votes' difference.

The loser bows, not in defeat but in recognition that the city, for better or worse, has spoken. In the agora, there is grumbling—some say too lenient, others too harsh—but none question the process. As the crowd disperses, a poet leans in to a friend: "They say justice is blind, but here she squints a little." They laugh, the sting of the phrase softened by the knowledge that, at least in Athens, the people are the law.

A thousand years onward, in a Roman basilica shaded by stone arches, the mood is altogether different. The air inside is thick with incense and the whispers of waiting men. Bronze lamps, fueled by bitter-smelling oil, flicker against the marble. At the head of the hall, three magistrates sit in crimson-striped togas, their faces severe, their hands gripping the bundled rods of authority: the fasces.

Defendants stand in a line, flanked by guards. Each accusation is read, not by the accused or accuser, but by a functionary in a voice so flat it might as well be a bird call. Theft of a horse. Damage to a neighbor's olive press. Lying under oath. The magistrates consult their tablets, the legal codes copied and recopied for centuries, their language rigid and precise.

When a verdict is reached, the senior magistrate stands. He raises the fasces and intones, "Let the law be done." Sometimes it is a fine, sometimes exile, sometimes the lash. The punishments are as meticulously scaled as a recipe.

In the upper galleries, plebeians strain to hear the sentences. They murmur approval when the law is upheld, shake their heads when it is not. The patricians in their reserved seats watch with detached interest, more invested in the maintenance of order than in the fates of individuals.

Between verdicts, a lawyer whispers to a scribe: "The written law never forgets, but it does not always remember the spirit." The scribe scratches the thought into his wax tablet, then prepares for the next case.

The echo of each pronouncement lingers in the marble. Justice here is not communal, not a matter of heated debate, but the cold ticking of statute, the smooth operation of empire.

Centuries shift again, and the scene moves to the echoing halls of a candlelit European castle. Here, justice is not a matter of vote or codex but of spectacle—sometimes, of terror.

In the great hall, a lord presides from a high-backed chair carved with lions. At his feet, the accused: three women, their wrists bound with rough rope. The charge is witchcraft—unseen curses, cattle blight, an unexplained fever in the lord's youngest son.

Villagers pack the benches, faces lit by the trembling glow of torches. The priest intones a prayer, then the steward reads the accusation. "By the ancient custom, let the ordeal reveal the truth."

The ordeal, in this case, is water. The women are led to a wooden tub, cold and greenish with well water. One by one, they are dunked and held under; if they float, they are guilty, for water, being pure, will not accept the unclean. If they sink—well, then they are innocent, but often drowned.

As the first woman is lowered, the crowd inhales as one. A whisper moves from ear to ear: "If she floats, may God have mercy." The woman emerges sputtering, clinging to the edge; the steward marks a tally. The lord's face betrays no emotion, his son at his side squirming, pale.

After each dunking, the accused are revived and set before the crowd. The villagers, by turns pitying and suspicious, stare into the women's faces, searching for any sign of otherworldly guilt. Most, though, are simply relieved it is not them.

When the ordeal ends, the steward consults with the priest. The verdict is delivered in a booming monotone: "Two found innocent, one condemned." The condemned is led away, and the crowd disperses, faces shadowed by the knowledge that justice, tonight, is as capricious as the weather.

In the flickering half-light, the remaining villagers huddle in small groups, muttering prayers and tallying the day's gossip. Far above, the castle banners snap in the night wind, indifferent to the spectacle below.

In the autumn of 1829, London is a maze of fog and flint. Lamplighters patrol the dusk, coaxing blue flames from street lanterns as the city's pulse slows to an evening hush. At the edge of Whitehall, a row of men in crisp blue tailcoats and rigid top hats assemble beneath a brass lamp. Their boots are mirror-bright, their faces scrubbed and unreadable.

Sir Robert Peel, broad-shouldered and relentless, emerges from his office in a dark greatcoat. The brim of his top hat is pulled low, lending him the look of a man both cautious and commanding. He stands before the line, shuffles a sheaf of parchment, and clears his throat.

"Gentlemen, these are your orders." The words echo in the cold. He reads each point with a lawyer's precision and a preacher's cadence:

"To prevent crime and disorder, as an alternative to their repression by military force." He lets the phrase hang, as if the air itself might challenge it.

"That the power of the police depends on public approval of their actions."

"That the test of police efficiency is the absence of crime, not the visible evidence of police action."

One by one, the nine principles are spoken into being, each a rule and a riddle. The constables, most barely out of adolescence, try to grasp the weight of it. They are not soldiers, nor spies, nor simply muscle for the crown. They are something new—policemen, guardians of the city's fragile trust.

Peel finishes his address, eyes his recruits. "Remember, the public are the police, and the police are the public." He signals a sergeant, who calls the squad to attention. Their blue coats catch the lamplight, and for a moment the line looks almost spectral, a row of shadows awaiting their future.

They march off in twos, truncheons at their belts, not swords. Some Londoners jeer from alleyways—"Blue devils!"—but many simply watch, curious to see if these men will be any different from the bailiffs or night watchmen of old.

Three decades later and an ocean away, the streets of Manhattan are lined with uniformed patrols, their boots crunching along the cobblestones. The precincts of New York City have borrowed Peel's blue, though the jackets are shorter and the hats less stately. The men wear standardized badges over their hearts and carry not clubs but printed notebooks. At the end of each shift, they file reports at sturdy desks made from the same wood as police batons.

The city is rowdier than London ever was—newsboys shout headlines, carriages jostle for passage, and the Irish quarter vibrates with laughter and brawls in equal measure. But the new police force brings a sense of order that was previously unknown. Robberies on the wharves fall. The number of public disturbances at the Bowery theaters dips. Word spreads that these men, though often poor themselves, cannot be bought for a bottle or a pocketful of coins.

One morning, a group of shopkeepers gathers outside Mulberry Street Station. A candy merchant with a handlebar mustache gestures with a licorice stick: "The day they walked a beat here, the kids stopped smashing windows. It's the uniform, I tell you. You see blue, you know you're watched."

A baker, arms floured to the elbow, chimes in. "They even checked on my daughter walking home after dark. She said they were polite, called her 'miss.'" There is laughter, then a pause as a pair of officers stroll past, not hurried, not prowling—just present.

Inside the station, officers queue up to file their reports. The sergeant reviews each sheet with the eye of a schoolmaster. Any error in grammar or spelling is marked in red. The discipline is relentless, but so too is the pride. Each man, no matter his station, knows the ledger is more permanent than a memory or a rumor.

By twilight, the city glows with lamplight and the movement of uniformed men. They are not yet beloved, and many still doubt their purpose, but the old ways—of vengeance, of private justice—grow distant with each passing week.

In the world's new capitals, the law walks upright, its face and intentions visible. The change is as subtle as the morning fog in London, or as sudden as the racket of New York's market, but everywhere the people feel the shift: a city, slowly learning to police itself.

The laboratory is a box of marble and tile, its air tinged with formaldehyde and the hiss of gas flames. In the heart of the room, a technician lifts a fragile glass slide under the scrutiny of a brass microscope. The lamp's blue glow casts his hands into sharp relief: the pale dust on his fingertips, the steady flex of his thumb as he rolls the next latent print.

Behind him, a table groans under the weight of evidence: shoes packed with clay, a silver locket with a blood-dark smudge, a pistol and the spent cartridge that may—or may not—fit its barrel. Each item is tagged with brown paper, looped through with twine, and stacked in the order it was received. There is no clutter, only the careful, relentless organization of a mind that distrusts chance.

A knock at the door. Two detectives enter, one in a high-starched collar, the other in a bowler hat and a gaze like cold steel. They approach the evidence table, hands behind their backs, and peer into the glass-topped cases where fragments are arrayed like museum curiosities.

"This is the thumbprint," the technician announces, sliding the card across the table. "And this is the print we lifted from the ledger at the crime scene."

The detectives bend close, compare the whorls and loops. The match is unmistakable.

From the far end of the lab, a white-coated scientist clicks the shutter of a boxy camera, immortalizing a bullet's peculiar rifling on a strip of glass plate. Another clerk, hunched over a desk, copies the day's findings into a black-leather logbook, pausing only to sharpen his pencil with a pocketknife.

The detectives confer in low voices, then signal their thanks and step out, carrying with them the weight of proof. The scientist resumes his careful work, each fingerprint, each photograph a brick in the rising edifice of forensic science.

Within a decade, the methods will spread—photographs at every crime scene, fingerprints logged and indexed, blood types cross-referenced and charted. The new science transforms the world of hunches and confessions into one of hard evidence and careful certainty. In the lab's steady glow, justice is no longer a matter of luck or lineage. It is a sequence, a pattern, a mark left behind.

When the last lamp is turned down, the technician places his slides in a wooden case and locks it. The key clicks home, the order absolute.

On a Saturday morning in 1974, the gymnasium at Maple Grove Community Center erupts with the squeal of sneakers and the clang of folding chairs. Vinyl banners—TEAMWORK, RESPECT, TOGETHER—droop from the rafters, their block lettering faded by years of sunlight and dust. The walls are the color of sherbet, and the faint aroma of popcorn lingers in the corners.

At half-court, a dozen kids in mesh jerseys scrimmage under the loose supervision of Officer Lopez, whose mustache is as impressive as his whistle. He calls fouls and encourages passes, sometimes pulling a prank—like swapping the game ball for a beach ball when nobody's looking. The parents on the sidelines, some still wary of the uniform, relax a little when they see him goofing around.

After the game, Lopez walks the kids home in a loose, laughing herd. He tips his cap to Mrs. Patel, helps Mr. Carter bring groceries up the porch steps, and listens with practiced patience as an elderly woman details her plan to catch the neighborhood's litterbug red-handed.

This is the new model—community policing—and it is not without skeptics. Some residents remember when the squad car's only visit meant a citation, or worse. Others see the block parties and "Coffee with a Cop" flyers as window-dressing, a way to soften hard realities with donuts and a smile. But the brass at City Hall is committed. They have a whiteboard to prove it.

Inside the community center, a corkboard above the water fountain displays a grid of charts. One tracks the number of break-ins by month—down, steadily. Another, more abstract, reports the results of a survey: "How Safe Do You Feel?" The line trends upward, from a meager 40% ("Very Safe") to almost 70% in just two years. The station takes this as gospel, and so does the local paper, which runs a human interest story every spring.

At the next block party, two officers grill hot dogs while the neighborhood kids compete in a tug-of-war. One mother, arms crossed, confides to her neighbor: "I never thought I'd let my son near a cop. But look at them—they're just people." Her friend laughs. "Wait until the budget cuts. They'll take away the barbecue first."

Still, the change is real. Kids wave at squad cars instead of hiding. More people show up at neighborhood meetings. The old guard, once suspicious, find themselves quoted in the station's quarterly newsletter, their complaints recorded, their ideas sometimes even adopted.

Forty years later, in a modern precinct house with tinted glass and ergonomic chairs, the morning briefing looks more like a tech start-up than a police station. A pair of giant screens dominate the front wall, one displaying a dashboard of crime statistics, the other a city map dotted with shifting, color-coded points.

Commander Park stands at the podium, remote in hand, toggling between charts. "We're trending down on burglaries, but uptick in catalytic converter thefts—hot spot here, here, and here." He points to the map, then glances at the assembled officers, half of whom type notes into tablets.

The data is real-time, piped in from call logs and patrols. A spike in suspicious activity? The system flags it. A new scam targeting the elderly? The detectives coordinate with social services and send out robocalls by noon. On the break room's refrigerator, a laminated sign reads: "Smart policing is safe policing."

In the squad room, a veteran officer recalls the old days, when most cases were solved by "shoe leather and a good barstool rumor." He shakes his head, grins. "Now it's algorithms and analytics. My daughter's in college, and she wants to intern here. Never thought I'd see the day."

At the end of the briefing, Commander Park summarizes: "We're not just chasing criminals. We're building trust, one call at a time." The phrase draws a few nods, a few eye rolls, but no dissent. The mission is clear, and the feedback loops are immediate.

In the city outside, the effect is subtle but persistent. Residents are quicker to report suspicious cars, and less quick to assume the worst of a uniform. At town hall meetings, people talk about "accountability" and "transparency" with the fluency of TED speakers. The line on the community safety chart continues its slow, upward climb.

Back at Maple Grove, the banners are new, the slogans updated, but the kids still play basketball on weekends. Sometimes Officer Lopez—now retired—drops by with his grandkids. He watches from the bleachers, content to see that the game goes on, and that, for once, the future doesn't need to be policed so much as trusted.

The conference room is all glass and angles, a shoebox of transparency perched on the top floor of the city's administrative center. Rows of reporters tap at tablets as the chief of police, a woman with streaks of white at her temples and a suit tailored to project confidence, faces the wall of cameras. Behind her, a screen flickers with bar graphs, each stacked column capped with a green arrow.

She begins: "Last year, our department adopted universal evidence protocols—chain of custody, independent audits, digital tracking from crime scene to courtroom." She lets the phrase settle. "Since then, community confidence in law enforcement has risen by twenty-five percent. More than that, we've seen a thirty percent increase in crime reporting from residents who, previously, wouldn't have trusted the system."

A reporter, notebook bristling with yellow tabs, raises a hand. "What's the metric for 'community confidence'?"

The chief smiles, a little brittle. "Standardized surveys, conducted by independent analysts. We measure not only trust in police, but willingness to cooperate and satisfaction with case outcomes."

There are follow-up questions, then a detour: a local crime blogger asks about a case in another district, a homicide with rumors of lost evidence. The chief does not blink. "That's exactly why we implemented these protocols. The public deserves certainty, not speculation. One failure erodes a hundred successes."

As the briefing adjourns, a city official lingers in the hallway. To a colleague, sotto voce: "Amazing what data does for people. They see a chart, and it becomes real." His counterpart shrugs. "Better than the old days, at least."

Elsewhere, a clip from a rural town's public access TV flickers into view. The county sheriff, sweat soaking his collar, faces a roomful of folding chairs and folded arms. "We did everything by the book," he insists, but the townspeople's voices are flinty and unyielding.

A retired teacher stands. "If the book is so good, why'd the Johnson boy rot in jail for a year before you cleared him?" A man in a feed cap grumbles: "My cousin got robbed, and nobody even took a statement."

The sheriff's face hardens, but the distrust is thick enough to taste. In the parking lot, neighbors talk openly about not calling 911. "What's the point?" one says. "They'll just mess it up again." The sting of failure is communal, not just personal.

In a cool, sterile laboratory two states away, Sharon Lee, age forty-eight, sits at a metal desk. She flips through case files, her lips pressed flat. The first is her own: a battered folder, the paper inside yellowed and soft at the edges. She spent six years in prison for a crime solved by junk science, the evidence later shredded by a law student with a borrowed microscope.

Now, she is part of a project—half academic, half crusade—to review possible wrongful convictions. On her wall, a dry-erase board lists the statistics in blocky red: 2,500 exonerations since 1989, an average of fourteen years lost per person, more than $300 million in compensation paid by taxpayers. But even that, she knows, is a poor measure of the true cost.

The case in front of her is familiar. She met the man once, at a conference. Ronald Cotton. Ten years gone, cleared by DNA evidence. She scans the summary, pauses at the victim's statement. Even after exoneration, the woman never fully believed in his innocence. Lee closes the file, eyes burning.

Next, she reads the profile of the Central Park Five: five teens, all under eighteen, pressured into confessions, decades wasted, families scattered and haunted. She thinks of how the city split along old lines—race, class, faith in institutions. When the real perpetrator confessed, no one seemed satisfied. The justice system had already extracted its toll.

The last file is thinner: Cameron Todd Willingham, executed in Texas after "arson" evidence was debunked by national fire experts. Lee makes a note in the margin: "Justice delayed, then denied." She wonders how many more like him have no one left to ask questions on their behalf.

The lab is silent but for the hum of the refrigerator and the tick of the old wall clock. Lee gathers the files into a stack, slides them into a bin marked "Follow-Up." She is scheduled to speak at a law school next week, tell her story, warn the students against the arrogance of certainty.

In a suburban kitchen, a woman pours coffee and folds the front page of the newspaper. The headline: "New DNA Tests Free Man Convicted in '91 Murder." She reads the article three times, thinking of the victim—her neighbor, years gone—and the accused, who lived three doors down. She wonders if anything would have been different, if anyone had just checked a little closer, asked another question, paused before closing the book.

In a small city, a man walks his daughter to school. He stops at the mural outside the precinct, painted with a montage of faces—officers, citizens, the names of the wrongfully accused. He points at a name, tells his daughter: "That's why we have to be sure. That's why it matters."

Everywhere, the same tension: justice as an ideal, justice as a fact. The charts and dashboards, the new laws and old scars, the stories told and untold. Each error tallied, each victory quietly filed away.

At the next press conference, the police chief opens with a new slide: "Average Case Resolution Time: Down 18%." She does not mention the exonerations, not yet, but she knows the number by heart. The goal, as always, is not perfection, but a system that can catch its own mistakes before it's too late.

She finishes her remarks and faces the crowd, the city outside flickering with a hundred possible stories, all waiting for justice—real, imagined, or simply hoped for.

CHAPTER 2

First Impressions: The Critical Nature Of Witness And Victim Statements

Justice is a structure, and like any structure, it stands or falls on its foundation. In criminal investigations, that foundation is rarely a smoking gun or a fingerprint dusted from a windowsill. More often, it is the unvarnished account of a witness or a victim—words spoken in a moment of stress, pain, or uncertainty, and preserved in the amber of official record. Despite the mythology of forensic drama, the vast majority of criminal cases are constructed not from physical artifacts, but from what people remember, believe, and are able to communicate.

The numbers are instructive. In a review of over 10,000 resolved criminal cases in the United States, more than 85% were decided primarily on the strength of testimonial evidence—statements from victims, witnesses, or suspects—while less than 15% hinged on physical evidence alone. Even in the era of DNA and digital surveillance, most crimes leave no clear biological or technological trace. In burglary, the rate of cases with recoverable fingerprints is under 10%; in sexual assault, less than one in five yield a testable DNA sample. In the remainder, justice depends on the recall of the people involved, and on the accuracy with which their recollections are gathered and preserved.

These initial accounts set the trajectory of entire investigations. The earliest version of a witness statement, even if offered through confusion or fear, can define which leads are followed, who is treated as a suspect, and whether a case makes it to court at all. An error or omission in that first telling is not easily unwound; the statement, once recorded, is reproduced in police reports, echoed in prosecutor's notes, and, if the matter proceeds that far, read aloud to a jury with the solemnity of scripture. Later contradictions are framed as inconsistencies or fabrications, further solidifying the power of the original narrative.

Consider the case of Case File 09-1872, a robbery-turned-shooting in a midwestern city. The first statement, collected by a patrol officer ten minutes after the event, recorded the witness as saying the shooter was "a black male, early 20s, tall, blue jacket." On this information, detectives canvassed nearby apartment complexes, conducted lineups, and ultimately arrested a man fitting the description, who lived within a mile of the crime scene. The witness identified him at trial. He was convicted and sentenced to fifteen years.

Years later, after new legal representation uncovered evidence of procedural bias in the original lineup, the conviction was vacated. The true perpetrator was found through later DNA testing; he was several inches shorter and had never owned a blue jacket, but shared a similar build and lived in the same neighborhood. In post-conviction interviews, the original witness expressed disbelief: "That's what I told them, but it all went so fast. They kept asking about the jacket, and I wasn't sure anymore." The error—subtle, human—had propagated through the system like a crack in a foundation, invisible until it became catastrophic.

This case is neither rare nor extreme. Nationwide, more than half of all wrongful convictions overturned by DNA evidence were originally built on mistaken or distorted eyewitness testimony. The cost of a single flawed statement is measured in years, reputations, and lives, and yet the mechanisms for collecting and verifying such statements remain inconsistent, shaped as much by tradition and resource limits as by science.

High-profile failures attract attention, but most errors occur in the shadows: a shaky recollection here, a leading question there, an unchecked assumption snowballing into certainty. In the heat of investigation, speed is prized and memory is fallible. Victims, asked to relive trauma, may unconsciously revise details to fit the questions posed to them. Witnesses, eager to help or simply to be done with the matter, offer what they think is wanted, not what is true. Investigators, pressed for closure, may see what they expect to see.

The stakes are plain. Every interview is a battle against time and entropy, a struggle to capture what really happened before it is washed away by fear, by rumor, or by the slow, inevitable drift of memory. The difference between justice and injustice is often no more than the phrasing of a single question, the way a room is arranged, or whether a pause is allowed to stretch before the silence is filled.

In the next sections, we will examine how statements are best gathered, how bias can creep in, and how technology and training can protect—or undermine—the fragile truths on which justice is built.

An effective interview room is engineered for neither comfort nor intimidation, but for candor. Enter the space: the walls are a matte beige or soft gray, colors chosen for their neutrality and absence of association. Lighting is bright enough to render faces clearly, but never harsh. The furniture is functional: two chairs, ergonomic but not indulgent, positioned at a slight angle to each other around a bare, lightweight table. There are no clocks, no windows, no art on the walls to draw the eye. The air is scrubbed of scent. Along one wall, a small, black camera lens is set just above eye level; a digital recorder, silent and flashing, sits unobtrusively at the table's edge.

This is not an accident. Research shows that both overtly coercive environments and those that are too casual can distort memory and undermine trust. The absence of distraction, combined with subtle signals of seriousness—a uniformed officer's posture, a notepad already open—prepares the mind to focus and, ideally, to speak with honesty. The recording equipment is never hidden, but its presence is introduced in plain terms: "For accuracy, we record all interviews. This protects everyone."

A skilled interviewer begins before any question is asked. The process opens with rapport-building, which is less about making friends than about establishing a baseline for communication. A greeting, a brief introduction of self and purpose, and an invitation to sit. The interviewer's first questions are often unrelated to the incident: "How was your drive in today?" or "Is the temperature okay in here?" These exchanges are not filler; they help the witness acclimate, signal that their comfort matters, and allow the interviewer to observe the person's normal speech and body language patterns.

The substantive interview begins with an open prompt: "Tell me everything that happened, from the beginning. Take your time." The phrasing is deliberate. The request for "everything" signals that nothing is too small or irrelevant; "from the beginning" sets the expectation of narrative rather than answer-and-response. The "take your time" is an explicit license for silence, an assurance that the process is not a test of speed or recall under pressure.

Once the witness begins, the interviewer's role is to listen—truly listen, without interruption or visible impatience. Even when the story slows or circles back, the interruption is held in reserve. The silence, if allowed to settle, often draws out additional detail: "Is there anything else you remember?" or "Take another moment, sometimes things come back after a pause." The body language here is key. Leaning forward at moments of hesitation can signal engagement, but too much intensity can feel predatory. A slight nod, a softening of the eyes, an occasional "mm-hmm" lets the speaker know they are heard and their words valued.

The contrast to poor practice is stark. A leading question—"The man was angry, wasn't he?"—offers the witness a narrative and subtly demands agreement. Even less obvious prompts, such as "Did you see the knife in his right hand?" can plant memories not previously present, especially if repeated by authority figures. The best interviewers are disciplined about phrasing: "How did the person seem to you?" or "What, if anything, was in his hands?" The difference is small but accumulates over the course of an interview, preserving the witness's ownership of the account.

Examples clarify the stakes:

Bad: "Did he threaten you before he took your wallet?"

Better: "What happened, if anything, before he took your wallet?"

Best: "Tell me about the moments leading up to when you lost your wallet."

With children, the need for neutrality is magnified. Instead of, "Did your teacher ever hit you?" the prompt becomes, "Tell me about your time at school." The art is in eliciting detail without foreshadowing it.

The tone of voice matters as much as the words. A question asked in the clipped, impatient manner of a bureaucrat can trigger defensiveness; the same words, spoken calmly and with genuine curiosity, are more likely to draw out true memory. Witnesses unconsciously mirror the emotional state of their interviewer: a relaxed, patient demeanor breeds calm, which is necessary for complex recall. Aggression or skepticism signals distrust and can cause a witness to withhold, hedge, or recant.

Even the seating arrangement is nontrivial. Psychologists have found that direct, face-to-face positioning—two chairs confronting each other across a wide desk—can provoke anxiety or feelings of confrontation. A slight angle, with the table as a shared surface rather than a barrier, produces more detailed and accurate statements. The room's lighting, by eliminating shadow on faces, reduces the chance of misreading emotional cues and helps later reviewers of recorded interviews to assess veracity.

Effective interviewers are also skilled in pacing. When a witness's voice trails off or their gaze shifts to the floor, the silence is held for a count of three before any prompt is given. This moment, uncomfortable for the untrained, is when the mind searches itself for additional detail. If the interviewer rushes to fill the silence, the window for deeper recall closes.

At the close of the interview, the best practice is to ask, "Is there anything else, however small, that might help us understand what happened?" The prompt is open-ended and respectful of the witness's agency. Even if nothing new is offered, the gesture communicates value and thoroughness.

The entirety of the session is documented—ideally in both audio and video, with backup copies stored in secure digital evidence lockers. Transcripts are prepared by staff trained to render speech faithfully, including pauses, filler words, and emotional inflections. This protects the witness from later distortion and preserves the integrity of their statement for every stage of the process.

In sum: the interview is not a checklist, but a choreography of attention, empathy, and discipline. The best practitioners treat each encounter as an experiment in memory, knowing that the success or failure of the case may hinge on the next word spoken.

Bias is the invisible hand in every interview room, guiding both question and answer with a touch that is often gentle and nearly always unacknowledged. Even the best-trained investigators—perhaps especially them—carry into the process a narrative, a suspicion, a need for the facts to fit together in a manner that is clean, plausible, and case-closable. This is not corruption, but a function of human cognition: our brains are not built for randomness, but for pattern and sense-making.

The most pernicious form is confirmation bias: the tendency to search for, interpret, and even recall information in a way that affirms what is already believed. A detective who has been briefed that "the suspect is probably a regular at the corner bar" will notice, recall, and record details that align with this story—perhaps to the exclusion of what is strange, ambiguous, or complicating.

Consider a set of interviews following a string of robberies. The lead investigator, convinced that the crimes are the work of a known repeat offender, frames her questions accordingly. A sample exchange, from the transcript:

INVESTIGATOR: "You said he looked familiar. Was it someone you've seen around the neighborhood before?"

WITNESS: "I—I think so, maybe at the gas station, or the bus stop..."

INVESTIGATOR: "Could it have been [suspect's name]? He's about your height, dark hair, usually wears a hoodie."

WITNESS: "It might have been. Yeah, I think he did have on a hoodie. And the hair was dark."

The witness's memory, already fragile, becomes a patchwork of the investigator's expectations and his own fleeting impressions. By the second or third iteration, what was once "maybe familiar" is a near-certain identification, repeated under oath. A week later, the witness reads in the newspaper that the suspect has been arrested. The next interview, he describes the suspect's walk, voice, and even a tattoo he never saw but now believes he did.

The bias is not always so direct. Sometimes it takes the form of question order. Studies show that the first facts introduced in an interview anchor the witness's sense of what is important and true. For example:

Transcript A:

INVESTIGATOR: "Start from when you entered the store."

WITNESS: "I walked in, and there was a man at the counter, I think buying cigarettes."

INVESTIGATOR: "Did you see anyone else?"

WITNESS: "There was someone by the magazines, but I didn't notice much."

INVESTIGATOR: "What was the man at the counter wearing?"

Transcript B (different witness, same event, different question order):

INVESTIGATOR: "Did you see anyone near the magazines when you entered?"

WITNESS: "Yes, there was a guy there, just standing, maybe waiting for someone."

INVESTIGATOR: "How about at the counter?"

WITNESS: "I saw someone, but I was more focused on the guy by the magazines..."

The order of questioning—whether the first anchor is "the man at the counter" or "the man by the magazines"—influences which detail becomes the centerpiece of memory. Witnesses, eager to cooperate and provide value, unconsciously magnify what they sense the interviewer cares about.

Leading questions further distort. A comparison:

LEADING: "He had a gun, right?"

NEUTRAL: "Did you see anything in his hands?"

LEADING: "Was it a revolver or an automatic?"

NEUTRAL: "Can you describe what, if anything, you saw in more detail?"

In a study of 500 real-world police interviews, leading questions accounted for nearly 30% of all prompts. More worryingly, witnesses who were asked leading questions showed a 40% increase in recall of details that never occurred—phantom memories, assembled from suggestion and desire to be useful.

The interviewer's status plays its own role. In laboratory settings, subjects shown ambiguous video footage are interviewed by people introduced as "lead investigator," "junior staff," or "outside consultant." When the "lead investigator" asks, "Did you notice the suspect's nervousness?" over 70% of subjects agree—even when the suspect in question appeared entirely calm. When the same question is asked by "junior staff," the rate drops below 20%.

The effect is even stronger in high-stakes environments. Witnesses in uniformed settings (police station, courtroom) are far more likely to defer to the framing of authority, changing their answers to match what they perceive is desired. A child witness, when asked "You're sure it was after lunch?" by a detective in uniform, will almost always nod—even if their earlier account had the event in the morning.

For most interviewers, the bias is invisible. They believe themselves to be neutral, even scientific. But language betrays intent: "Was the car going fast?" instead of "How fast do you think the car was going?" or "What color was the car?" instead of "Did you see the car at all?" The difference is small but cumulative, shaping the statement in ways no checklist can easily capture.

Other, subtler biases play out. Social desirability bias: the witness tailors their story to match what they think the interviewer wants or expects, especially on issues of race, class, or motive. Repetition bias: the more times a fact is rehearsed (especially if written down or repeated back), the more certain it becomes, even if false. Cultural bias: questions worded for a particular dialect or reference set can confuse or mislead those outside it, resulting in errors that are mistaken for deception.

One internal memo from a major metropolitan police force, reviewing 100 exonerations, concluded: "Most errors began with a mis-framed interview; once the story was shaped, the system reinforced it at every stage." The original statement is cited in every subsequent report, and any deviation is flagged as inconsistency. The effect is a ratchet: every bias, once introduced, is locked in and amplified.

Mitigating these effects is possible, but requires vigilance and humility. Some agencies now require interviewers to script their opening prompts and to have all interviews reviewed by an outside panel for bias language. Others rotate interviewers to avoid familiarity, or train officers in active listening and neutral phrasing. The goal is not to eliminate all bias—an impossible task—but to recognize it, compensate for it, and document every step so that later reviewers can see where the process may have gone astray.

In the end, the most powerful defense is awareness: to remember, always, that memory is as much a function of context as of content, and that every word spoken in the room is a potential vector for distortion. Justice demands nothing less.

Between incident and interview, memory is not preserved in glass but battered by the winds of rumor, repetition, and external influence. The interval may be as brief as an hour or as long as several days, but in that space, recollection is shaped as much by outside forces as by the truth of the original event. Far from being a static record, memory is an active process—one that reconstructs, reinterprets, and sometimes wholly rewrites what was seen, heard, or felt.

The research is unambiguous: human memory is astonishingly malleable. In controlled experiments, subjects who witnessed a simulated theft were later exposed to a brief newspaper article describing the crime—with a handful of small, intentional errors. More than 60% of subjects incorporated at least one false detail from the article into their later accounts, even insisting, when pressed, that they had "seen it with their own eyes." In real-world settings, where witnesses are bombarded with news coverage, online speculation, and the opinions of neighbors, the effect is even greater.

Media is not the only culprit. Group discussion among witnesses can be equally, if not more, contaminating. Psychologists call this phenomenon "memory conformity." When multiple people witness the same event, their recollections often diverge at first—one recalls the assailant's hat, another the color of the getaway car, a third the sequence of shouted words. But after a single round of group discussion, these differences collapse. The most confident or persuasive person's version becomes the dominant narrative, even if it is inaccurate.

A case study from a university town in the Midwest: Following a late-night brawl outside a campus bar, police interviewed five student witnesses. All initially described the suspect as "medium build, wearing a gray sweatshirt." But in the hours before formal statements were collected, the witnesses spent time together, comparing notes and rehashing the story. By the time of the official interview, all five agreed on a new detail: the suspect had a "distinctive dragon tattoo on his forearm." This description was broadcast to the campus and included in the police report.

Days later, security camera footage surfaced. The suspect wore a long-sleeved jacket the entire time, with no tattoo visible on either arm. When confronted, the witnesses were adamant: "I know what I saw." Yet, in initial interviews, not a single mention of a tattoo had been made. The detail was born in the cauldron of discussion, then reinforced by repetition until it achieved the solidity of memory.

The timeline of memory degradation is shockingly fast. Studies show that within 24 hours of an event, up to 30% of specific details may be lost or altered, even without outside interference. Add the influences of news stories, social media posts, and casual conversation, and the original memory can be almost entirely replaced. The longer the delay before a witness gives an account, the more vulnerable their statement is to contamination.

An infamous example: The bombing of a downtown train station in the 1980s. In the chaos that followed, eyewitnesses were interviewed at intervals—some within an hour, others after a day or more. Those interviewed earliest provided accounts that, though incomplete, were largely corroborated by surveillance footage and physical evidence. Later witnesses, exposed to a blitz of news coverage and rumors about a "lone man with a duffel bag," repeated this detail with utter confidence—even those who had not noticed any bag at the scene. In the end, the bag did not exist. The narrative, constructed by the media, was more powerful than the original perception.

Witnesses are rarely aware of these influences. The process feels organic, even helpful—after all, discussing a shocking event with others is a normal response, a way to process and make sense of what happened. But every exchange, every headline, every overheard theory is a vector for new information to insinuate itself into the memory trace. Once present, it is almost impossible to distinguish the original from the introduced.

This is not to say that witnesses are unreliable; rather, their reliability is highly dependent on context and timing. The best practice, supported by decades of research, is to conduct interviews as soon as possible after an event, in isolation from other witnesses and with minimal exposure to external narratives. Even a brief waiting period, filled with speculation or discussion, can degrade the accuracy of a statement beyond easy repair.

Some agencies now employ "memory isolation" protocols, directing witnesses to avoid all discussion of the event until their statement is recorded. In major incidents, they may sequester witnesses on site or provide written instructions to remain silent about details, even among friends and family. Such measures may seem extreme, but the alternative—statements shaped by rumor, groupthink, or media—has proven disastrous in too many cases to count.

Modern technology has not solved this problem; if anything, it has exacerbated it. The constant presence of phones, social networks, and twenty-four-hour news means that witnesses are rarely left alone with their thoughts. Information flows in, unfiltered and relentless, warping the fragile record of what really happened.

In one high-profile case, a witness's account of a bank robbery changed four times in as many hours, as she consumed updates from television, Twitter, and texts from friends. The final, official version bore little resemblance to her first impression—but it was the latter that made its way into the court record, where it was treated with the same gravity as physical evidence.

The lesson is clear: in the battle for the truth of a moment, time is both ally and enemy. Swift, protected collection of statements is essential; any delay opens the door to suggestion, contamination, and the slow drift of memory toward fiction.

It is, as always, a race against forgetting—and against the stories that others, intentionally or not, plant along the way.

The integrity of a statement is only as strong as the paper, tape, or file that preserves it. Without rigorous documentation, even the truest account can be compromised, questioned, or simply lost to the entropy of a crowded caseload. The process may seem bureaucratic, but every step—every signature, every time-stamp, every recorded pause—is a bulwark against the errors and manipulations that have haunted the history of criminal justice.

The first rule is absolute: capture every statement as verbatim as possible. Gone are the days when a detective jotted down the "essentials" in a spiral notebook, distilling hours of testimony into a page of bullet points. Research shows that even minor rephrasings can introduce bias, omit nuance, or inadvertently transform the witness's meaning. If audio or video recording is possible, it must be continuous, high-quality, and without gaps or edits. The equipment is tested before each use—a dead battery or missing SD card is, in practical terms, a destroyed memory. Every session begins with a clear time, date, and location marker, spoken aloud and visible in frame if video is used. The same goes for the names of all persons present, their roles, and, if applicable, any observers or legal counsel.

During the interview, the device is never stopped, paused, or muted. Interruptions are noted in real time; if a break is required (for comfort, legal advice, or emotional distress), the camera or recorder keeps rolling, with the reason for the break clearly stated. In the event of technical failure, a secondary device runs as backup, and any gap is documented with obsessive care in the written record.

When the interview is finished, the file is exported, labeled with a unique identifier, and immediately entered into a digital evidence management system. No statement is ever stored on a personal device or shared by unsecured email. Digital files are “hashed”—that is, converted into a unique, tamper-evident code that will change if the file is altered in any way. This hash is logged alongside the original, creating an audit trail that can survive any later dispute over authenticity.

For written statements, the protocol is equally precise. Whenever possible, the witness writes their own account, in their own handwriting, on numbered pages provided for the purpose. If literacy or language is a barrier, the interviewer writes verbatim, reading back each line for confirmation, and both parties sign or initial each page as it is completed. Any correction is made by striking through the error with a single line, writing the change above or beside, and having the witness initial the alteration. Erasures, white-out, or unmarked rewrites are strictly forbidden; even a single unacknowledged change can cast doubt on the entire document.

Every page of a statement, whether handwritten or typed, is dated, timed, and signed by both witness and interviewer. In some jurisdictions, a notary or second officer witnesses the signing, adding a further layer of validation. Once completed, the statement is photocopied or scanned, and the original stored in a secure evidence locker—never a desk drawer, never a case file folder that can be misplaced or pilfered.

Chain of custody is not a mere formality. It is a living history of every hand, every office, every moment the evidence is touched or moved. Each transfer—from interview room to case officer, from precinct to court, from archive to appeal—generates a new line in the log, signed and dated. This record, though tedious, is the only defense against accusations of tampering, fabrication, or "lost" documents—a scenario that has toppled more than one high-profile conviction.

Modern technology has added new layers to the process, but also new vulnerabilities. Cloud storage and encrypted databases reduce the risk of loss, but increase the risk of unauthorized access. For this reason, most departments maintain dual systems: digital files for rapid access and sharing, and physical or "cold" backups, isolated from any network and stored in climate-controlled vaults. In the event of a cyber-attack or data breach, the original statements remain untouched, ready to be re-verified by hash and physical comparison.

Documentation, at its core, is about trust—not just in the statement, but in the system that preserves it. Every safeguard, every redundant check, is a response to past failures, from the infamous shredded notes of a 1970s corruption scandal to the more recent "disappeared" emails and altered logs that have brought entire investigations into disrepute.

It is easy to see the paperwork as a burden, a distraction from the real work of investigation. But to those whose lives depend on the accuracy and permanence of their words, each line in a logbook is a thread in the safety net. The process may feel impersonal, but it is the last and best guarantee that what was said, in that fleeting moment, will not be forgotten or misrepresented.

Justice, in the end, is written in the record. It is a fragile inscription, one that can be erased by carelessness or malice. But if protected with rigor—with time-stamps, signatures, hashes, and chains of custody—it can endure the assaults of error, doubt, and even deliberate attack.

In the silent stacks of evidence lockers and encrypted servers, the truth waits, immutable as law. The system may be flawed, but the record, if cared for, is eternal.

CHAPTER 3

Breaking Points: The Psychology And Ethics Of Coercive Interrogation

The interrogation room is engineered for discomfort. Its walls, painted an ashen hue that seems to absorb light, meet in hard angles at the corners. The only window is not a window at all, but a slab of mirrored glass set flush in the wall: a one-way lens that conceals more than it reveals. At the room's center, a metal table anchors the scene. It is bolted to the floor, its surface scoured clean by solvents and long use, and the steel is always cold, no matter the season. Above, the fluorescence is tuned to a spectrum that drains warmth from skin and flattens every shadow, so that faces blur into masklike planes and eyes are always rimmed in blue.

Across from each other, in the hard-edged geometry of the space, a suspect and two detectives play out their roles. The suspect—a man in his early thirties, jaw stubbled, hands folded and unmoving—stares at the tabletop as if it might yield answers. The detectives sit in chairs slightly higher than his own, a detail intentional in its asymmetry. Their note pads remain closed. There is no water pitcher. The air, scrubbed of scent, has the texture of dust.

The design is not accidental. The architecture of interrogation has been refined by decades of experiment and failure, each element meant to exert a pressure that is both visible and invisible. In the words of one procedural manual: "The room must strip away the illusion of control. Only then is truth possible."

Yet the record of what emerges from rooms like this is troubled. In a nationwide analysis of exoneration cases, more than 20% of wrongful convictions involved a confession later proven false by physical evidence or the testimony of the actual perpetrator. In cases involving juveniles or individuals with cognitive vulnerabilities, the rate is even higher: more than 40% of exonerated minors had confessed to crimes they did not commit, often in exhaustive and graphic detail.

The causes are neither simple nor new. Modern police interrogation borrows freely from methods developed for military use, particularly those refined in the middle decades of the twentieth century. During World War II and the Cold War, intelligence officers studied how to break the will of a captive, how to induce the revelation of secrets by pressure, repetition, and fatigue. These techniques migrated into domestic law enforcement, stripped of their overt brutality but not of their psychological power.

The tools of coercion are subtle now, but their effect can be devastating. Most departments forbid direct threats of violence or promises of reward, but the allowable margin—what is called "psychological leverage"—remains vast. "The room is the first instrument," says Dr. Irene Caldwell, a forensic psychologist who has testified in more than seventy cases of alleged confession coercion. "But the second is the narrative: the story the detectives tell, and the way they invite the suspect to climb inside it."

Three techniques dominate the playbook. The first is minimization—downplaying the seriousness of the offense, or suggesting that anyone in the suspect's position would have acted the same. It is the gentle prod, the sympathetic ear. The second is maximization—exaggerating the strength of evidence, the severity of potential punishment, the inevitability of conviction. It is the hammer that follows the velvet touch. The third is the narrative trap: constructing a story of the crime so detailed and plausible that the suspect, weary or confused, comes to believe in it themselves. Sometimes they repeat it verbatim. Sometimes they elaborate, adding detail not in the original script.

Critics argue that these methods, while effective at eliciting admissions, often cross the boundary between persuasion and manipulation. "There's a line between allowing a suspect to explain themselves, and putting words in their mouth," says criminal defense attorney Sonya Li. "The best interrogators know exactly where that line is. The worst pretend it doesn't exist."

Even among law enforcement, the debate is ongoing. A training officer in a major metropolitan department describes the goal as "getting to the truth by any means short of a constitutional violation." But recent court rulings and the rise of video-recorded interrogations have complicated the calculus. "Now, we have to be able to explain every tactic, every question," the officer says. "If it looks bad on tape, it probably is."

In the current room, the detectives begin with the well-worn choreography. The first asks about the suspect's day, the weather, whether he's eaten lunch. The second sits silent, arms crossed, radiating quiet threat. The suspect answers in monosyllables, never raising his eyes. The overhead light, reflected off the table's surface, flickers with the rhythm of the building's HVAC.

Outside the glass, in the observation booth, a rookie officer is told to watch and learn. "This is where most cases are won or lost," his supervisor says. "Not in the lab. Not in the courtroom. Here."

As the session stretches into its second hour, the suspect's speech slows. He fidgets with his jacket sleeve. The first detective leans in, voice soft: "You're not a monster. You just made a mistake. We can work with that." The second detective flips through a manila file, letting the silence balloon. Both know the pattern, the sequence of pressure and release. What they want, more than anything, is a story that fits.

Whether that story is true is another matter.

The three primary techniques—minimization, maximization, and narrative construction—are not simply methods; they are philosophies. Minimization seeks to lure a confession by making it seem painless. Maximization tries to bludgeon the truth out by making resistance seem impossible. The narrative trap closes around those who, under strain, come to doubt their own memory and substitute the script provided for the one they cannot retrieve.

"Ethically, we're at a crossroads," says Professor Andre Frumkin, who studies interrogation at the University of Michigan. "Either we admit that the system is not infallible and change how we extract confessions, or we keep burying the mistakes along with the innocent people we convict." He points to the case of the Beatrice Six, a group of Nebraskans who, after marathon interrogations, confessed in vivid detail to a murder none of them had committed. Their confessions, secured by alternating cycles of reassurance and threat, were so persuasive that even the victims' families believed them, until DNA evidence intervened decades later.

As the detectives cycle through their tactics, the suspect begins to talk. The first details are halting, disjointed. He doesn't remember, he says. He wasn't there. He might have been, but only by accident. The detectives nod, never challenging, only steering. Soon the fragments become sentences, the sentences become a story.

In the observation booth, the rookie officer watches the transformation with fascination. "Is that really how it works?" he asks.

His supervisor shrugs. "Most of the time, yes. Sometimes you get the truth. Sometimes you just get a story."

The debate is not academic. In the United States alone, more than one hundred people have been exonerated after confessing to crimes they did not commit—each case a monument to the power of suggestion, fatigue, and the architecture of pressure. The names of these cases fill legal journals and are studied in police academies, but the methods endure. There is always another suspect, another room, another confession to be harvested.

As the session draws to a close, the suspect signs his statement, hands trembling slightly. The detectives thank him, pack their folders, and leave him alone at the metal table, where the overhead light continues to bleach the color from everything it touches.

In the next rooms, the same rituals unfold, each shaped by the invisible hand of technique, habit, and the enduring hunger for closure. The techniques of minimization, maximization, and narrative entrapment remain, unchallenged and refined.

Whether justice is served—or simply satisfied—is the question that lingers, unanswered, in the chill of the room.

The script of minimization is older than most of the detectives who perform it. At the desk, the veteran detective leans in, elbows splayed, voice tuned for sympathy rather than threat. The suspect—barely more than a kid, hair matted, eyes hollow—has been in the room for two hours. The first hour was silent, the second slow and gentle, a peeling away of reluctance in thin, transparent strips.

"Look," the detective says, pushing aside his notepad as if to underscore the absence of formal process. "I'm not here to ruin your life, okay? I know people make mistakes. I've been at this job a long time, and I've seen worse. Hell, I've done worse." A pause, weighted with manufactured camaraderie. "This isn't the end of the world. You just have to help me understand what happened."

The kid blinks, uncomprehending. He picks at a seam in his sleeve, then shakes his head. "I didn't—I mean, I was just there. I didn't do anything."

The detective shrugs, disarming. "You were there, sure. That's what people are saying. But nobody's going to believe you if you don't tell your side. The thing is, if you explain it now, it's way better for you. Prosecutors go easier on people who admit it up front. That's just how it works."

This is the heart of minimization: the crime is reframed as a minor stumble, an understandable lapse, the kind of thing anyone might do. "No one got seriously hurt, right?" the detective continues. "You didn't mean for things to get out of hand. We can fix this. But only if you're straight with me."

What happens next is not a contest of strength, but of exhaustion. The kid's resistance is not overcome, but coaxed to collapse under the weight of an easier story. The detective offers him a way out—one that appears painless, even smart. "It's always better to tell the truth," he says, "before someone else tells it for you."

The research is unequivocal. Minimization works not by threat, but by relief: the prospect of a softer landing, the suggestion that honesty now will purchase leniency later. In laboratory studies, suspects subjected to minimization were twice as likely to confess—even when innocent—than those questioned with neutral prompts. When minimization was paired with the illusion of "cutting a deal," the confession rate tripled. Innocent participants, exposed to repeated assurances that "everybody makes mistakes," signed detailed confessions in more than 30% of cases, often inventing plausible but false explanations for acts they had never committed.

The psychological mechanism is straightforward. Under stress, the brain seeks escape routes. When the options are continued anxiety or a promise of safety, even a phantom safety, the logic is simple. "Confessing becomes the path of least resistance," explains Dr. Lydia Castell, a cognitive scientist who studies memory and compliance. "Especially for people who have been conditioned to believe that authority is there to help, or that small transgressions are forgivable."

Real life is rarely as clean as the experiment. In the landmark case of Michael Crowe, a fourteen-year-old boy from Escondido, California, minimization was weaponized with surgical precision. After his sister was murdered, Crowe was brought in as a witness, but hours of gentle prodding, appeals to family loyalty, and repeated assurances that he "wasn't a bad person, just confused" produced a confession so detailed and remorseful that even his parents believed it. Only later, when another suspect was linked to the crime by DNA, did the truth come out: Crowe had invented the memory under pressure, desperate to end the relentless kindness of his interrogators.

Another case, less famous but no less tragic: In a Midwestern suburb, a single mother was brought in after her infant's accidental death. The detective told her, "You're not a monster. You just made a mistake. We can help you, but you need to help us." The woman, sleep-deprived and grieving, eventually admitted to acts she never committed, describing in vivid detail how she "must have" dropped the baby even though no physical evidence supported the claim. She later recanted, but the confession had already cemented itself in the minds of police, prosecutors, and the public.

Back in the room, the kid at the table nods slowly, as if agreeing with his own defeat. "I guess—I guess I messed up," he says. "But it wasn't all me. It was just—just a stupid thing."

"That's what I figured," the detective says, voice smooth. "Nobody's going to throw the book at you for a stupid thing. We just want to get it on the record."

He presses the record button on the tape deck, the only loud sound in the room. The kid clears his throat and begins, "I was just hanging out, and—"

The rest of the story, true or not, is secondary. The confession is the artifact, the object of value. On paper, in the report, it will read as spontaneous, uncoerced. There will be no mention of the careful diminishment, the suggestion that a life-altering admission is merely paperwork.

Legal scholars have debated the ethics for decades. "Minimization is so insidious because it doesn't feel coercive," writes defense attorney

Paul Banerjee. "It feels like mercy, even when it's the opposite." The courts, slow to adapt, continue to allow such statements as evidence, reasoning that promises of leniency are not technically threats.

But the numbers are hard to ignore. In a study of more than 1,000 exoneration cases, minimization was present in at least 30% of known false confessions. The language varied, but the theme was constant: a gentle nudge toward an easier, less frightening future, if only the suspect will agree to take the blame.

Back in the hallway, the rookie officer turns to his supervisor. "Isn't that kind of... unfair?" he asks. "Telling them it's not a big deal, when it kind of is?"

His supervisor shrugs, the gesture weary and practiced. "It's not about fair. It's about getting the story. Everyone's got one."

In the next room, the kid signs his name at the bottom of the confession, letters cramped but legible. The detective thanks him, then leaves, closing the door with a click soft enough not to echo.

Justice, such as it is, has taken another confession. Whether it is true is left as an exercise for the next department, the next lawyer, the next court.

But in the record, it is fixed: a moment of surrender, carefully minimized, carefully preserved.

Maximization is the blunt instrument. If minimization is a soft word and a gentle nudge, maximization is the raised voice, the threat veiled only by procedure. The switch, when it comes, is abrupt: the door slams, the chairs scrape closer to the table, the air itself seems to contract.

The suspect this time is older, a laborer with hands swollen by work. His knuckles are raw, and his brow beads with sweat under the glare of the fluorescent lights. He's been in the room since dawn; his watch, confiscated at intake, ticks unseen in the property bin. The first hours are a blur of questions, none of which he answers. Then the detectives return, together, and the temperature in the room drops.

"We've got a problem, friend," says the first detective, tossing a manila folder onto the table. "You know what's in here?" He doesn't wait for a reply. "Forensics. Prints. Witness statements."

The second detective, taller, circles behind the suspect's chair, then stands so close that his shadow falls across the table. "I don't think you understand how serious this is," he says, voice just above a whisper. "We're talking life in prison. No parole. Unless you start talking, right now."

The suspect shrinks into his chair, but there's nowhere to go. The first detective opens the folder, pulls out a sheet of paper with a single line of text, and places it in front of the man. "Your prints, right here. On the door handle."

The man stares at the paper, lips trembling. "I never—I was never—" His words evaporate under the twin beams of accusation.

"It's over," the second detective says, leaning so close their noses are nearly touching. "You want to make it worse? Keep lying."

This is maximization: not just the threat of consequence, but its palpable, inescapable presence. Everything is dialed up—the volume, the proximity, the certainty of guilt. The detectives do not question; they declare, and the suspect is left to navigate the shrinking territory of denial.

The literature on maximization is grim reading. Studies show that prolonged exposure to loud, aggressive questioning triples the rate of confessions, but it also triples the rate of false confessions. In conditions of sleep deprivation—common in extended interrogations—subjects lose the ability to distinguish between hypothetical and actual events. "The exhausted brain is a confabulating brain," notes Dr. Angela Kim, who researches cognitive breakdown under stress. "Faced with overwhelming evidence, even when it is fake, people start to believe their own guilt."

In the Chicago study known as the "White Room Experiment," volunteers were kept awake for thirty-six hours and subjected to cycles of accusatory questioning. By the end, nearly half of the innocent participants confessed to acts they never committed. Many began to reconstruct plausible narratives to explain their supposed actions, filling in memory blanks with imagined detail.

Back in the room, the older man's resistance unravels in real time. The detectives alternate shouts and silence, never letting the suspect settle into a rhythm. When he asks for water, he is told to wait. When he asks what time it is, they ignore him. The folder on the table grows fatter, though no new evidence appears.

"Look, we have three witnesses who put you at the scene," the first detective says. "We can walk you through every second of that night. You're done."

"I was home," the suspect whispers. "I told you."

The second detective slams his palm on the table, the sound echoing off the cinderblock. "You think anyone's going to believe that? You think a jury's going to buy your story, when we've got you dead to rights?"

He leans in, so close the suspect recoils. "Your best chance—your only chance—is to come clean. Otherwise, you're going away forever."

The suspect's hands flutter on the table, searching for an anchor. "I don't remember," he says, voice barely audible. "Maybe—I was drunk. Maybe I went out, I don't know."

The opening is all the detectives need. "That's more like it," the first says, his tone softening just a fraction. "No one's going to fault you for being honest. People do stupid things when they're drunk. You just have to admit it."

The man's face crumples, and he starts to cry—first in silent tremors, then in noisy, gasping sobs. The second detective slides a box of tissues across the table, but the comfort is performative. "Take your time," he says. "But we need this on the record."

The cycle of accusation and isolation continues. For the next hour, the suspect is left alone, the door closed, the only sounds the hum of the building's air and the ticking of a distant clock. When the detectives return, they resume the assault. "We've got your DNA. There's no way out."

"Why do you keep lying?" "What are you hiding?" "Are you really going to let your family down like this?"

Eventually, the man stops protesting. He begins to nod when they accuse him. He signs the statement, even though it implicates him in a way he cannot comprehend. Later, when shown the video of his own confession, he insists he has no memory of giving it.

This is not an aberration. In the case of Juan Rivera, an Illinois teenager accused of murder, detectives told him they had ironclad physical evidence, including semen samples and fingerprints—none of which existed. After days of isolation and aggressive interrogation, Rivera confessed to every detail, including elements of the crime scene only known to police. The jury convicted him, twice. Only years later did new DNA testing exonerate him completely.

In another case, Anthony Capozzi of Buffalo, New York, was accused of a string of rapes. Police told him his mother's car was seen at the scene, that fibers matched his clothing, that multiple victims had picked his face from a lineup. None of it was true, but after repeated cycles of confrontation, Capozzi confessed in detail. He served twenty-two years before the actual perpetrator was caught—confessing instantly, without maximization.

In the hallway, the rookie officer watches the playbook in action. "Do you think he actually did it?" he asks.

The supervisor watches through the glass, noncommittal. "Doesn't matter. They've got a confession."

"But what if it's not real?"

The supervisor sighs. "That's not our job. We just collect the statements. Let the lawyers figure it out."

In the aftermath, the suspect is escorted out, shoulders bent as if bearing invisible weight. The room is cleaned, the table wiped down, the next folder already in the inbox.

Maximization is efficient. It breaks down the will not by argument, but by attrition. The suspect's voice, at the end, is always the same: weary, hollow, a final echo of the person who entered the room.

Outside, the sky is a flat gray, matching the walls of the room and the weight in the suspect's chest.

Tomorrow, the detectives will run the same playbook. And tomorrow, another confession will be entered into the record—true, false, or something in between.

The narrative trap is the slowest, most insidious of the three. Unlike minimization or maximization, which press the suspect toward confession, the narrative trap invites them to inhabit a story of the interrogator's choosing—a story that may, over time, become indistinguishable from their own memory.

The suspect is a woman in her late twenties, picked up after a fight in the parking lot of a strip mall. She is disheveled, mascara streaked in twin lines down her cheeks, hands cuffed in front of her like a penitent. The initial interview yields nothing. "I don't remember," she says, over and over. "I was drinking. It's all a blur."

The detective, a woman herself, sits across the table. She doesn't push, not at first. She lets the silence expand, filling it only with the soft ticking of her pen against the pad. When she does speak, her tone is gentle, almost maternal.

"It's common, you know. When people are under stress, or using, the brain shuts down to protect itself. Things get foggy. Sometimes people wake up and can't piece together the hours."

The suspect nods, relieved to have her blankness normalized. "Yeah. I just remember the lights, and then, nothing."

The detective smiles, careful. "Maybe it's better that way. But sometimes, things come back. Bits and pieces."

For the next hour, the detective sketches a rough outline of the incident. The suspect's ex-boyfriend is in the hospital. There are witnesses who saw her screaming, throwing bottles. Security footage shows her in the lot, clutching something in her hand. "It looks like you tried to get away," the detective says. "Maybe you didn't mean for things to go that far. Maybe you just wanted him to stop hurting you."

"I—I don't know," the suspect whispers. "He was yelling. I wanted him to stop."

The detective takes a long breath, leans forward, and places her hand on the table. "It's okay. We think you blacked out. We think you didn't even realize what happened until it was over." She glances at the one-way mirror, then lowers her voice. "If you want, we can help fill in the gaps. Just tell us what you do remember, even if it's only feelings."

This is how the narrative begins. Over multiple sessions, the detective layers on detail. First, the feelings: anger, fear, confusion. Then, flashes of sensory data: the sound of glass breaking, the taste of blood, the distant warble of police sirens. "That's good," the detective says, encouraging each new fragment. "You're doing great. It's coming back."

Eventually, suggestion becomes memory. The suspect, unsure of where her own recall ends and the detective's script begins, starts to reconstruct a plausible version of events. "Maybe I pushed him.

Maybe I picked up the bottle. I don't know—I just wanted him to stop." The statements are tentative at first, then firmer with repetition.

By the fourth session, the woman is able to narrate the entire incident, beginning to end. She can describe the color of the boyfriend's jacket, the angle at which she swung, the cold shock of the bottle breaking against his head. She apologizes, sobbing. "I never meant to hurt anyone," she repeats. "I'm not that kind of person."

The research on memory implantation is clear and chilling. In controlled studies, subjects can be led to believe, with utter certainty, that they committed acts—stealing, cheating, even violence—that never occurred. The mechanism is repetition: each time the false memory is rehearsed, especially with encouragement from authority, it becomes more real. "Memory is a collaborative process," explains Dr. Martin Greene, a neuropsychologist specializing in trauma. "If you're unsure, and someone offers you a story that makes sense, your brain is more likely to adopt it. Especially if you need that story to explain things you can't remember."

This effect is magnified in those with a history of substance abuse or mental health challenges. For them, the boundaries between reality and suggestion are especially porous. One study found that among suspects with diagnosed bipolar disorder or PTSD, false memory implantation rates were as high as 60% after only three sessions of suggestive interviewing.

The literature is full of haunting examples. In the Norfolk Four case, four Navy sailors confessed in detail to a rape and murder after detectives spent weeks rehearsing the "most likely" sequence of events with them. The men began to recall, with increasing vividness, the sights, sounds, and actions of a night they never lived. It was only after DNA evidence excluded all four that their confessions were called into question.

Another case: Henry McCollum, a teenager with cognitive impairments, was accused of a brutal crime in North Carolina. The interrogators spent days feeding him bits of the crime scene—what the victim wore, the location of evidence, the sequence of blows—until he was able to recount the narrative almost verbatim. Years later, when asked, McCollum insisted the memories were true. Only the discovery of the real perpetrator's DNA at the scene exonerated him.

In the interview room, the suspect's own story takes shape slowly, fragment by fragment. "I must have done it," she says, weeping. "That's what everyone says. I just—I just wish I could forget."

The detective pushes the confession across the table, pen uncapped. The suspect signs, hands trembling.

Later, in jail, the woman will call her mother and say, "It's all my fault." She will tell her cellmate, "I remember it now. I remember everything." Even though, in the beginning, she remembered nothing at all.

The rookie officer, observing from the next room, is shaken. "She really didn't know, did she?"

The supervisor closes the case file with a sigh. "Doesn't matter. She confessed."

"But—isn't that dangerous? Making someone believe they did something they didn't?"

The supervisor shrugs, as if to brush away the question. "People want closure. The law wants closure. Memory—memory's just along for the ride."

In the files, the confession is clean, detailed, and self-incriminating. The district attorney will read it, the judge will hear it, and the woman will never be able to untangle the story from the truth.

For the vulnerable, for those with fractured or fragile memories, the narrative trap is more than a technique. It is an erasure and a rewriting, a theft of agency as profound as the crimes it seeks to solve.

The system moves on, satisfied. The detective receives a commendation for her empathy, her patience, her ability to "get to the truth."

But the suspect, released years later on appeal, will never quite trust her own mind again.

For every false memory created, there is a real one destroyed. And in the end, the record holds only the version written by the strongest hand.

The cost of confession is not paid at the table. For the suspect, the worst is yet to come.

Decades of research chart the aftermath of coercive interrogation with the precision of forensic autopsy. In a survey of over a thousand former suspects—both those convicted and those later exonerated—more than 70% reported ongoing psychological distress attributed not to the crime, but to the process of questioning itself. The effects are not fleeting. They are carved into the days and nights that follow: insomnia, panic attacks, the relentless replay of events, real or suggested, in the theater of the mind.

For some, the trauma manifests immediately. One man, accused and cleared in a high-profile fraud case, described it this way: "They say you walk out when it's over. But I never left that room." The air, the light, the voice of the detective—he dreamed them for years, waking each night with the sensation of being watched. He never returned to his old job, never trusted another closed door.

Others bear the scars more quietly. In a study of 120 false confessors later exonerated by DNA evidence, more than half reported symptoms consistent with post-traumatic stress disorder: avoidance of reminders, flashbacks, difficulty maintaining relationships. A third attempted suicide within five years of release. Many could not hold a steady job, or withdrew from family and friends.

The shame is a special kind of poison. For the innocent, the memory of capitulation—of having surrendered, against all logic, to a story that was not theirs—gnaws at the self. "It's like losing your soul," said one exoneree, who confessed to a crime he could not have committed because he was hundreds of miles away. "You doubt everything. Your own memory. Your own mind."

Even among the guilty, the process is corrosive. The knowledge that the confession was extracted—not given—tarnishes whatever sense of closure or redemption the justice system intends. "It wasn't me talking," a convicted felon recalled in a group therapy session. "It was the voice in that room. The one that told me who I was, and what I'd done. After a while, you start to believe it."

Clinical studies support these accounts. Subjects exposed to simulated interrogation environments showed elevated cortisol levels and abnormal heart rhythms for hours, sometimes days, after the event. Those with prior trauma, mental illness, or substance use histories were the most affected. "Coercive interrogation is a perfect storm," says Dr. Clarissa Boone, a psychiatrist specializing in legal trauma. "It attacks not just the facts, but the fabric of selfhood—memory, identity, agency. For people who are already vulnerable, it can be devastating."

This devastation is not limited to suspects. Family members, friends, entire communities feel the ripple. The mother who cannot believe her son would confess unless he was guilty. The spouse who replays the recording, trying to hear some note of resistance, some proof that the person she loved was not broken. The children, grown now, who read about their parent's "admission" in a cold line of newsprint, never quite able to put it aside.

Testimony from exonerees is often haunting in its sameness. The man who spent eighteen years in prison for a crime he confessed to, despite knowing the truth, described his release as "being born without a past." He could not answer questions about his life before, could not imagine a future. "I live in a kind of fog," he told a reporter. "I know I didn't do it, but I also know I said I did. Sometimes I wish I could just erase it all."

Another, a teenager at the time of her confession, developed crippling anxiety that persisted long after her name was cleared. She could not sleep without every light on, could not walk into a room unless she could see the exit. "I'm not scared of people," she said. "I'm scared of being believed. Of being trapped by my own words."

The literature documents these wounds in chilling detail. One study compared the mental health of false confessors to that of military veterans returning from combat. The rates of PTSD were nearly identical; the rates of major depression were higher among the former suspects. "The difference," the study noted, "is that the trauma of interrogation is internalized as shame, not heroism."

This is the unspoken cost of the techniques. The confessions are entered into the record, cited in court, quoted by the news. The wounds, less visible, fester in silence.

The system, for its part, is slow to recognize the harm. Police manuals and legal training still frame the extraction of a confession as a necessary evil, justified by the higher good of justice. "We're not therapists," one detective said. "We're here to solve crimes." But the line between solving and creating is easily blurred, especially when the methods work so well.

There are exceptions. Some jurisdictions now require all interrogations to be recorded, from start to finish, in hopes that transparency will serve as a check. Others train detectives in "trauma-informed interviewing," a practice that avoids the old cycles of isolation and pressure. These measures help, but the larger machine grinds on.

The question, then, is ethical as much as practical. Is the information gained worth the price paid? For every confession that leads to a genuine resolution, how many false ones destroy the life of someone innocent, or erode the dignity of the person who confesses? Is the system protecting society, or is it simply replicating the trauma it claims to remedy?

Legal experts are divided. Some argue that the occasional miscarriage is inevitable, a tolerable byproduct of a functioning justice system. Others see it as a failure so fundamental that it cannot be offset by any number of correct convictions.

"The legitimacy of law depends on the legitimacy of its methods," says Professor Mona Vasquez, an ethicist at Georgetown. "If we destroy people in the pursuit of truth, we have achieved neither justice nor truth. We have only performed a ritual of violence, sanctioned by the state."

The final irony is that the system is often indifferent to the very information it extracts. Confessions are prized for their efficiency, for their ability to close cases and clear dockets. Whether they are true is sometimes secondary. The record, so carefully constructed, becomes the measure of reality—even when reality is elsewhere.

For the person at the center, the cost is permanent. The memories of the room—the light, the voices, the click of the pen—are woven into every day that follows. The struggle is not just for freedom, but for the reclamation of the self.

In the end, the mission of justice must be to protect not only the safety of the community, but the dignity of all who pass through its doors. Anything less is a betrayal of the name.

The record is eternal. But so, too, is the damage it leaves behind.

CHAPTER 4

Interviews Versus Interrogations: Purpose, Process, And Presumption

The classroom is tiered in gentle steps, each row of seats equipped with a slender desktop, a discreet lamp, and a port for the charging of devices. At the front of the room, a panel of touchscreens lines the wall above a massive digital projection screen. The décor is pure municipal: carpet the color of old oatmeal, ceiling tiles mapped with tiny acoustic holes, an air of scrubbed sterility that manages to be both impersonal and intimate. Rows are filled with police cadets, civilian crime analysts, and a handful of uniformed officers from smaller towns where budgets do not stretch to such amenities.

The instructor, Detective Sergeant Whitaker, sets her phone to silent and addresses the class with practiced efficiency. Her hair is cropped close in a style favored by those with neither time nor tolerance for the distractions of fashion. She wears plain clothes, but her badge—clipped to her belt—sends its own signal.

"Today we'll be comparing two basic tools of the trade," she begins, voice amplified just enough to cut through murmurs but not enough to startle. "Interviews and interrogations. If you think they're the same thing, you're in the right room."

A couple of the younger cadets shift, embarrassed or amused. Whitaker doesn't smile. "Let's get straight to it."

The lights dim, and the projector throws up a split-screen video. The left side is labeled "INTERVIEW: Witness A, Post-Theft." The right: "INTERROGATION: Subject 17, Suspected Theft." Both screens show the same woman, a grocery store clerk with neat hair and a cardigan too bright for the setting.

Left side: the room is softly lit, furnished like a bland office, with a pair of plush chairs angled toward each other and a carafe of water on the table. The interviewer, mid-thirties and blandly pleasant, starts with small talk. "Thanks for coming in. I know your schedule's tight."

The clerk nods, relaxing her hands in her lap.

Whitaker taps her remote and the video pauses. "Note the body language. Open, relaxed, slight smile. This is not accidental. The witness knows she's not under suspicion. She's here to help."

A line of text appears below the left screen: "Goal: Elicit full, untainted recall."

Whitaker toggles play.

"Can you walk me through what happened after lunch?" the interviewer asks.

The clerk starts slow, then gains momentum. "I finished stocking the bread aisle, checked out a couple customers, and then I noticed the register was off. The drawer felt—lighter, I guess. I didn't want to accuse anyone, but..."

"Was anyone else near the register?" The question is asked neutrally, the interviewer's pen moving but eyes fixed on the clerk's face.

"Yeah—my supervisor, and the guy from produce, Mike. He comes up front sometimes. But I didn't see anyone actually touch it."

"Anything unusual about their behavior?"

A pause, then a head shake. "No, not really. Mike was talking about baseball. My supervisor was on her phone most of the time."

Whitaker pauses again. "Classic open-ended questioning. Note the lack of assumptions. No leading, no suggestions of guilt, just a chronological build. The key is letting the witness organize the memory themselves."

She highlights the left video's sidebar: "Open prompt. Neutral affect. Minimal interruption."

A hand goes up in the back. "What about memory contamination?" asks a cadet with a jawline cut from recruiting poster stock.

Whitaker nods. "We'll get there. But first—watch the contrast."

She turns to the right screen.

Here, the lighting is harsh, the furniture cheap and hard-edged. The same woman sits at a metal table, shoulders hunched, fingers locked together. Across from her, a detective in rolled shirtsleeves leans forward, elbows on the steel.

Whitaker lets the first thirty seconds run in silence. The difference is immediate: the suspect's eyes are downcast, her breathing shallow. The detective's voice is low but forceful.

"I know you've been through a lot," he says. "We're just trying to get to the bottom of this. You and I both know why you're here."

The clerk stares at her hands. "I—I don't know. I just—I did my job."

He leans in closer. "We have statements from two employees saying you were alone with the register. Security camera shows you at the till right before the money went missing." He lets the implication hang. "You're a good person, right? But people make mistakes. Happens every day."

Whitaker freezes the video. "Minimization, classic form. Framing the crime as a mistake, not a character flaw. But listen for the pivot."

She rewinds ten seconds and plays again.

"You're a good person, right? But people make mistakes. Happens every day. I'm not saying you planned it. But maybe you were desperate. Needed the money for something important."

The clerk's face pinches, eyes welling. "I didn't—I swear, I didn't take anything."

"But if you did, it's better to admit it now. We can work with that."

Whitaker overlays a red circle on the detective's face: "Watch the micro-expressions." The class leans in as the video loops: the subtle hardening of the jaw, the flicker of the eyes toward the file folder, the calculated sigh.

"Notice the difference?" Whitaker asks.

A row of analysts in matching blazers whisper and nod.

She advances the video five minutes. The tone escalates.

"You're not leaving until you tell the truth," the detective says. "We can call in your supervisor. We can get the tapes. If you want to protect yourself, you need to be honest."

The clerk trembles, voice thready: "I didn't do it."

The detective stares. "It's not about what you did. It's about what you're willing to admit. I'm giving you the chance to explain it before someone else does."

Whitaker cuts both videos and brings up a blank slide.

"This is why the distinction matters," she says. "An interview is for information-gathering. No presumption, no adversarial energy. It's about opening up a memory, not shaping it. An interrogation is the opposite: it's about closing options, narrowing the focus, pushing toward a single version of events—usually one that matches the theory of the case."

She turns to the trainees. "What did you notice about the clerk's body language in the second video?"

A woman in the second row answers: "She got smaller. Defensive. She looked like she was waiting for it to be over."

"Exactly. Accusatory pressure induces stress, which impairs recall. But it's worse: under enough stress, people will say whatever gets them out of the room fastest. That includes admitting to things they didn't do."

A young analyst, skeptical, raises a hand. "Isn't that only with really aggressive tactics?"

Whitaker shakes her head. "No. Even low-level pressure can create false confessions, especially when the suspect is tired, scared, or confused about the evidence. The data is overwhelming."

She runs a montage: a series of news clips and documentary interviews with people who confessed to crimes they never committed. Faces flicker on the screen—some angry, some haunted, some numb. The overlay tallies percentages: "23% of exonerations involve false confession. 60% involve minors or cognitively vulnerable individuals."

Back to the classroom. "Questions?" Whitaker asks.

A cadet leans in. “So what’s the right approach?”

Whitaker clicks her remote, bringing up a checklist:

- Open prompts

- Chronological retelling

- No leading questions

- Wait out silences

- Avoid confrontation unless all evidence is corroborated

“First, you get the story in their own words. Only after that do you start testing for inconsistency or exploring alternate explanations. And even then, you avoid any statement that signals ‘we already know you did it.’”

She pulls up two more clips: one of a child witness being interviewed about a playground fight (“Tell me what happened at recess, start to finish”), and one of a burglary suspect being interrogated (“We have your prints. If you want to help yourself, tell us why you did it”).

The class watches, absorbing the contrast.

Whitaker circles back. “For those of you going into the field: you will be under pressure to close cases. You will be told, directly or indirectly, to get confessions, to move on. Resist that. The risk of error is too high.”

A silence settles in the room, punctuated only by the faint hum of the climate system and the blinking cursor on the wall display.

She ends with a final slide: a composite mugshot, half innocent, half guilty, the border smeared and indistinct.

“Your job is not to decide who is which. It’s to get the story—the real story—without writing it for them.”

The lights come up, and the class remains quiet, the lesson settling over them like a fine dust.

Whitaker checks her watch and calls a break, but no one is in a hurry to leave. Most stare at the screen, replaying the split images in their minds, the way a single approach can tilt an entire investigation.

Outside, in the corridor, the sun is climbing past the upper windows, a sharp white line dividing shadow from light.

Break ends with a brittle click of the lights and the shuffle of returning bodies. Sergeant Whitaker stands at the whiteboard, marker in hand, as the last of the students settle. The screen now shows a grayscale scan of a police case file, the name and face of the accused blacked out with digital ink.

"We're shifting gears," Whitaker announces. "This is a robbery case from three years ago. Pay attention to the sequence—the point at which the interview crosses over into interrogation, and what changes from that moment forward."

She gestures to the side table stacked with battered copies of "Inbau & Reid: Criminal Interrogation and Confessions," paper flags bristling from every other page. The classroom whiteboard is already lined with key phrases: "Presumption of Guilt," "Confirmation Bias," "The Reid Technique—Nine Steps."

Whitaker toggles the projector to a transcript view.

"At the top, you'll see timestamps and speaker tags. At the bottom, I'll annotate significant departures from best practice. Here's the context: Male, late twenties, stopped for matching a vague description—'tall, dark hair, blue jacket'—taken in for questioning after a liquor store stickup. Evidence? Circumstantial at best."

She sets the pointer to 00:00.

INVESTIGATOR: Thanks for coming in. Mind if we record this?

SUSPECT: No, that's fine.

INVESTIGATOR: Just routine. Want some water?

SUSPECT: Sure.

"Note the calm, the rapport-building," Whitaker says. "First ten minutes are pure cognitive interview. Goal is open narrative."

At 00:10:17, things start to shift.

INVESTIGATOR: Can you walk me through your afternoon, starting when you left work?

SUSPECT: Yeah, I went straight home. Took the bus. Got there around six, I think.

INVESTIGATOR: Anyone see you on the bus?

SUSPECT: Not that I know of.

The annotation flashes: "Noncommittal alibi = increased suspicion." Whitaker underlines it in red on the board.

"Watch the progression," she says. "Here, the investigator is gathering, not yet presuming. But listen to the next sequence."

INVESTIGATOR: So you got home at six. What happened then?

SUSPECT: Watched TV, made some food.

INVESTIGATOR: Alone?

SUSPECT: Yeah, just me.

"Textbook. The interviewee is not providing independent verification, which is common, but from this point, the investigator's questions tighten."

She skips to 00:15:42.

INVESTIGATOR: Thing is, we have you on camera near the store around 5:55. Any reason you'd be in that area?

SUSPECT: I transfer buses there, every day.

INVESTIGATOR: Okay. So you admit being near the store.

Whitaker pauses. "This is called an assumptive close. The language switches from possibility to certainty: 'You admit.' Not 'Did you see the store?' but 'You were there.'"

The transcript resumes. The investigator now leans on sequence.

INVESTIGATOR: A witness says you ran from the scene.

SUSPECT: I didn't run. I was just catching the bus.

INVESTIGATOR: Can you see why that looks suspicious?

The whiteboard marker scrapes out: "Reid Step Four—Confrontation." Whitaker draws a line under it.

On screen, the video shifts to a two-shot, both faces visible. The investigator's posture is forward, elbows on the table, gaze locked on the suspect's face. The suspect shrinks back, arms crossed, eyes darting.

Whitaker freeze-frames. "Body language tells the story: dominance and retreat. The investigator is now physically signaling suspicion."

At 00:21:00, the transcript accelerates.

INVESTIGATOR: We have a witness. We have you at the scene. What are we missing?

SUSPECT: I don't know. I didn't do anything.

INVESTIGATOR: You expect us to believe you just happened to be there?

The annotation pops: “Shift from evidence-gathering to narrative imposition.”

A cadet in the front row raises a hand. “Isn’t that the point, to pressure them once you’re sure?”

Whitaker shakes her head. “Pressure is only justified if the facts support it. Here, the ‘witness’ is unreliable, the camera evidence is ambiguous. But listen to what happens next.”

She highlights the transcript in yellow.

INVESTIGATOR: You seem like a good guy. I think you’re just scared. If you tell us what really happened, you’ll feel better.

SUSPECT: I already told you. I went home.

INVESTIGATOR: You realize we can get bus footage, right? We will. Might as well be honest now.

Whitaker circles the line: “Bluffing about evidence = risky.”

She switches to the video: the investigator is now inches from the suspect, voice lowered, every phrase a challenge. "This is where the presumption of guilt crystallizes. From this point, all information is filtered through the lens of 'how does this support my theory?'"

At 00:27:16:

INVESTIGATOR: Look, we already know what happened. You're not in trouble if you tell the truth. We just want to hear your side.

SUSPECT: I didn't do it. I swear.

INVESTIGATOR: You're digging yourself deeper. Why not just say you needed the money?

Whitaker annotates: "Suspect's denials are reinterpreted as resistance, not as possible truth."

She turns to the whiteboard and writes, in block letters: "CONFIRMATION BIAS."

"Everything after the fifteen-minute mark is about confirming the investigator's belief, not testing it. Every denial is a lie, every inconsistency is proof. This is where most wrongful convictions start—not with malice, but with tunnel vision."

A row of trainees nod. One flips through the flagged pages of his Inbau & Reid manual.

The transcript continues, now marked with frequent "interruption" notes.

INVESTIGATOR: Why don't you just admit it? People respect honesty.

SUSPECT: Because I didn't do anything!

INVESTIGATOR: The longer you lie, the worse it looks. This is your chance to be a man about it.

Whitaker points with her marker. "Notice how the tone escalates? It moves from inquiry to challenge to character attack. The suspect is now responding emotionally, not cognitively."

The video shows the investigator's body language: arms now spread, hands splayed on the table, face inches from the suspect. The suspect has stopped making eye contact, hands gripping the chair's edge.

"Physical dominance," Whitaker says. "Every inch of space taken is a psychological cue: 'You're trapped.'"

A woman in the back raises a hand. "Isn't some of this necessary if you think they're lying?"

"Necessary, perhaps. But dangerous if you're wrong," Whitaker replies. "This is how innocent people get railroaded—because every tactic that works on the guilty also works, sometimes better, on the innocent. They become confused, exhausted, desperate to escape."

She advances to the next key segment.

INVESTIGATOR: We've had people in here before. Most confess after a couple hours. The smart ones, anyway.

SUSPECT: I really don't know what else to say.

INVESTIGATOR: You're going to let this ruin your life?

A pause. Then, quieter:

SUSPECT: No.

The investigator sits back, satisfied. "You'll talk eventually."

Whitaker clicks the remote, freezing the video with both faces visible: one smirking, one defeated.

"This case never went to trial. The actual perpetrator was caught two months later. But for a long time, this suspect was the prime target. His denials were treated as proof of guilt, his every action reinterpreted to fit the narrative."

She draws a bracket around the section of transcript where the switch occurs, then underlines "Presumption" three times.

A trainee in the front: "So how do you avoid this? If you have a theory, you're always going to see things that way."

Whitaker erases the board with a single swipe, then writes: "DELIBERATE SKEPTICISM."

"You test every theory against the facts. You write down alternative explanations, even the ones you hate. You have a partner play devil's advocate. You re-interview, without confrontation, after you get new evidence. And you document, document, document."

She looks around the room. "The goal is not to trick suspects. The goal is to uncover what happened—even if it means giving up on the easy answer."

On the side wall, a panel of "Ten Commandments for Interviews" flickers to life. The first: "Assume nothing." The last: "Check yourself, always."

Whitaker closes the file on the projector and faces the class.

"Any questions?"

A hesitant hand. "What's the most common mistake new investigators make?"

"Confirmation bias," she says, without hesitation. "And believing the playbook is foolproof."

A ripple of laughter, then a quiet, sobering pause.

She moves to the back wall, where reference books and old case binders line the shelves. She pulls down a worn file and holds it up.

"This is a record of every interview I ever did where I was wrong. I reread it before every new case. Keeps me humble."

The students watch, some nodding, some uncertain. But the message is clear: the techniques work—until they don't. And when they fail, the cost is measured not in closed cases, but in ruined lives.

Whitaker glances at the clock, then signals the break.

The classroom empties in slow clumps, the cadets and analysts lingering to glance at the transcript, the playbook, the cautionary folder of mistakes.

Outside, the sunlight is fading behind the administrative block, the sharp white line on the corridor now diffused and pale, as if the day itself were warning: beware of shadows that look like truth.

After break, the classroom lights return at half-strength, and the ambient hum is replaced by the shuffling of bodies and the dull thud of evidence boxes on particleboard tables. Sergeant Whitaker presides from a corner, but this phase is less lecture and more autopsy. The room is arranged in pods: each cluster of students receives a stack of redacted police reports, facsimiles of crime scene photos, and a manila folder of court documents, each stamped "CASE FILE: JOHNSON."

Projected across the main wall is a mosaic of the case—timeline, location maps, witness lists. At the center, a grainy booking photo of a young Black man, expression stony, eyes rimmed with exhaustion. The slide reads, in block capitals: "Case Study: State v. Johnson (2003–2017)."

Whitaker claps hands once, sharp and clean. "This is not a puzzle to be solved," she says. "The conviction was overturned three years ago. Your job is to walk back every step and find where the truth left the process."

A murmur passes over the room as the first page of the file is read aloud:

"On the night of March 14, 2003, two masked individuals entered a liquor store at closing time. The clerk was shot, the register emptied, and the suspects fled in a gray sedan. Johnson was arrested within forty-eight hours, based on eyewitness identification and his proximity to the scene."

On the tables, evidence is arrayed: time-stamped photos, typed witness statements, sketches of the crime scene. Students sift through the packets, annotating with green and red highlighters.

Whitaker moves among the pods, pausing at the table nearest the front. "Start with the alibi," she instructs. "What did Johnson claim, and how was it handled?"

A trainee reads from the transcript: "He said he was home, watching TV with his sister. The officers interviewed the sister but didn't follow up when her account differed on what show was on."

"Why not?" Whitaker asks.

"Because the detective wrote: 'Alibi not credible due to inconsistency in minor details.'"

A chorus of pens scribbles in unison. "Minor details," Whitaker repeats. "Confirmation bias at work. The investigation seeks out, and locks onto, what supports the theory. Everything else is noise."

On the projection screen, the timeline advances:

- 10:07 p.m.: Robbery occurs.

- 10:15 p.m.: Gray sedan reported by off-duty officer three blocks east.

- 10:22 p.m.: Johnson stopped for rolling stop at intersection, released.

- 10:40 p.m.: 911 call places Johnson at his mother's apartment.

"Next," Whitaker says, "look for physical evidence."

A woman in a navy hoodie raises a gloved hand. "There's nothing tying Johnson to the store. No prints, no DNA. The shell casing didn't match his uncle's registered handgun, which was the only weapon they checked."

"Correct," Whitaker affirms. "Yet note the language in the case summary: 'Johnson's lack of physical evidence at the scene is inconclusive, as gloves and mask were worn.' In other words, absence of evidence is reinterpreted as evidence of cunning."

A burst of nervous laughter from the pod. Whitaker lets it fade.

At the next table, a student points to a highlighted passage: "Alternate suspect. An informant tipped that a local gang member bragged about 'robbing the bottle shop' days after the murder. That line is crossed out in the detective's notebook, with 'not relevant' in the margin."

Whitaker underlines the phrase on the whiteboard: "NOT RELEVANT."

She addresses the class. "How does information become not relevant?"

A trainee in the back shrugs. "If it doesn't fit the story you're building."

"Exactly. The more invested the investigator, the less likely they are to chase down lines that complicate the picture. Now, watch what happens in the interviews."

She pulls up a video segment, timestamped 2:04:16, and queues the playback.

The interview room is familiar now: blank walls, battered metal table, a single chair occupied by Johnson. He sits straight-backed, hands folded. Two detectives face him, one silent and looming, the other speaking in the bland, steady tones of practiced authority.

DETECTIVE: "You were seen driving a gray sedan near the store."

JOHNSON: "It's my mom's car. I was coming home from work."

DETECTIVE: "We know you were there. Two witnesses ID'd you from a lineup."

JOHNSON: "I never went in. I swear to God."

DETECTIVE: "If you admit it now, it goes better for you. If you keep lying, you're looking at life."

The playback freezes as Whitaker annotates on the board: "Reid Step Five—Offer Moral Excuse."

She advances the video.

DETECTIVE: "Look, you're not a bad guy. Maybe you just needed the money. Maybe you got scared. But this is your chance to help yourself."

Johnson shakes his head, voice flat. "I didn't do it."

Whitaker turns to the class. "Every denial is reframed as defiance, not doubt. By this point in the investigation, the presumption of guilt is total. Listen to the next sequence."

The video resumes:

DETECTIVE: "You know what we think? We think you got in over your head. We think your friend pulled the trigger, and you freaked out."

JOHNSON: "I don't know anything about it."

DETECTIVE: "We can put you at the scene, we can put you in the car, we can put the gun in your hand. You want your family to hear that in court, or do you want to explain it yourself?"

There is a long, strained silence. Johnson looks down. "Can I call my mom?"

"Not until we get your side," the detective says.

The class watches as the tactics escalate—softer at first, then relentless. In the transcript, as in the room, the pressure is insidious, wrapped in paternal concern.

A student at the far table looks up from the file. "Is this legal?" she asks.

"In most jurisdictions, yes," Whitaker replies. "The rules allow for deception—within limits. But the real danger isn't in the lie; it's in the certainty. Once a theory is fixed, every fact is bent to fit it."

The next evidence packet goes around: a printout of the prosecution's summary, with key lines highlighted.

- "Johnson placed at the scene by two eyewitnesses, despite conditions being 'dark and visibility poor.'"

- "Johnson's statement contained several 'inconsistencies' with known facts, though these were minor."

- "Johnson failed a polygraph administered after twelve hours in custody."

Whitaker comments, "Twelve hours of sleep deprivation, no food or water documented for the last four. Polygraph as anxiety meter, not truth detector."

A student raises a hand. "Did they ever find the actual shooter?"

"Yes," Whitaker says. "DNA on the dropped ski mask matched a parolee picked up six years later for a different robbery. He confessed to three other jobs, including this one. Said Johnson was never there. He didn't know the name."

Silence, then a slow exhale from several students.

Whitaker opens the floor. "Let's walk through the five biggest places the system failed. One: Alibi witness dismissed for trivial discrepancies. Two: Physical evidence ignored or rationalized away. Three: Alternative suspect erased from consideration. Four: Timeline contradictions left unresolved. Five: Forensics not fully explored—only checked against a weapon they already linked to Johnson."

She slides a court transcript onto the document camera, showing the final nail.

PROSECUTOR: "The defendant's refusal to confess, despite overwhelming evidence, demonstrates consciousness of guilt."

Whitaker flips to the appeals court ruling, finger tracing the lines.

"Mr. Johnson was wrongfully incarcerated for twelve years before DNA evidence exonerated him. The original investigators have since retired."

A hush settles over the room. The students sit motionless, some still clutching highlighters, others with hands resting on the stark white of the table.

Whitaker closes the folder, slow and deliberate. "You may never be the smartest person in the room. But you can always be the most careful. If you do nothing else—if you take nothing else from today—let it be this: Doubt your own certainty. If you can't do that, you shouldn't be in the job."

A man at the window clears his throat. "Is that what happened to Johnson? Everyone just got used to being right?"

Whitaker lets the question hang. "Being right is addictive," she says. "You'll never get more praise than when you close a tough case. But the only thing worse than being wrong is not knowing you were."

The class lingers as the evidence is reboxed, the documents stacked for the next cohort. Some students wander the perimeter, reading the sticky notes and margin scribbles from those who came before, as if a residue of caution can be learned by osmosis.

At the door, a woman in a pressed shirt and sharp ponytail pauses. "What happened to him? Johnson."

"He's free," Whitaker says. "But he missed his twenties and most of his thirties. His mother died while he was inside. The system gave him a settlement, but it doesn't fix much."

A moment's silence, then the woman nods and exits.

The classroom empties, leaving only the hum of the projector and the shadow of the booking photo, now faded to near-invisibility.

Outside, dusk has settled. The last sunlight is gone, replaced by sodium streetlamps casting their own imperfect, yellowed light on the concrete paths below.

Inside, the tables are bare again—save for a single folder, left open to the first page. At the bottom, under the list of charges and arresting officers, someone has scrawled in pencil:

"BE CAREFUL. THE NEXT JOHNSON IS WAITING."

No one moves to erase it.

CHAPTER 5

Theory Before Evidence: The Dangers Of Deductive Investigation

The lecture hall is an amphitheater of attention, its semicircle tiers trimmed in particleboard and navy upholstery, all angled toward a lone projection screen at the pit's center. There, under the cool buzz of ceiling cans and the occasional chirp of laptop keys, a hundred students fan out in concentric waves, waiting for the next item to drop on the agenda.

At the front, Professor Edie Benham perches at a high lab table, one elbow on its edge, pointer in hand, hair in a disintegrating bun. The screen above her flashes: "INVESTIGATIVE METHODS: DEDUCTION vs INDUCTION." Next to the title, a comparison table:

Deductive Investigation	Inductive Investigation
Begin with a theory	Begin with evidence
Test with evidence	Build theory from facts
Discard the irrelevant	Gather all, filter late
Suspect first	Who, what, why later

Benham raps the pointer twice on the table. "You're detectives now," she says, "so you live or die by process." A pause, just long enough to let the words break the room's surface tension. "Let's walk through these two ways of thinking. Deduction, on the left. What's the first step?"

A few hands hover, but she points to a young man in the second row, navy hoodie, thick glasses. "Start with a suspect?" he offers.

"Start with a theory," Benham corrects, but nods. "That theory is usually a suspect, a scenario, or a motive. Then you look for evidence to prove or disprove it. Right?"

Heads nod. Notes are made.

"Induction?" She points at a woman with earbuds still looped around her neck.

"Collect everything first. Build a theory from what you find."

"Good," Benham says, voice even, precise. "Induction is more about open collection—see what the facts suggest, and only then start building your scenario. You don't try to make the puzzle pieces fit a picture you already have in your mind."

She leans forward, resting both palms on the table's edge. "Now, why does this matter? Anyone?"

The class is silent except for the faint shuffle of feet and the settling of lecture-hall air.

Benham points back to the table. "Because this"—she circles the words 'Deductive' and 'Inductive' with her pointer—"decides whether you get the right answer, or just the answer you want."

On the screen, she advances to the next slide: a simple timeline. "Let's do a test case. You roll up to a house—burglary call. Back door's kicked in, electronics gone, one neighbor saw a tall figure in a hoodie running down the street at 2:12 a.m. The first patrol officer finds a bike abandoned in the alley, and shoe prints by the fence. You have twenty minutes before the scene is swarmed by neighbors and news vans."

She faces the class. "Deductive approach—walk me through it."

A student in the back, arms crossed, calls out: "Start by canvassing for tall guys in hoodies. Find out who in the neighborhood matches. See if the bike was stolen."

Benham nods. "Classic. You fix on the hoodie, the height, maybe the bike, and you build your theory—tall guy, probably local, probably rode in on the bike, left it to escape faster." She taps the screen. "What's the risk?"

"Tunnel vision," someone mutters up front.

"Exactly," Benham says, clicking to the next slide—a GIF of an actual police lineup, three men in hoodies under harsh light. "If you lock in too fast, you ignore what doesn't fit. You discard evidence that doesn't confirm your theory. You risk missing the truth because you're only seeing what you expect to see."

She moves to the next bullet: "Inductive approach."

This time, the student with the earbuds raises her hand. "You'd collect everything—like, log every shoe print, maybe check for fingerprints on the door, get video from all the houses, see who's missing a bike in the whole area?"

Benham grins. "You're making more work for yourself, but yes. Inductive means you let the evidence lead. Maybe the shoe prints belong to a kid who lives next door—maybe the bike was ditched by someone else hours earlier. You don't know yet. You don't assume. You don't filter out details because they seem off."

She looks up at the lecture hall, scanning for resistance, boredom, or the glint of actual interest. "So, which is better?"

A shrug ripples across the rows. One hand in the back. "Depends on the case?"

"Always," Benham agrees. "But here's the real trick: most real-world investigations mix the two. Nobody is purely one or the other. The danger is when you forget you're doing deduction, and start to treat your theory like a fact. That's where mistakes happen."

She shifts tone, voice sharpening. "Let's talk about confirmation bias. Anyone define it?"

A voice in the middle: "It's when you only see what supports your theory, not what challenges it."

Benham lets the answer settle. "It's more than that. It's when your own mind tricks you into sorting, weighting, and even remembering things in a way that keeps your story on the rails. Cops are as bad as anyone, sometimes worse. Once you have a suspect, every new detail gets sorted into 'helps my case' or 'doesn't matter.' Even exculpatory stuff."

She scans the room, making eye contact with at least a dozen students, letting the discomfort hang. "If you're not careful, you will railroad the wrong person—maybe more than once. Happens every year in every city in the country."

A slide appears on screen: "Case Study: The Innocent Project, 1997–2019." Below it, a statistic in bold: "72% of overturned convictions involved some form of investigative bias."

Benham glances at the stat, then at her class. "Seventy-two percent. That's not a rounding error. That's a design flaw."

She flips back to the first slide, the comparison table. "Let's play with the edges. Deductive isn't always bad. If you have a serial pattern, or rock-solid forensic leads, it's efficient. Inductive isn't perfect—collect too much and you drown in noise. The key is knowing when you're sliding from one mode to the other."

A hand goes up in the front. "How do you catch yourself?"

Benham turns, considering the question. "You check your own assumptions, constantly. You have a colleague play devil's advocate. You write down your theory and then spend time trying to break it. You look for the detail that screws up your favorite scenario."

She raps the table again. "And you never, ever treat a confession, a positive ID, or a gut feeling as the last word. You treat it as a new branch in the tree, not the trunk."

She advances to the final slide: "Best Practices," in blunt capitals.

- Never discard evidence as irrelevant until all theories are tested.

- Seek disconfirming as well as confirming evidence.

- Use team review to challenge case narrative.

- Maintain separate files for alternate suspects.

Benham reads them aloud, voice flat but final. "You will be judged by your process, not your hunches. If you shortcut, someone pays—sometimes with decades of their life."

She lets the weight of the lesson hang, then clicks the projector off. The hall, once blue-lit and focused, snaps back into warm daylight and quiet murmurs.

"See you Thursday," Benham says, gathering her things. "Bring questions."

The students begin their ritual of closure: laptops stowed, notebooks zipped, conversations revived. But as the crowd thins, a few linger by the front, eyeing the comparison table still visible as a ghost image on the dark screen.

The lesson, for now, has landed.

The next session opens with the lights dimmed, the hum of the projector a metronome for the silence. Professor Benham stands at the podium, hands clasped behind her back. The screen is all white at first, then flickers to a single line of black text: "Case Study: Ronald Cotton, 1984–1995."

There is no preamble. The class, remembering the last session, comes to quiet quickly.

Benham advances to the first slide: a grainy black-and-white mugshot. Below it, a name and number. "This is Ronald Cotton," she says. "He spent eleven years in prison for a crime he did not commit. Let's break down how that happened."

She toggles the screen, revealing a side-by-side of two faces: Ronald Cotton, and the man whose crime he served time for, Bobby Poole. At a glance, they could be cousins. Benham lets the class take this in.

"Here's the story," she begins. "In 1984, a woman named Jennifer Thompson was assaulted in her apartment in Burlington, North Carolina. She was brave—fought back, memorized every detail she could. Later, at the hospital, she gave the police a description: Black male, early twenties, athletic, close-cropped hair, no facial hair. The composite sketch they generated looked a lot like Ronald Cotton, a local man with a minor record."

She flips to a timeline. The first segment is fat, labeled "Initial Investigation." Dots branch out: witness statements, composite sketches, lists of local men with records. One dot—"Cotton, R."—is circled in red.

"They did a photo lineup first," Benham narrates. "Thompson picked Cotton. Then they did a physical lineup. Thompson picked Cotton again. Each time, the officers told her she was doing great, that she'd helped move the case forward. This is what we call reinforcing feedback."

The class watches as the timeline branches again—this time thinner, more focused. The other names fade, Cotton's is underlined.

"At trial, Jennifer Thompson testified. She was confident, clear, unwavering: 'There is no doubt in my mind,' she said. The jury convicted in under an hour."

A hand in the fourth row goes up. Benham nods to the student, a young woman with a blue spiral notebook.

"Was there any physical evidence?" the student asks.

"Great question," Benham answers. "None. No fingerprints, no DNA—this was pre-DNA era for most labs—no fibers or hair linking Cotton to the scene. Just the eyewitness ID, and Cotton's record."

She switches to a chart labeled "Alternate Suspects." Names are listed: Poole, B.; Smith, D.; Wilkes, T. Each with a series of plus and minus signs next to attributes: age, build, criminal record, alibi. Benham taps her pointer on Poole's row.

"Now, here's where it gets interesting. During the investigation, Bobby Poole was flagged by several locals as a possible match. He was the right age, lived nearby, and had a reputation. But because the witness ID was already so strong, and because Cotton fit the narrative so well, the investigation didn't really pursue Poole."

She pauses, letting the screen hang on Poole's faded row. "Even when rumors started spreading in prison that Poole was bragging about the crime, no one outside took it seriously."

She clicks forward: "Second Assault." "While Cotton is awaiting trial, a second, nearly identical assault occurs, same method, same location. Thompson sees the composite sketch and says, 'That's the same man who attacked me.' But because Cotton is already arrested, the system treats the second case as unrelated. No one asks Thompson to compare the two men side by side."

A new visual: a narrowing funnel, wide at the top with "All possible suspects," tight at the bottom with only "Cotton, R." Benham traces the narrowing with her pointer.

"This is called filter failure. At every stage, the investigation gets more and more certain, less and less open to contradiction. Even when Poole is arrested, even when he confesses to multiple rapes, nobody links him to the Thompson case until years later."

The next slide is a copy of a police report, with passages highlighted:

- "Cotton has been positively identified."

- "No credible alternative suspects."

- "Alibi not corroborated."

Benham points to the phrase "No credible alternative suspects." "This is classic deductive closure. The evidence was never tested against Poole. The possibility was not even entertained in the reports. It was as if the other names never existed."

She advances to a photo: a faded picture of the courtroom, Thompson on the stand, Cotton at the table. "Thompson's testimony was rock solid, because the system had reinforced her confidence at every turn. Studies show that witness confidence goes up—not down—with each positive ID, even if the initial match was shaky. Memory becomes more certain with repetition."

The screen goes black, then a single word fades in: "1995." Below it, "DNA Evidence Available."

Benham's voice is soft. "Eleven years later, DNA testing finally exonerates Ronald Cotton. The real perpetrator was, of course, Bobby Poole."

She clicks to a final timeline. This one is thick at both ends, thin in the middle. "This is the arc of the case. Broad possibilities at the beginning, total focus by the midpoint, then—years later—broad possibilities again as the truth comes out. The tragedy is what happens in the thin part."

A hand in the back row. "Did anyone get in trouble for the mistake?" a male student asks.

Benham shakes her head. "No one was disciplined. No one lost their job. The process was followed, just a little too tightly."

She looks around the room, the kind of stare that is more challenge than invitation. "So. What would you have done differently?"

Silence at first. Then the student with the blue notebook offers: "Re-check the alibi. Interview everyone about the alternate suspects."

Benham nods. "And?"

"Have a second team review the evidence, without knowing the lead suspect," someone else says.

"Exactly," Benham says, a hint of satisfaction in her voice. "The problem wasn't malice. It was commitment. The team was so certain about Cotton that every new piece of evidence was seen through that lens. When exculpatory facts showed up, they were either minimized or ignored."

The screen now shows a side-by-side of Cotton and Poole, this time in color. The resemblance is striking. "The brain loves patterns," Benham says. "But the more you love a pattern, the more likely you are to fit everything to it—even the things that don't belong."

She lets the class take in the images for a long moment. "You need skepticism not just for others, but for your own process. Every time you lock in, ask what you're locking out."

She closes the session with a single slide: "11 years lost. 0 physical evidence. 1 witness, reinforced."

"Learn from this," Benham says, voice low and insistent. "You are the only thing standing between someone's life and the slow machinery of error."

The room stays still for a few seconds after she walks out, as if the gravity of the numbers hasn't quite finished dropping.

The following week, the seminar moves to a smaller classroom, the kind with moveable tables and glass walls. The vibe is less lecture, more forensic workshop: crime scene maps, colored markers, stacks of anonymized case folders. Professor Benham stands at a rolling whiteboard, diagramming what she calls "the pipeline of error."

"Let's walk through how an investigation gets tunnel vision," she says, drawing a long rectangle on the board. "At the very top, you have an incident—a robbery, a shooting, a fraud. Within hours, sometimes minutes, there's a working theory."

She writes "Initial Theory" in black at one end of the rectangle.

A few students shift in their seats, some already making notes, others waiting for the case study to drop.

"The theory isn't random," Benham continues. "It's based on what's in front of you: a suspicious neighbor, an ex-spouse, the last person seen with the victim. Sometimes the theory is suggested by a superior, or pulled from a hunch, or even a rumor."

She draws a triangle below the rectangle, narrowing to a point. "This is how attention funnels. First, you look for evidence that supports your theory. That's not always wrong—if the theory is good, you can build a case fast. But here's the catch." She taps the board. "Every new piece of evidence gets categorized as either 'supports my theory' or 'irrelevant.'"

She writes the categories in red: "ON THEORY" and "NOT RELEVANT."

"Suppose you have a burglary. The working theory is that the teenage son did it to buy drugs. So you start there. If the son has a history, if he hangs with bad friends, if he was out late the night before—it all goes in the 'on theory' bucket. But if his alibi is solid, if there's physical evidence that points to a different person, if a neighbor saw a different suspect, those get less weight."

She looks around. "Anyone want to push back?"

A student at the edge raises her hand. "Isn't it still the job to investigate the other leads?"

Benham grins. "Absolutely. But time and again, the research shows that once a theory takes root, even smart investigators start bending new information to fit. Not out of malice, but out of habit. Confirmation bias is sticky."

She slides a folder across the table. "Here's a real case, anonymized. A string of pharmacy robberies in a medium city, same M.O.—masked guy, uses a note, threatens violence, never caught on camera."

She opens the file, spreading out incident reports. "The initial theory was an ex-employee. The first detective spent weeks digging up his old HR file, looking for motive, questioning former managers. When the DNA on the robbery note didn't match, it was labeled as 'inconclusive'—the paper could have been contaminated, maybe the robber wore gloves. When a witness said the robber sounded female, it was 'possible confusion due to stress.' The ex-employee, meanwhile, had an ironclad alibi for two of the three robberies, but the focus didn't shift. It took a year and three more robberies before the pattern broke and a completely different suspect was caught."

Benham points to a spot in the timeline. "Here's where the error locked in. After the second robbery, all new evidence was interpreted in light of the ex-employee theory. That's tunnel vision."

She invites the students to mark up the board. Soon it's covered in arrows, highlights, and post-it notes: "Ignored lead," "Alternate suspect never followed up," "DNA not persuasive."

Benham sits on the edge of a table, letting the class work for a minute. Then she asks: "What's the fix?"

A young man in the back offers, "Have a team review the evidence fresh, like a cold case squad."

"Good," Benham says. "Peer review is one solution. Another is to deliberately look for evidence that breaks your theory, not just what fits. It's called 'falsification,' and it's the only real way to guard against self-deception."

She erases the triangle, then redraws it—this time, with the narrowing point interrupted by a big red X. "Anytime you catch yourself binning evidence as 'not relevant' because it doesn't fit, you should stop and ask: what if my theory is wrong? What would this evidence mean then?"

She clicks to a slide of a pie chart: "Investigative Blindness—Sources." The largest wedge is "Initial Theory Bias (46%)," with the next "Confirmation by Peer (22%)," followed by "Resource Constraints (18%)," and "External Pressure (14%)."

"The big slice," Benham says, pointing with her marker, "is still the working theory bias. It's easy to say, 'Not me, I'm careful,' but even the best get trapped."

She shares an anecdote. "A detective I know spent years teaching that you should 'follow the evidence, not your gut.' Then his own case blew up—he'd ignored a key phone log because it contradicted his timeline. When the error came out, he realized he'd never even written it down. The mind edits as it goes."

She cues up a video: a clip from a police bodycam, muted and captioned. Two officers interview a robbery victim who insists the suspect was “really short, maybe five-four.” The officers nod but ask her again and again, “Could he have been taller? Six foot or so?” The victim shakes her head each time. The next morning, the suspect—six foot one—is arrested, and the statement is written as “Height: Uncertain.”

Benham lets the clip play out, then pauses. “Even eyewitnesses get bent by what the questioner wants. The problem is contagious.”

A hand in the front row. “How do you keep from falling into the trap?”

Benham answers with practiced crispness. “First, keep an open file for every alternative theory, no matter how weird. Second, have at least one team member whose job is to attack the main theory—argue the other side, devil’s advocate style. Third, at regular intervals, do a blind review: have someone uninvolved go over the case and see what jumps out.”

She lists them on the board, bold and underlined:

- Alternate Theories File

- Devil's Advocate Role

- Blind Review Protocol

She adds a fourth: "Be suspicious of certainty. The moment you feel 100% sure, you are probably missing something."

A low chuckle moves through the room.

Benham brings up the last slide: a quote from a wrongful conviction report—"The biggest danger is not what you don't know, but what you know for sure that isn't so."

She looks at the room, softer this time. "Your job is not to be right. Your job is to be correct. If that means starting over, so be it."

The class breaks into clusters, each group dissecting the case files in front of them, looking for places where the theory bent reality. Benham circles the room, nodding as students point out blind spots, debate motive, sketch out alternate timelines.

She knows the real test will come years later, when these students have cases of their own, budgets to watch, quotas to meet. For now, she just wants them to be a little less certain.

The session ends not with applause, but with the scribble of notes, the silent promise to try and do better next time.

The reform, when it comes, starts small. A pilot program in a mid-size department, a handful of detectives told to run every case as an "open evidence" file, no matter how obvious the culprit seems. There are grumbles—about paperwork, about slowing things down—but the captain, a convert to the new gospel, is relentless.

The detectives meet around a battered conference table, coffee gone cold in styrofoam cups, the air heavy with the day's accumulation of old sweat and printer ink. Each investigator brings a case file, but also a separate binder: "Alternate Theories."

First, they walk the room. Each case gets a five-minute summary, but then the rest of the table asks questions—deliberately, sometimes aggressively, pushing for holes in the story. The lead investigator is required to list at least two plausible alternate suspects, or if the case is too tight, to explain why all other options have been eliminated.

After the walk-through, every scrap of collected evidence is logged—printouts, videos, scribbled notes, anonymous tips. Nothing is discarded. If a witness makes a statement that sounds bizarre, it goes in the log, flagged for context but not filtered out. If a suspect has an alibi, it's chased down with the same urgency as any accusation. The evidence log is a living document, time-stamped, with each addition signed off by the person who added it.

At set intervals—one week, two weeks, every new major break—the case goes up for review by an independent peer, someone with no skin in the game. The peer's job is to try to poke holes, to champion the ignored possibilities, to act as "the defense" before the actual defense ever sees the file.

This is the inductive approach in practice, and it is, at first, a mess. The logs swell with information, the board in the squad room fills with sticky notes, and the weekly reviews run twice as long as before. But something else happens, too. Investigators catch their own errors sooner. The "slam dunk" cases get double-checked, and sometimes, a whole theory is tossed before it even gets to the prosecutor. In the first year, the unit overturns two internal "solves" before charges are filed—one, a mistaken ID by a traumatized victim, the other, a burglary pinned on a neighbor with a record, later shown to be out of state at the time.

In the training seminars, Benham returns as a guest, walking the new recruits through the protocols. She lays out the golden rules, each one carved from the failures of the past:

- Log every fact, whether it makes sense or not.

- Never treat a theory as a fact until it is confirmed from multiple, independent lines of evidence.

- Schedule regular "break your own case" sessions, where someone else attacks your theory.

- Keep alternate suspect files alive until all are disproven.

- Celebrate every time you prove yourself wrong—because it means you got it right in the end.

In the room, the veterans are at first skeptical, but over time, the tone shifts. A detective who once bristled at being second-guessed now volunteers for the peer review slot. Another, famous for her "gut," starts each case with a checklist taped to her dashboard: "What am I missing? Who else could it be? What doesn't fit?"

They start to see the benefits in real time. A domestic assault case, seemingly airtight, is paused when a review reveals the lead witness changed her story after an off-the-record call with the investigating officer. The detail triggers a secondary interview, where the witness admits to fabricating part of her story out of fear. The wrong person, it turns out, would have been convicted—and nearly was.

A cold case is revived when an overlooked note, logged but ignored, points to a new pattern. The log, once a burden, becomes the best tool for finding what others missed.

When reporters ask about the new approach, the captain sums it up: "We're not in the business of closing cases. We're in the business of getting it right. Sometimes that's slower, but it's better for everyone."

The department tracks the numbers. In two years, clearance rates remain steady, but the number of post-arrest corrections—cases dropped before trial, exculpatory evidence found late—falls by half. Complaints about bias and "railroading" drop, too.

The real payoff is harder to measure. The detective who lost a conviction when his theory was busted doesn't take it as a defeat; he brings the story to the next academy class, warning the cadets not to get "drunk on your own brilliance." The squad rooms are a little less tense, the reviews a little less adversarial. No one calls it perfect, but no one wants to go back.

At the end of a particularly long review session, the board is covered in lines of colored yarn, sticky notes curling at the edges. Benham, packing up her slides, sees a new addition to the squad's bulletin board:

"BE SKEPTICAL. BE THOROUGH. BE HONEST."

Underneath, someone has drawn a cartoon detective with a magnifying glass, staring at his own feet.

As the sun sets behind the administrative block, the only thing left in the room is the hum of the evidence fridge, the slow accumulation of lessons learned, and the growing conviction that real justice takes time—and more than a little humility.

CHAPTER 6

Words As Weapons: How Suggestive Questioning Alters Reality

The conference room is designed for authority. Its walls, soundproofed in navy felt and ringed with LED uplights, give off an antiseptic glow. Four dozen law enforcement professionals occupy the arc of modular chairs: lieutenants and detectives, a handful of prosecutors in trim suits, two techs in polo shirts sporting agency crests. At the center of the horseshoe, a digital screen the size of a pool table floats above a slender podium, waiting for the speaker to begin.

At 0900 sharp, Dr. Miranda Chen steps to the podium. Her hair is clipped back in a severe barrette, and her suit is charcoal, the only adornment a white enamel pin shaped like a question mark. She speaks into the room's ambient array, her voice coming from everywhere and nowhere.

"Thank you for coming," she begins, hands resting on the edge of the plexiglass lectern. "Today's workshop: 'Language, Suggestion, and the Engineering of Memory.' If you think this sounds theoretical, don't worry. By the end of the day, we'll be talking about your own casework—past, present, and future."

A scatter of skeptical laughter from the back row. Dr. Chen ignores it, flicking the first slide into existence:

EVIDENCE IN QUESTION: HOW WORDS SHAPE WITNESS MEMORY

The title is followed by an old black-and-white photograph: a group of 1970s college students, one arm in a sling, standing in front of a battered Ford Mustang. The caption: "Loftus et al., 1974."

"Most of you know her name," Chen says, "but let's begin at the beginning. Elizabeth Loftus. Stanford. The mother of the modern false memory movement. In the early studies, she showed a room of volunteers a short film of a car crash—two vehicles, a stop sign, a spray of broken glass. Immediately after, she split the volunteers and asked them two versions of the same question. Group A: 'How fast were the cars going when they hit each other?' Group B: 'How fast were the cars going when they smashed into each other?'"

She advances to the next slide, a table of results:

Question phrasing	Mean estimate (mph)
"hit each other"	34
"smashed into each other"	41

"The only difference was a single word—'smashed' instead of 'hit'—but it increased the average speed estimate by seven miles per hour. More importantly: a week later, when asked if they remembered seeing broken glass at the scene, the 'smashed' group was twice as likely to say yes, even though there was none."

A few hands jot notes. Others fold arms or exchange wary glances.

Chen smiles, the kind of smile that means the real lesson is coming. "You might think, 'So what? People misremember details all the time.' But here's the point: that detail was not simply forgotten or guessed. It was constructed—built from a suggestion, made real by the power of language." She advances to a short video clip, a reenactment of the original Loftus experiment. The voices are dubbed, the colors slightly washed, but the effect is the same: a parade of college kids, each more certain than the last that there was glass, that it must have been there, that it would have made sense.

"Fast forward fifty years," Chen continues, "and these same mechanisms are at work in every interview room, every courtroom, every police report you write. The words you use—consciously or not—build memories in your witnesses' heads. Sometimes, those memories are more real to them than what they actually saw."

A sergeant in the third row raises a hand. "You're saying our questions make people lie?"

"I'm saying your questions can manufacture memories out of nothing," Chen replies. "The distinction between lying and confabulation is important. A liar knows the truth and hides it. A confabulator believes the memory completely, because it was built in response to the language you used."

She clicks to the next visual: a split-screen of two police interviews from a decades-old case. The left side is transcript only; the right, a video feed.

INTERVIEWER: "Did you see the man's gun?"

WITNESS: "Yes. He had a black pistol, I think."

INTERVIEWER: "And how would you describe it?"

WITNESS: "It was shiny. Maybe a revolver."

Chen points with her laser. "This is what we call presupposition. The question assumes a fact not yet in evidence—that the suspect had a gun. More than half the time, witnesses confronted with presuppositions will conform to them, even if they never saw the thing in question."

She scrolls down to the second transcript.

INTERVIEWER: “Did you see anything in the man’s hands?”

WITNESS: “No. I wasn’t looking there.”

INTERVIEWER: “Could he have had something?”

WITNESS: “Maybe. I can’t be sure.”

“This version,” Chen says, “is neutral. It doesn’t front-load the memory with expectation. The difference? The first interview produced a suspect description so convincing that it led to a ten-year sentence. The second—same event, different witness, neutral language—produced nothing useful for prosecution. The ‘gun’ was never found, because it never existed. But the first witness would have bet her life on it.”

She advances to a scatterplot of wrongful convictions, each dot mapped by year and source of error. The largest cluster is labeled “eyewitness error—suggestive language present.”

“As of last year, more than three-quarters of wrongful convictions in violent crime cases involved tainted or suggestively constructed eyewitness testimony. Most of those witnesses had no reason to lie. The problem was in the questions, not the answers."

The crowd quiets, pens stilled in midair.

Dr. Chen steps from behind the lectern, using her hands to punctuate the air. "Now, I want to teach you two terms. Both come from the language sciences, but you'll see them in your daily work."

She writes on the digital whiteboard:

WORD INTEGRATION

WORD SUBSTITUTION

"Word integration is when a new detail, not present in the original memory, is inserted during questioning and later recalled as if it were always there." She plays a clip from an experiment:

EXPERIMENTER: "Did you see the children getting on the school bus?"

SUBJECT: "Yes, there were two or three."

(But the original film had no bus at all.)

"In hundreds of trials, subjects exposed to these subtle inserts not only reported seeing the bus, but could describe its color, the number of windows, even the sound of its engine. The memory, once planted, felt as solid as the rest."

Chen gestures to the audience. "Anyone here never heard of word integration?" A few hands half-rise; most stay down. "Good," she says. "Now, word substitution is even sneakier. It happens when a detail is not invented outright, but replaced with a different one, subtly redirecting the witness's entire recall."

She flips to a photo array: a man in a blue jacket, a man in a black jacket, a woman in a red coat. "In lineup studies, if the interviewer refers to the suspect as 'the man in the blue jacket' during pre-lineup questioning, witnesses are nearly twice as likely to pick the blue-jacketed suspect—even if, in the original event, the perpetrator wore gray. This works with hair color, car models, even the time of day. Language primes the witness, and the memory shifts to accommodate the prompt."

A prosecutor in the back row calls out, "Isn't this just semantics?"

"Semantics is the whole point," Chen says. "A memory is not a video tape. It's a living, language-driven narrative that updates every time you access it. If you change the words, you change the story—sometimes forever."

She turns back to the room, catching the eyes of several officers who look less skeptical now, more uneasy. "So when you ask a witness, 'What was the man wearing when he pointed the gun at you?' you're doing two things: you're assuming a gun, and you're assuming the witness saw both the gun and the clothing at the same time. If they didn't, their brain will often fill in the gaps. Most won't even realize they're doing it."

Chen lets the silence settle, then advances to a final slide: a highlighted passage from a real-world case file.

OFFICER: "Did you see the white van near the bank before or after the robbery?"

WITNESS: "After, I think. It was parked by the side street."

But in the raw surveillance footage, there is no white van. None of the other witnesses mention one, until the first testimony goes public. After that, more than a dozen people remember seeing the van, and several even describe its make and model. The van becomes real in the mind of the investigation, triggering a search for a vehicle that never existed.

Dr. Chen turns off the projector. The room is quiet. She steps forward, arms relaxed at her sides.

"The lesson is simple, but not easy: Every word you choose shapes the witness's memory, for better or worse. Your job is to capture the facts, not rewrite them. The integrity of your case—of every case—depends on it."

A detective near the front raises a tentative hand. "What's the fix, then? How do we avoid doing this?"

Chen smiles, the hard kind, a warning and a reassurance in one. "We'll get there. But first, you need to see the problem as it really is. Tomorrow, we'll review how suggestive language has shaped actual convictions—and how it can be undone. For now, go back through your own interviews. Look for the places where you built a memory instead of finding one."

She checks her watch, then surveys the room. "That's all for this morning. See you at thirteen hundred."

As the chairs scrape back and the professionals file out, the screen remains dark, the digital whiteboard still displaying the two terms:

WORD INTEGRATION

WORD SUBSTITUTION

They hang in the air, a quiet indictment, waiting for the next session.

The next session opens with the click of LED panels brightening to surgical white. Dr. Chen stands not at the podium, but at a rolling display board, where she has mounted a series of transcript excerpts, each one highlighted in surgical blue. There is no preamble. The first line projected is a simple question:

Did you see a broken headlight?

She draws a rectangle around it, then, below, writes the alternate:

Did you see the broken headlight?

"Let's break this down," Chen says, marker in hand. "First, the neutral prompt. 'A broken headlight'—it's open, it allows for the possibility, but doesn't assume it exists. Now, see how it changes: 'the broken headlight'—that's a presupposition. It plants the idea that such a thing already exists, that it's a fact just waiting for recall."

She flips to the first transcript pair.

Transcript A:

INTERVIEWER: Did you see a broken headlight?

WITNESS: I'm not sure. I didn't notice one, but there might have been.

Transcript B:

INTERVIEWER: Did you see the broken headlight?

WITNESS: Yes, I think the one on the right was smashed.

Chen pauses. "Two otherwise identical witnesses. In lab settings, 46% of 'a broken headlight' subjects say yes. For 'the broken headlight,' that jumps to 74%. When you bring them back a week later, the difference is even larger. In the second group, almost all are certain there was a broken headlight, and many can recall which side it was on."

She calls up the raw data on the side screen:

- Neutral prompt: 46% recall, mostly tentative ("maybe," "not sure").

- Presupposed prompt: 74% recall, mostly confident, with new details ("right side," "looked fresh").

A hand from the audience, a detective with a salt-and-pepper mustache. "So it's just a trick of memory?"

Chen nods. "Not a trick—an engineering. You're shaping the structure of the memory as you ask. If the prompt is neutral, the memory stays tentative. If the prompt presupposes, the brain fills in to match."

She moves to the second pair.

How fast was the car going when it contacted the other vehicle?

How fast was the car going when it smashed into the other vehicle?

She circles "contacted" and "smashed," then underlines "the other vehicle" in both.

"In the original Loftus experiment, the mean speed estimate for 'contacted' was 32 mph. For 'smashed,' it was 41. But more than that, the word 'smashed' doubled the odds that witnesses remembered broken glass at the scene—even though there wasn't any."

She projects the paired transcripts.

Transcript C:

INTERVIEWER: How fast was the car going when it contacted the other vehicle?

WITNESS: Maybe 25, 30. It didn't look that bad.

Transcript D:

INTERVIEWER: How fast was the car going when it smashed into the other vehicle?

WITNESS: Oh, 45, maybe 50. It was a really bad hit.

Chen overlays the results:

Verb Used	Mean Speed (mph)	% Recalling Broken Glass
contacted	32	12%
bumped	34	14%
collided	38	32%
smashed	41	32%
hit	34	14%

"The only thing that changed was the verb. Every other detail in the scenario, every cue to the witness, was identical. But with a more violent verb, the event becomes more violent in the mind."

She lets the chart hang, then sweeps her pointer across the audience. "This is not theory. It's an empirical effect. The words you use calibrate the memory. If you use a more intense word, you get a more intense event—every time."

Another hand, a woman in a burgundy pantsuit. "But what about real witnesses? People on the scene, not in a lab?"

Chen advances to a third example, this one drawn from an actual field interview.

First, the neutral:

Was the man carrying anything?

Then, the loaded:

Was the man carrying a weapon?

She pairs two transcripts from a real robbery case.

Transcript E:

INTERVIEWER: Was the man carrying anything?

WITNESS: I don't think so. Maybe a bag, but I can't remember.

Transcript F:

INTERVIEWER: Was the man carrying a weapon?

WITNESS: Yes, he had a gun. Or a knife—something black, I think.

Chen highlights the crucial lines:

In the neutral prompt, 18% of witnesses said yes, but most were vague or unsure. In the suggestive prompt, 64% said yes, with a majority specifying a "gun," "knife," or "black object." In reality, security footage showed the suspect carrying nothing at all.

She presents the summary:

- Neutral prompt: 18% recall, most responses tentative.

- Suggestive prompt: 64% recall, most responses confident, often with fabricated detail.

She adds, "This effect holds even when the witness is a trained observer—a security guard, an off-duty cop. Suggestive language works on experts and civilians alike."

The room is quieter now. Several attendees flip through their own notebooks, making small marks.

Chen returns to the display. "These are not isolated incidents. We see the same effect across dozens of studies, hundreds of field cases. Every word you use either preserves the original memory, or builds a new one on the fly."

She scrolls to a final chart: a meta-analysis of 47 experiments on suggestive questioning. The line is stark, a diagonal ramp from "neutral" to "loaded" to "presupposed," each step up matched by a jump in witness certainty and inaccuracy.

A man near the aisle raises his hand. "So even asking a leading question once can change the memory?"

"Once is often enough," Chen says. "Repeated questions—especially with escalating language—can rewrite the whole event. But a single presupposition, at the right moment, sticks."

She lets the data linger. "You'll hear more about the consequences in the next session. For now, know this: Your language is a tool. Use it carelessly, and you contaminate the evidence. Use it precisely, and you protect the truth."

She scans the audience. "Questions?"

A long moment, then the room is still.

Chen caps her marker, sets it aside.

"Lunch in fifteen," she says. "Bring your own transcripts after break. We'll see how they measure up."

As the session breaks up, the transcript pairs remain on the board, blue rectangles around each prompt. On the screens, the data glows: verbs, percentages, and a warning in every number.

The room is dimmed to a bluish half-light. Attendees return from lunch with folders and laptops, some holding annotated case files, most looking alert in the afterglow of caffeine. On the main screen, a title slide reads:

CASE STUDY: THE BRENTWOOD CONVENIENCE STORE SHOOTING (2006–2015)

Dr. Chen waits until all are seated, then cues the next slide. "Today, we'll walk through a real case. Some of you may have read about it in the journals, but the lesson is in the details—especially the language of the interviews. This is not a simulation. Every transcript is from the actual investigation."

She advances to the first document: a police interview summary, dated two hours after the crime. A sidebar photo shows a young woman—early twenties, hair in a neat braid, face blank with exhaustion.

"The witness is Nicole Parsons. She worked the register at the Brentwood Food Mart. On May 2, 2006, two men robbed the store. During the scuffle, the owner was shot and killed. Nicole was in the cooler, stocking sodas, when it happened."

A bullet point summary:

- Two suspects, both masked

- Witness did not see the shooting

- Initial description: "Loud voices, one male, one possibly female"

Dr. Chen zooms to the first transcript.

INTERVIEW #1

DETECTIVE: You said you heard the voices before you came out?

PARSONS: Yes, yelling. I thought it was a fight.

DETECTIVE: You didn't see the shooters?

PARSONS: No, I was in the back. I only saw after, when they ran out.

DETECTIVE: What did you see then?

PARSONS: Two people, both wearing dark hoodies. One was taller than the other.

DETECTIVE: Anything else?

PARSONS: The shorter one had red shoes.

Chen annotates: "Notice the open prompts, the tentative recall. No leading questions yet."

She scrolls to INTERVIEW #2, three days later.

DETECTIVE: When you saw them running out, did you notice which one had the gun?

PARSONS: I don't know. Maybe the tall one? I think he was in front.

DETECTIVE: Could you see the gun in his hand?

PARSONS: Not really. Just, they were running.

DETECTIVE: Some witnesses say you saw the gun directly.

PARSONS: I... maybe. I was scared. I'm not sure.

Chen highlights: "Now we see mild presupposition—'which one had the gun' assumes a fact. Also, reference to 'other witnesses,' though at this stage there were none."

She brings up INTERVIEW #3, one week after the event.

DETECTIVE: Let's walk through it again. When you came out, where was the tall man?

PARSONS: At the front, by the door.

DETECTIVE: And the gun—was it pointed at you, or at the owner?

PARSONS: At the owner, I think.

DETECTIVE: Was it a big gun? Did you see the color?

PARSONS: Um, silver maybe? It was big, I remember that.

DETECTIVE: Was it a revolver?

PARSONS: Maybe. I don't really know guns.

Chen draws a digital box around the lines: "Gun appears in the testimony for the first time. Note: In forensic review, store video never showed a weapon, and the owner's wounds were consistent with a concealed derringer, not a large-caliber revolver."

She switches to INTERVIEW #4, after a suspect is arrested. The man in question, Antonio Graves, is nineteen, five-ten, with no record of firearms use.

DETECTIVE: Take a look at these photos. Do you recognize the man?

PARSONS: Maybe. He's the right height.

DETECTIVE: He has a history of armed robbery. When you saw him, did you think he looked dangerous?

PARSONS: I guess, yeah.

DETECTIVE: Did you see him holding a gun?

PARSONS: Yes—I mean, I think so. He was holding something.

DETECTIVE: Did you see a silver revolver in his hand?

PARSONS: Maybe. Yes. It must have been.

Chen lets the slide linger, then annotates in red: "Classic word integration and substitution. 'A gun' becomes 'a silver revolver,' seeded by prior questions. Certainty increases with each retelling."

She steps to the side. "At trial, Nicole Parsons testifies with conviction: 'Antonio Graves had a silver revolver, pointed at the owner. He threatened to shoot if the register wasn't opened.' There is no physical evidence—a gun is never recovered. But the jury finds Graves guilty, and he is sentenced to twenty-five years."

A voice from the audience, subdued: "Did he do it?"

Chen presses a key. "Eight years later, DNA from a dropped glove matches a different suspect, a parolee named Vernon Deeds. Deeds confesses, describes the weapon in detail—a derringer, stolen from a pawn shop, not a revolver. Graves is exonerated and released."

She brings up a final interview, conducted after Graves' release.

INTERVIEWER: How did you feel when you heard the testimony against you?

GRAVES: I didn't blame her. I could tell she believed it. The words sounded like the truth.

INTERVIEWER: What do you remember most about the interviews?

GRAVES: They asked the same questions, over and over, but each time the words were different. They started adding things. After a while, I thought maybe it really was me, or maybe I'd just forgotten everything.

Chen turns back to the audience. "The witness, Nicole Parsons, underwent therapy for years. She never understood how her memory changed. Even after the exoneration, she stood by her account—because it had become hers, even if it was built on suggestion."

She pauses, then speaks quietly. "This is the cost. A man lost eight years. A witness will never trust her own mind again. And all it took was a series of careless words."

The room is silent. Dr. Chen closes the slide deck, leaving only the title screen, blue and unblinking.

She addresses the group: "Every one of you will be in a position to plant a memory, or protect it. The language you use is the difference."

There are no questions. The case file sits, projected and still, as a warning and a charge.

The final session is a practicum. The room is reconfigured with round tables, each stacked with notepads, colored pens, and laminated cards. The walls are covered in butcher paper grids, labeled "PROMPT," "PITFALL," and "NEUTRAL FORM." Dr. Chen moves among the clusters, coaching, listening, correcting in real time.

On the main display, a heading:

GUIDELINES FOR NEUTRAL QUESTIONING

Chen addresses the group, voice firm. "We've seen how memory is shaped by language. Now, we'll learn to build questions that guard against contamination."

She cues the first side-by-side example.

LEFT: "Did you see the suspect's weapon?"

RIGHT: "Did you see anything in the suspect's hands?"

She circles the left prompt. "Problem: Assumes a weapon was present, even if the witness didn't see one. This is a classic presupposition. It can manufacture a false memory."

Then the right. "Neutral: Leaves open the possibility of nothing, or of something non-threatening. No assumptions."

She gestures for teams to practice rewriting. Voices overlap, some in agreement, others debating the finer points of phrasing.

Another pair appears on the wall.

LEFT: "Was the car going fast when it ran the red light?"

RIGHT: "How would you describe the car's speed?"

Chen annotates: "The first version introduces two biases: 'going fast' and 'ran the red light.' The second is open-ended and collects the witness's own impression."

A hand rises. "What if you need to clarify a point?"

Chen nods. "Always echo the witness's language before introducing new terms. For example—if a witness says, 'He was moving quickly,' ask, 'When you say quickly, what do you mean?' Do not paraphrase as 'So he was speeding?' unless they use that word."

She leads a rapid-fire round, reading problematic prompts and having the groups suggest neutral forms. The air is lively; the corrections, precise.

- "Did you notice the blue sedan at the intersection?" becomes "Did you see any cars at the intersection?"

- “Did you hear the suspect threaten the clerk?” becomes “Did you hear anything the suspect said to the clerk?”

- “Did you smell alcohol on the driver?” becomes “Did you notice any odors coming from the driver?”

Chen provides a list of red-flag words to avoid:

- “the” (when it presupposes existence)

- “weapon,” “gun,” “knife” (unless raised by witness first)

- “speeding,” “fleeing,” “attacking” (leading verbs)

- “before or after” (implies sequence witness may not have observed)

- “must have,” “obviously,” “clearly” (editorializing)

She hands out a checklist, laminated for durability:

NEUTRAL QUESTIONING CHECKLIST

- Use open-ended prompts ("Tell me what you saw," "Describe what happened")

- Avoid leading language or presuppositions

- Echo the witness's exact terms when following up

- Do not introduce details not volunteered by the witness

- Pause after the answer; allow witness time to elaborate

- If clarification is needed, restate in the witness's own words first

- Review transcripts for red-flag words before submission

On the side display, she brings up recent research. A chart shows "Statement Consistency" and "Wrongful Conviction Rate" for three midwestern police departments over five years. The units that adopted the neutral questioning protocol saw a 40% drop in retracted or revised statements, and a 28% decrease in cases referred for potential wrongful conviction review.

Chen notes: "These aren't just numbers. Every improved interview is a life less disrupted, a case less likely to collapse under scrutiny."

She cues a recorded interview as a capstone. The screen shows a calm interviewer, hands folded, using open prompts throughout.

INTERVIEWER: Can you walk me through what happened, in your own words?

WITNESS: I was across the street. I saw two people arguing.

INTERVIEWER: Tell me more about what you saw and heard.

WITNESS: One of them, the shorter person, raised his hand, but I didn't see anything in it. The other yelled and ran.

INTERVIEWER: Did you notice any objects, or what the raised hand was doing?

WITNESS: Just waving, I think. No objects.

The display splits: the original witness recall, and the final report. They match almost perfectly.

Chen underlines the result. "This is what we aim for. Unfiltered memory, collected with care."

She closes the session. "The only safeguard against suggestion is vigilance. Every word you use is a tool—wield it with intent."

The attendees gather their notes, some still murmuring over best practices and checklists. On the wall, the butcher paper grids are filled with clean, neutral prompts. There are fewer red flags now, more green circles and underlined improvements.

As the group disperses, the neutral questioning checklist is visible on every table, clipped to folders or tucked into pockets.

Chen lingers at the board, erasing stray marks, then pauses. She adds one final line to the top of the checklist, in marker:

BE HONEST—WITH THEM, AND WITH YOURSELF.

She caps the marker, steps back, and surveys the room.

In the end, the record is only as good as the questions that built it.

CHAPTER 7

Exploiting The Vulnerable: Interrogation Tactics And Disadvantaged Suspects

The room is designed for confession. Four cinderblock walls, painted a shade of blue so flat it could be an absence, meet in the middle at a metal table. Fluorescent tubes overhead buzz so faintly they might be inside your own skull. There are no windows, just the hollow presence of a one-way mirror. The recording equipment sits in the corner, lights dark, cable unplugged from the wall.

Marcus is seated at the table, palms down, eyes locked on the scuffed stainless surface. He is twenty-two, short, with the broad face and almond eyes of Down syndrome. His hair is cropped tight to the scalp, and the right sleeve of his sweatshirt is chewed to string by anxious teeth. He wears shoes with Velcro straps and a name badge on a lanyard—MARCUS, in black block letters, a faded smiley face next to it.

Across from him, two detectives arrange themselves in careful geometry. The older one, stubble-gray and heavyset, leans back in his chair, hands folded across his belly. The other is younger, clean-cut, with eyes like chipped marble. They introduce themselves as Officer Paul and Officer Vince, their names spoken slowly and loudly, as if Marcus is not just hearing impaired but foreign to language itself.

The first words out of their mouths are not questions, but instructions:

"We're just going to talk for a while, Marcus. Okay? Just talking. Nothing to worry about."

Marcus nods, eyes on the table.

"You know why you're here, right?" This is Paul, the heavyset one, enunciating each syllable.

Marcus shakes his head. "No," he says, voice thin and barely audible.

Vince leans in. "It's about the store. The one on Main. You were there that night, weren't you, buddy?"

Marcus blinks, unsure. "No, I—I don't go there."

Paul claps his hands together, startlingly loud. "We have you on camera, Marcus. You're not in trouble, but we need to know what happened. You get that?"

Marcus's left foot begins to bounce under the table. He glances at the glass wall, then at the door, then back down. "Can I have water?" he asks.

Vince stands, crosses the room, and returns with a cone of water from the cooler. He places it just out of Marcus's reach, then slides it across the table with a practiced flick. "Here you go, pal."

Marcus sips, spilling most of it down his sweatshirt.

Paul resumes. "You were there with your friend, right? Jake? You guys went after work."

Marcus nods reflexively. Then hesitates. "Jake is my friend," he agrees. "But I go home after work. I eat dinner."

Vince makes a show of jotting this down. "But sometimes you hang out, right? After you finish at the center?"

A pause. "Yes. We go to the movies sometimes."

"But this time, you went to the store. At night. After hours."

Marcus fidgets with the lanyard. "I don't think so."

Vince: "It's okay if you don't remember. Sometimes it's hard. But it's good to tell the truth. That's the only way to make things better. You want to make things better, don't you?"

Marcus nods, barely.

Paul folds his hands. "Let's go slow, Marcus. Just yes or no."

A beat, then: "Did you go to the store after it was closed?"

Marcus shakes his head.

Paul: "Are you sure? It's okay to say yes."

Marcus nods, then shakes his head again, looking between them, unsure which is the right answer.

Vince smiles. "You're doing great, Marcus. Really good. Sometimes people just get confused. Maybe you were with Jake, and Jake wanted to go in. You just wanted to help, right?"

"Jake said he needed a snack," Marcus says, voice even smaller. "I was waiting."

"There you go!" Vince says, loud enough to make Marcus wince. "So you waited outside, while Jake went in?"

A long silence. Marcus tries to remember the script of his day, but the question sits on his tongue like wet cotton.

Paul supplies the answer. "So maybe you saw Jake go in, and then he called you to help. Maybe he was scared. Did you go inside, Marcus?"

"Yes," Marcus says, nodding now, desperate for approval. "I went inside."

Paul writes this down in block capitals. "You're a good kid, Marcus. No one's mad at you. We just want to know what happened next. Did you see what Jake did?"

Marcus shrugs. "He took chips. And soda."

Vince: "Did he break anything?"

A frown. "I don't think so."

Paul: "You didn't see him break the register?"

Marcus hesitates. "No. Maybe. He said it was open."

Vince leans in, conspiratorial. "It's better if you just tell us, Marcus. Did you and Jake take the money?"

"No," Marcus says, then, when both detectives stare at him, "I think he did. Not me."

Paul: "But you were there."

Marcus nods, then shakes his head. "I was at home. I eat dinner with my house."

The two detectives exchange glances. Paul circles back.

"Okay, Marcus. Here's what we have. You and Jake go to the store. It's closed, but Jake wants chips. Jake goes in, you follow. Jake breaks the register, takes money. You see him do it, right?"

Marcus licks his lips, which are dry and cracked. "Yes," he says, voice hollow.

Paul: "That's good, Marcus. We know it's scary. But telling the truth is always better."

Vince: "If you just sign here, we can help you get home. You want to go home, right?"

Marcus nods.

Paul slides a form across the table, already filled out. "Just write your name on the line. You know how to do that?"

Marcus picks up the pen, his grip childlike, tongue protruding in concentration as he scrawls "MARCUS" in shaky, careful letters. He is sweating now, sweat collecting in the folds of his neck and on the backs of his hands. His foot bounces again under the table, double-time.

Vince caps the pen for him. "Great job, Marcus. We're almost done."

Paul glances at the unplugged recorder, then at Vince. "One more thing, Marcus. We need to read you your rights, just to make it official. Do you understand what it means when someone reads you your rights?"

Marcus, face blank, nods.

Paul recites the Miranda warning in slow, segmented language. "You have the right to remain silent. That means you don't have to talk to us if you don't want to. Do you understand?"

Marcus nods.

"Anything you say can and will be used against you. That means what you say can be used in court. Do you understand?"

Another nod, this one slower, more hesitant.

"You have the right to an attorney. That means a lawyer. If you can't afford a lawyer, one will be given to you. Do you understand?"

"Yes," Marcus says, because that is what he is supposed to say.

Vince smiles, kind and false. "You're really smart, Marcus. Most people don't get it the first time."

Paul: "So you understand that you can talk to us, or not talk to us. It's up to you."

"Yes," Marcus repeats, softer now.

Paul closes the folder. "That's all we need, Marcus. You did good."

They leave him alone in the room, door shut, recorder still dark. Marcus sits for a long time, staring at the name he has written. He is not sure what he has confessed to, only that he has done what was asked of him.

In the hallway, the two detectives stand in silence. Vince says, "Open and shut," and Paul nods, satisfied.

Inside the interrogation room, Marcus pulls at the edge of his sleeve until the fabric comes away in soft, unraveling threads. He picks at the paper cup, crushing it until the water leaks out and runs in a thin line across the table. When the door finally opens, and a uniformed officer comes to walk him out, Marcus wipes the tears from his face and says, "Thank you," as he has been taught.

The confession, signed and dated, is left behind. It sits in the file, clean and perfect, a monument to the precision of the process.

In another room, the detectives record the summary of the case. The confession is highlighted, double underlined.

There is no mention of the contradictions, or the way Marcus's answers were shaped like wet clay.

The case, for all practical purposes, is closed.

The auditorium is half full, though the air has the density of a complete sellout. Students, faculty, and the occasional uniformed observer cluster in padded rows beneath a battered gold crest: State University, Founded 1919. On the front wall, the projection screen flickers with the opening slide:

False Confessions and the Vulnerable Mind

Dr. Elena Vasquez stands at the lectern, hands braced on either side. Her hair is jet black, her glasses horn-rimmed and severe. She wears a tailored blazer in forensic gray. Behind her, the first slide morphs into a bar chart, its data points painted in bright, condescending colors.

"Let's start with the numbers," she says, voice clipped but not unkind. "In studies conducted between 2003 and 2019, people with intellectual disabilities were four to five times more likely to make a false confession than their neurotypical peers."

She lets the stat hang, shifting to the next slide: a heat map of the United States, certain states pulsing with a sickly orange.

"Most of these cases," Dr. Vasquez continues, "involved the same basic pattern. A suspect with limited cognitive ability is subjected to standard interrogation protocols. These protocols were never designed with vulnerability in mind."

She clicks the remote. A bullet-point list appears:

- Extended questioning

- Suggestive language

- Repetition of false evidence

- Simplified, sometimes misleading, explanations of legal rights

She points with the remote. "The combination is devastating. In almost every documented case, the suspect tried to comply with what they thought the police wanted to hear. Not because they understood the accusation, but because they wanted to please the authority in the room."

On the side wall, a row of grad students tap notes into laptops, the rhythm as precise as a metronome. In the fourth row, a uniformed officer writes in longhand, underlining the word "suggestibility" three times.

Dr. Vasquez advances to a new slide: a photograph of a standard police interview room—blue cinderblock, metal table, digital recorder.

"Here's what happens," she says. "The suspect—let's call him A.—is brought into the room. The officers start with open-ended questions, but quickly, as A. struggles to provide detail, they shift to leading prompts."

A video window opens on the slide. A young man, broad face and thick wrists, sits at a table. He is asked about a robbery. At first, he shakes his head, says he was home. The officers smile and nod, then repeat the question, slightly altered: "You were at the store that night, right?" A. hesitates, nods. The officer brightens, says, "That's okay, just tell us what happened." By the end of the tape, the suspect is confessing to everything, even though the timeline shows he was nowhere near the scene.

Dr. Vasquez freezes the frame, then zooms on the suspect's face. "This is what we call 'acquiescence bias.' The tendency to agree with authority, especially under pressure."

She turns to the audience. "Anyone here ever heard of 'interrogative suggestibility'?"

A hand rises in the back, a middle-aged man in a faded corduroy blazer. "That's when a person's memory or statement is changed by how the question is asked?"

"Close," Vasquez says. "It's not just memory. It's the whole narrative. People with high suggestibility will alter their entire account to fit the interviewer's expectations—even if it means contradicting themselves. Especially if they feel it will please the authority figure."

She brings up another slide: a Miranda card, the legal warning in bold type.

"Now, Miranda rights. For most people, these are hard enough to understand. For someone with an intellectual disability, they're essentially meaningless. The reading level is college sophomore. The concepts—self-incrimination, right to silence—are so abstract that even many adults don't fully grasp them."

She clicks to a video split-screen. On the left, a standard recitation of rights to a typical suspect. On the right, the same script delivered to a young man with cognitive impairment.

Left side: The suspect nods, asks if he can have a lawyer present.

Right side: The young man blinks, nods, and says "Yes" after every line, even as he fails to process the meaning. When asked if he wants a lawyer, he says, "No, I don't want to get anyone in trouble."

Dr. Vasquez pauses the video. "The purpose of these warnings is to protect the suspect. But in practice, for vulnerable populations, they function as a formality—something to get past so the questioning can proceed. The safeguards are only real if the person understands them."

She transitions to a new slide: "Case Study—The Dillard Interview, 2014."

A transcript is projected, side-by-side with annotations in red.

OFFICER: Did you kill the man?

SUSPECT: No.

OFFICER: Are you sure? We have witnesses who say you did.

SUSPECT: I don't remember. Maybe.

OFFICER: Did you stab him with the knife?

SUSPECT: Yes, I think so.

OFFICER: Why did you do it?

SUSPECT: I'm sorry.

Each statement is bracketed: "Contradiction," "Compliance," "Yielding to Suggestion."

"This is the sequence, every time," Dr. Vasquez says. "Denial, suggestion, acquiescence, confession. For suspects with cognitive limitations, the threshold for confession is much lower, and the likelihood of retraction after legal counsel is nearly universal."

In the front row, a law student whispers to a neighbor, both staring at the slide with the air of those who have just discovered a cheat code for a rigged game.

Vasquez toggles to a comparative video. First, an interrogation of a neurotypical adult, who resists pressure for hours before finally requesting a lawyer. Next, a session with a suspect flagged as "mildly intellectually disabled." The suspect caves within thirty minutes, admitting to acts he never performed.

She lets the video roll, then stops at the twenty-minute mark. "Note the techniques: repeated questions, exaggerated gestures, the use of simplified statements—'We know you did it,' 'Your friend already told us,' 'You won't get in trouble if you say it now.' All of these are devastatingly effective on a vulnerable mind."

She steps away from the lectern, hands now open. "What's the takeaway?"

A hand, near the middle. "Standard techniques don't work on everyone."

"Exactly. The justice system relies on procedures developed for average, competent adults. But a huge segment of the population—up to 15%, depending on how you define vulnerability—falls outside that category. For these people, confession is not evidence. It's a symptom of a broken process."

She clicks to her final slide: a line graph charting exonerations of vulnerable suspects over the past decade. The line climbs year by year, a silent indictment.

Dr. Vasquez closes the laptop, folding her hands on the lectern. "Until we redesign our procedures to account for cognitive difference, we will keep producing false confessions. We will keep convicting the innocent. And we will keep telling ourselves it's a fair process."

The room holds its breath. Then, a slow, reluctant applause builds from the front row, spreading outward, as if the audience is uncertain whether this is a presentation or a warning.

As the crowd filters out, Dr. Vasquez remains at the lectern, answering questions from a small knot of law students and a reporter from the campus newspaper. Her tone is calm, almost resigned. She has given this talk a hundred times. The data never changes.

At the back of the hall, the uniformed officer closes his notebook, tears off a page, and stares at the word he has underlined.

Suggestibility.

He folds the note and pockets it. Out in the hallway, the rest of the world moves at regular speed.

Inside, the record keeps building, case by case, confession by confession, just as the numbers say it will.

The interview room is two sizes too small, windowless, with the stale chill of air recycled through a hundred interrogations. A recording unit, blinking red, is the only decoration. The table is dented steel. On one side sits Mrs. Nguyen, seventy-three, spine bent to a comma, hair swept into a neat bun. She wears a cardigan over a house dress, and her hands—fine-boned, trembling—are folded tightly in her lap.

Opposite her, Officers Mills and Rourke scan a printout of the incident report. Mills is older, his voice permanently hoarse from years of shouting over bad radios. Rourke is newer, with a cop's haircut and an air of forced patience.

"Okay, Mrs. Nguyen," Mills begins, speaking at half speed, "we want to talk about what happened last Thursday. Do you understand?"

Mrs. Nguyen smiles, hesitant, and nods. "Yes, yes. Thursday. Very—very much trouble."

Mills checks the box on the intake form marked "English Proficiency: Limited." Department policy requires an interpreter if the interviewee requests one or if communication proves difficult. Mills has decided neither is the case.

"Can you tell us, in your own words, what happened with your neighbor?"

Mrs. Nguyen's accent is thick, vowels clotted together. "He come to my house, very angry. Bang door. He say—he say I make too much noise. I say, not me. He shout. He try open door. I—" She makes a shoving gesture, then hesitates, searching for the word. "I... push?"

Rourke: "Did you push him, or did you threaten him?"

She blinks, not understanding the distinction. "He is—he is very angry. I afraid. I just say go home."

Mills leans in, voice louder. "Mrs. Nguyen, did you threaten your neighbor with a knife?"

Mrs. Nguyen's eyes widen. "Knife? No, no. I cut vegetable. He see, maybe, but I not threaten. I just cooking. Knife in hand, yes, but not for him. For—" she pantomimes chopping, "for cabbage."

Rourke scribbles in his notepad: "Admits to holding knife."

Mills: "So you had the knife in your hand when you opened the door?"

Mrs. Nguyen: "I—door open, yes. Knife in hand, yes. Because I cut. But not threaten, no."

Mills repeats, slower: "You. Had. The. Knife. When. You. Saw. Him."

Mrs. Nguyen nods, eager to show she is paying attention. "Yes, yes. But not for him. For me—my food."

Mills: "But you admit you had a knife."

"Yes, yes," she says again, smiling, hoping this is the right answer.

Rourke sets down his pen. "Okay, Mrs. Nguyen, did you say anything to your neighbor that sounded like a threat?"

She cocks her head. "Threat? What meaning, please?"

Mills exchanges a look with Rourke, then pantomimes a stabbing motion. “Did you do like this?”

Mrs. Nguyen recoils, startled. “No, no, no. Never. I just say, go, please. I scared.”

Mills: “But you had the knife. And you opened the door. And you shouted at him?”

Mrs. Nguyen, voice quavering: “He so loud. I afraid. I say go home. Only this.”

The interview limps forward. Every question is repeated, each time louder, as if volume is a bridge across the language gap. Mrs. Nguyen grows more anxious, nodding and agreeing to anything that seems to end the questioning. When Mills asks, “Did you threaten him?” she says, “Yes, yes,” because that is what he seems to want.

“See? Got her,” Mills mutters to Rourke, who grunts in agreement.

They push the confession form across the table. “Sign here,” Mills says, then pantomimes a pen in the air.

Mrs. Nguyen hesitates, then scrawls her name in trembling English letters. She smiles, hopeful for approval.

Mills stands, satisfied. "You can go home now, Mrs. Nguyen."

She nods, gathers her bag and leaves, pausing at the door for a last uncertain glance. The hallway is cold and empty.

Inside the room, the officers review the recording.

"Classic case," Mills says. "They never say it straight, but you just gotta break it down for them."

Rourke nods. "She definitely threatened him. Confessed, even."

They close the file. No mention is made of the missing interpreter, or of the policy requiring one. The recording will be enough for prosecution, they assume.

Mrs. Nguyen rides the bus home, hands still shaking. She cannot remember what she has admitted, only that she has failed to make herself understood.

The next day, the confession is entered into evidence, one more unassailable brick in the wall of the case.

In the training manual, under "Best Practices for Non-Native Speakers," the advice is clear: Use simple language. Repeat as necessary. Obtain confession.

But nothing in the manual covers the space between words, or the chasms opened by silence.

For Mrs. Nguyen, the memory of the knife is nothing compared to the sharpness of her own confusion.

It will be months before she realizes what she has signed.

The room is windowless, painted the color of institutional neglect. A bare bulb hums overhead, casting shadows on cinderblock. On one side, a plastic chair bolted to the floor. In it sits Ryan, thirty-five, not tall but broad, his face drawn with the slackness of exhaustion. He is handcuffed to a steel ring, though he can barely sit upright.

The detective is named Keller, a man who has spent two decades learning the minute gradations between discomfort and suffering. He wears a windbreaker over a cheap suit, and sits across from Ryan with a spiral notebook and a bottle of water. The bottle is unopened.

Ryan shakes, his hands vibrating so badly he cannot hold still even with the cuffs. His shirt is damp with sweat, and his breath comes in short, shallow bursts. He is in day two of detox, and the fever is starting to eat the edges of his vision.

Keller offers a cigarette. Ryan says nothing, just stares at the filter. Keller withdraws it.

"Let's talk about the fight," Keller says, voice even. "You were at O'Malley's, after midnight."

Ryan closes his eyes. "Need a doctor," he mumbles.

Keller ignores this. "You remember what happened?"

"Need a doctor," Ryan repeats, louder now, his voice almost a plea.

"We'll get you help as soon as we finish here," Keller says, making a note in the spiral. "The faster we do this, the faster you get out of here. Deal?"

Ryan swallows, Adam's apple bobbing. "Deal," he says.

Keller opens the file. "Security footage shows you at the bar. We know you got into it with the victim. Just need you to walk me through it."

Ryan's eyes roll in his head. He is sweating through the plastic chair, and the shaking is worse. "Didn't want to fight," he says. "Just wanted a drink. He—he pushed me."

"That's what he says," Keller replies. "But witnesses saw you throw the first punch. You see how that looks?"

Ryan's teeth are chattering. He says, "Just want to sleep. Just—please."

Keller unscrews the water, sets it on the table, just out of reach. "Tell me what happened, and you can have this."

Ryan focuses on the bottle. "He pushed me. Called me a bum. I—" He stops, fighting nausea. "I didn't mean to."

"But you did it. You hit him."

"Yeah," Ryan says, the word nearly a sob. "I hit him."

Keller slides the bottle closer. "Was that the only thing you did? Or did you hit him after he went down?"

Ryan shakes his head, but the motion is so weak it could be agreement or denial. "Just once. I think. I don't—"

"Your memory's fuzzy," Keller says, sympathetically. "That's the withdrawal. Makes it hard to remember."

Ryan nods. "Makes everything hard," he whispers.

Keller leans in. "You want to go to the hospital, right?"

Ryan nods again, violently.

"Okay," Keller says. "Just tell me you started the fight. You were angry, right? You lost control."

Ryan's lips tremble. He can barely form words. "I started it," he says. "I was angry."

Keller writes this down. "See, that wasn't so bad. One more thing: did you mean to hurt him?"

Ryan is weeping now, though he doesn't know why. "No. I swear."

Keller hands him the water. "I believe you."

The interview ends. Keller stands, closes the file, and waves in the nurse. Ryan is taken to the infirmary, where he vomits twice and passes out. When he wakes up, he is in a holding cell. He has no memory of what he said, only that the pain is less and the lights are not as bright.

Two days later, the confession is typed and submitted to the court.

Three weeks after that, security footage is retrieved. It shows Ryan trying to break up the fight, not start it. But by then, the statement is on the record, and Ryan has signed his name to it.

The detective moves on to the next case. In the logbook, under "Confession Obtained," Keller makes a checkmark and closes the day's entries.

Ryan is released from jail with a warning, his record amended but his trust in memory permanently scarred.

The room is cleaned, the chair wiped down, the handcuffs reset. By evening, another suspect will sit in it, shivering, waiting for the pain to end.

The system is efficient. It knows how to extract what it needs.

And sometimes, it knows how to wring the truth from agony.

The courtroom is cathedral-quiet, its walls paneled in dark wood, the ceiling crosshatched with beams the color of old coffee. At the far end, under the seal of the state, Judge Harriet Chen presides from a raised dais. She is in her early sixties, hair silver, expression unreadable behind wire-rimmed glasses. On her left, the American flag; on her right, the state's. The gallery is packed with law students, their laptops open, ready to score every maneuver.

At counsel table, the defendant sits between his attorneys. He is called James in the transcript, but his file lists three other names—aliases, or perhaps artifacts of a fractured identity. He is gaunt, with eyes that dart at invisible cues. His hands flutter on the tabletop, never at rest.

Judge Chen brings the hearing to order. "We are here today to consider the admissibility of the defendant's confession," she intones. "The defense will proceed."

Michael Okonkwo, lead defense counsel, stands. He is a big man, with a resonant baritone and a gift for measured outrage.

"Your Honor, we contend that the confession obtained from Mr. James was the product of coercion and—more importantly—of his diagnosed schizophrenia. We submit that the statements were involuntary and, by every standard, unreliable."

He calls his first witness: Dr. William Reeves, forensic psychiatrist.

Reeves is brisk, almost military in his bearing. He takes the stand, recites his credentials—Harvard, three books, a lifetime on the expert circuit. Okonkwo leads him through the basics: diagnosis, history, symptomatology.

"Dr. Reeves, can you explain how Mr. James's mental illness might affect his responses to questioning?"

Reeves nods. "Schizophrenia is a disorder of both perception and cognition. In a psychotic episode, the individual's ability to distinguish reality from delusion is severely compromised."

"And would this affect his understanding of, say, a police interview?"

"Profoundly," Reeves says. "He may interpret neutral questions as threats. He may experience auditory hallucinations that instruct him to comply. Or—" Reeves glances at the jury box, making sure to capture the law students' attention— "he may be so overwhelmed by internal stimuli that he will say anything to stop the process."

Okonkwo: "Are people with schizophrenia more likely to confess falsely?"

Reeves: "Much more likely. Their impulse is to relieve distress, not to communicate truth. This is especially true if the interrogator employs pressure or appeals to delusional beliefs."

Okonkwo approaches the stand. "You reviewed the video of Mr. James's interrogation. What did you observe?"

Reeves shifts in his seat, then begins: "The officers quickly picked up on Mr. James's paranoia. He believed he was being targeted by a government conspiracy. Rather than correct this, the detectives leaned in—they told him that 'admitting to the crime' would help them protect him from the others. This tactic—while not illegal—was, in my view, an exploitation of his psychosis."

He glances at the judge. "It is not a voluntary confession if the suspect believes that confession is necessary to survive."

Judge Chen scribbles notes, never looking up.

The prosecutor is named Jacobs. She is sharp, sharp-voiced, and never misses a gap.

"Dr. Reeves, you agree that the confession contains facts only the perpetrator would know?"

"Some facts, yes. But many were fed to Mr. James during questioning. Others are details drawn from his own delusions."

Jacobs: "But he knew where the knife was hidden."

"That was suggested to him multiple times during the interrogation," Reeves replies. "He was led to the answer, often by accident."

Jacobs tries again: "You're not saying the police acted in bad faith?"

"Not at all," Reeves says. "But the methods were not designed for a suspect in psychosis."

Jacobs thanks the doctor, returns to her table.

Judge Chen motions Okonkwo to sum up. He stands, voice heavy. "The case law is clear. If a confession is not voluntary—if it is the product of mental disease or coercion—it is not admissible. The question is whether Mr. James had the capacity to understand what he was saying, and whether the officers respected his limitations."

He sits.

Jacobs rises, her face set. "The state submits that Mr. James was Mirandized, that he gave a detailed confession, and that his statements were corroborated by physical evidence."

Judge Chen nods, then calls a recess to consider.

The gallery erupts in murmurs. Law students debate the merits, some betting on exclusion, others on a split ruling. The bailiff hushes them with a glare.

After forty minutes, Chen returns.

"Having reviewed the record, the transcript, and the testimony of Dr. Reeves, the court finds as follows: The reliability of confessions obtained from mentally ill suspects without proper safeguards is fundamentally questionable. The detectives, though acting in good faith, failed to recognize the severity of the defendant's impairment."

She pauses, lets the silence fill.

"This court cannot admit the confession into evidence. The motion to suppress is granted."

A flash of surprise from the prosecution. Okonkwo's jaw tenses, but his relief is visible.

James does not react, his gaze fixed on a point in the middle distance. It is unclear whether he understands what has happened.

In the gallery, a law student types, "Mental illness = confession suppressed," and underlines it twice.

Judge Chen adjourns. As the parties file out, the only sound is the shuffle of paper and the scrape of chairs.

Outside, the sky is dark, the city lights reflected in the polished glass of the courthouse. Okonkwo stands with Dr. Reeves, both speaking in low tones. Jacobs walks alone to her car, already plotting the next angle.

Inside, the room is reset for the next case. The confession, so painstakingly extracted, is rendered moot by the process.

But the precedent is made. And in the files of a hundred defense attorneys, the ruling is printed out, highlighted, and underlined for future use.

On the record, the victory is narrow. But for James, and those like him, it is the only protection the system allows.

Judge Chen lingers on the bench, reviewing the next day's docket, her face the same as when she delivered the ruling: precise, and without visible regret.

The justice system grinds on, but the rules have shifted, just a little.

And for now, that is enough.

The classroom at the police training center smells of dry-erase ink and yesterday's coffee. Rows of modular desks face a wall-mounted projection screen, and the air hums with the tension of forty officers who would rather be anywhere else. At the front, Captain Robert Torres checks the time, then slaps a stack of laminated cards onto the podium.

"Let's get started," Torres says. He has the build of an ex-linebacker, a close-cropped mustache, and a voice that can clear a bar at last call. The wall behind him flashes with the title slide: INTERROGATION PROTOCOLS: VULNERABLE POPULATIONS.

He paces the front row. "By now, you've all heard about the new rules. But it's one thing to read a policy; it's another to do it right, under pressure. Today, we're going to make sure you know the difference."

A groan ripples through the room. Torres ignores it.

He points at the first bullet on the screen: ALL CUSTODIAL INTERVIEWS MUST BE RECORDED, START TO FINISH.

"That means no more 'off the record' chats," Torres says, glaring at a sergeant with a reputation. "You roll tape before the suspect walks in, and you keep it rolling until they walk out."

He waves a remote, and a training video stutters to life. Two actors in uniform demonstrate how to set up the AV equipment—camera placement, microphone check, timestamp confirmation. The officers in the room watch with a mix of boredom and envy for the actors' easy day.

Torres clicks the next slide. "Let's talk about Miranda. Everyone in this room has it memorized. Now you're going to learn how to say it so anyone—no matter their background—can understand."

He holds up a card, reading slowly: "You do not have to answer questions. If you want to, that's your choice. You can stop anytime. If you want a lawyer, just ask. One will help you, even if you don't have money."

A hand goes up, half-mocking. "Captain, that's baby talk."

Torres grins, not kindly. "That's the point. Last year, we had two confessions thrown out because the suspects couldn't read past third grade. If you want your case to stick, you speak at their level, not yours."

He divides the class into pairs. "Role-play time. One of you is the officer, the other is a suspect flagged for possible intellectual disability. Read the warning. Make sure they can repeat it back in their own words."

Reluctant at first, the officers cycle through the script. Some stumble over the simplified language; others get into character, dropping to a careful monotone.

Torres walks the aisles, correcting technique. "Keep it short. No legal jargon. If they can't explain it back, you start over."

After twenty minutes, he signals for quiet.

"Next up," he says, "interpreters and advocates."

The screen fills with a checklist:

- Certified interpreter must be present for non-native speakers.

- No family or friends in the room as substitute.

- Advocate required for suspects with documented cognitive or mental health diagnoses.

"Having a family member translate is not sufficient," Torres says, "unless you want your interview thrown out on a silver platter. Use the interpreter bank. They're trained to recognize legal terms, and they know how to flag when the suspect doesn't understand."

He passes out the laminated cards. Each has a flowchart: IF VULNERABILITY IS SUSPECTED, THEN...

Torres waits while the officers inspect the cards.

"These aren't just for show," he says. "You keep it in your wallet. Every time you question someone, you ask yourself: Can they follow what I'm saying? If not, you call in help."

A detective in the third row raises a hand. "What if we don't know? Some of them fake it."

Torres nods. "That's why we record the whole thing. If it's on video, and you did it by the book, no one can say you railroaded them. But if you cut corners—skip the interpreter, skip the advocate, or feed the suspect the story—you'll be out of luck, and probably in front of I.A."

He shifts gears. "Final point: the two-interview protocol."

On screen, a diagram: Interview One—Information Gathering. Interview Two—Confrontation.

Torres explains. "First interview, you ask open-ended, neutral questions. Get their version, without accusation. No confrontation, no pressure. Only after that, if the evidence supports it, do you move to confrontation. Keeps the statements clean, and helps weed out false confessions from people who just want to please."

He gestures to the board. "It's more work, but it works. Departments that piloted this cut their false confession rates by half in six months."

Torres lets the numbers hang in the air.

The room is quieter now. Some officers are still skeptical, but most are listening. Torres can tell by the way they hold their pens, the way their eyes narrow at the details.

He walks to the back, picking up stray copies of the old policy manual. "Look," he says, softer now. "I know it's a culture shift. But the world is watching, and so are the courts. You get it right here, or you get burned out there."

He dismisses the class with a wave. "You've got the cards, you've got the protocol, now go practice. Next week, we do it live, with actors. If you blow it, we start over."

The officers file out, some muttering, some silent. The cards go into wallets, pockets, a few tossed in the bin by the door.

Torres remains behind, flipping through the attendance sheet. He knows most won't change right away. But a few will. And every year, more of them show up knowing this is the new normal.

He locks up the room, turning off the projection screen. The blue glow fades, replaced by the flat white of the overheads. Torres lingers a minute, staring at the flowchart still etched in his mind.

He thinks about the old days—about the shortcuts, the confessions squeezed out before anyone could contest them.

He thinks about the cases that went sideways, and the people who never should have ended up in the system at all.

Torres leaves the building, passing a glass case filled with photos of past police chiefs. He wonders if one day they'll put him there, the first to make the new rules stick.

He doubts it. But he'll settle for knowing he was the first to try.

Outside, the night is cold, the parking lot empty. The cards in the officers' wallets will outlast him, he hopes.

Back inside, the training room waits, its tables already set for the next group, the next chance to do it better.

In the end, the record never stops. It just waits for the next hand to shape it.

CHAPTER 8

Blackout Confessions: Manufacturing Memories In Substance-Impaired Suspects

The suspect is a man named Stuart. He is forty-three, with hair slicked in runnels over a pale, blunt head, eyes muddy and slow. He sits slumped at a metal table, wrists lashed to a steel ring by a pair of zip ties, knuckles purpling against the chill. The room is cubic and hypoxic, walls blank concrete, air so still it turns each breath into a ripple. A single bulb pools over the table, its light so concentrated it peels the edges off shadows.

In the glassed-off observation cubicle, a woman in a linen blazer watches through a one-way. She scribbles something into a spiral notebook, then nods to the pair seated across from the suspect. One is Detective Sofia Dobrev, hair scraped back so tight it sketches the lines of her skull, voice pitched for maximum control. Next to her, a junior—Trainee Carter—eager enough that he has already inked two full pages of notes.

Dobrev opens the file. There are four photographs: two from a cell phone, two from what looks like a security camera. All show the same event—a narrow vestibule, a quarrel, a splay of limbs against a newsstand. None of them clearly capture a face. The only constants are the grainy timestamp in the lower corner and a blur of navy windbreaker. Next, Dobrev removes a document titled "WITNESS STATEMENT—DRAFT" in all caps, pages crisp, never once folded.

She begins as the tape clicks on.

"Stuart," she says, and lets the name sit for a moment. "Do you recall what happened last Friday night?"

He lifts his head, stares at the wall behind her. His jaw works, but nothing comes out.

Carter is ready with the primer: "Sometimes, when people have a lot to drink, their brains—" he taps the side of his own skull, as if to demonstrate— "stop making memories. It's called a blackout. Not passing out. You can still walk, talk, even do things you normally wouldn't. But the next day, there's nothing there. A gap."

Stuart shrugs, sullen.

Dobrev recites from the folder: "You left the Ripcord Lounge at 11:14 p.m., after seven drinks." She glances at the junior, who murmurs, "Vodka, neat." Dobrev continues: "You were seen in the alley behind the closed bodega at 12:06. Then again at the QuickGo on Fulton. Every camera shows you walking, sometimes running. Do you remember any of that?"

Stuart closes his eyes. His fingers clench and unclench, useless against the ties. "No," he says. "I remember leaving the bar. That's it."

Dobrev clicks the first photo onto the table, flipping it so it faces Stuart. "This is you in the alley, 12:08 a.m. Is that your jacket?"

He squints. "I guess so."

"Looks like you, doesn't it?" Carter says, not unkindly.

Stuart says nothing. His chest moves with slow, effortful breaths.

Dobrev places the next photo, this one of a scuffle at the QuickGo. The figure in the windbreaker blurs against another, who is half-collapsed, arm shielding his face.

"This was at 12:18," Dobrev says. "Do you know the person in the hat?"

Stuart shakes his head, eyes fixed on the table. "No."

"That's the victim," Carter supplies. "His name is Joshua Klein."

Dobrev lays out the witness statement. It's an assembly of leading questions and yes-no answers, most of them one word. The statement is unsigned, but there's a highlighted quote: "It was the man in the blue jacket. He hit me, then ran."

Stuart keeps his gaze on the paper. A tremor works its way up his forearms.

"Here's the thing," Dobrev says, folding her hands. "You don't remember, and that's not your fault. Blackouts are like that. But the evidence says you did this. So we need your help to figure out why."

Stuart's voice, when it comes, is frayed. "I would never do that. I'm not—I'm not violent."

"No one's calling you violent," Carter says. "It's just—when people drink, they do things. They're not themselves. Maybe something happened that set you off. Maybe you were provoked."

Dobrev leans forward, face softening just enough to look maternal. "If you tell us, it can help. The court understands blackouts. If you don't remember, you can still be honest. Did you have a reason to be angry?"

Stuart presses his lips together, a white line forming across his mouth. He shakes his head, then stops. "I don't remember. I really—" He swallows, voice catching. "If I did something, I don't know it."

Dobrev slides the last photo forward: a still of Stuart, profile clear, windbreaker zipped high, the jaw taut in a way that looks predatory. "This was right after. You're leaving the scene."

He looks at it, then away. "That's me, I guess."

"Stuart," Dobrev says, "you were found two blocks from the store, asleep on a bench. You had blood on your jacket. Your hands were scraped. The victim ID'd you. The DNA will match, we both know that. But what matters is intent. If you can tell us what happened, we can explain it. If you can't, the court will make up its own story, and it won't be good."

A silence follows, so dense the ticking of the wall clock sounds like a typewriter from the next room.

Carter, gentle, almost whispering: "Maybe you were scared. Maybe you thought someone was coming for you. That happens. You were in the army, right? Sometimes people react out of instinct."

Stuart's brow furrows. He looks at the photo, at his hands, at the officer's badge. "I—" He breathes, slow and shallow. "I don't know."

"Can you walk us through what you do remember?" Dobrev says. "Even if it's just fragments?"

A pause, then: "I remember... drinking. I was upset. Got into it with someone at the bar. Not a fight, just words. I left. I walked. Then nothing."

Dobrev nods. "That's common with blackouts. There's just—nothing. So what do you think happened in the alley?"

Stuart's jaw tightens. "I must have—I mean, if you say I did it—"

Dobrev interrupts, soft. "We're not saying, Stuart. We're showing you the evidence. The photos. The statement. The blood. Is it possible you attacked the man? Even if you don't remember?"

Stuart squeezes his hands so tight the knuckles blanch. "I don't want to believe it."

"Nobody does," Carter says. "But sometimes, the body just goes on autopilot. The memory isn't recorded, but the actions still happen. It's not who you are—it's the blackout. That's why they call it that."

Dobrev adds, "The victim's not pressing for maximum penalty. He just wants the truth. If you admit it, it shows you're not a danger. You're someone who made a mistake."

Stuart lowers his head, stares at the tile, then back to the photo. "Maybe I did do it," he says, the words at first a whisper, then stronger. "Maybe I did. I just—I can't remember."

Dobrev nods, as if this is what she hoped for. "Thank you, Stuart. That helps a lot."

Carter writes the statement, then reads it back, line by line. Each time, Stuart nods or mumbles assent.

By the end, his shoulders are hunched so low it's as if the bones inside him have begun to dissolve.

Dobrev stands, gathers the evidence, and slides the witness statement forward for a signature.

Stuart signs, letters jagged and dark, then slumps back in the chair.

Dobrev and Carter leave him alone under the light. Through the one-way, the woman in the linen blazer closes her notebook, satisfied.

On the tape, Stuart's last words are a ghost of a confession, echoing against the hollow room.

"Maybe I did do it. I just can't remember."

The briefing room at city headquarters is less auditorium, more seminar pit. Fifty officers, a spectrum of uniform and plainclothes, arrange themselves in a shallow crescent, notepads ready, coffee steaming in paper cups. Sun knifes through the clerestory windows, cutting hard angles into the navy carpet. At the front, a projection screen glows an eerie blue.

The neurologist is Dr. Nina Mirzoyan, imported from the university for the day. She wears a navy blouse under a white coat, sleeves rolled to the elbow, hair in a disciplined French twist. Her pointer is a carbon-fiber wand, which she flicks at the screen with surgical precision.

Slide one is a triptych: three renderings of the human hippocampus, each rendered in cartoonish color. The left panel glows green—normal, awake. The middle is gray and stippled—ethanol saturation. The right is a lunar void, dotted only by the dim sparks of neurons under benzodiazepine and GHB.

Mirzoyan taps the first panel. "Baseline: This is you, sober. The hippocampus here is the seat of memory formation. It is your live feed, your digital recorder."

She shifts to the second. "Alcohol, even at moderate levels, begins to fuzz the input. At high doses—what we call binge intoxication—the hippocampus shuts off completely. No new memories are stored. The hard drive is disconnected. This is amnesia by design."

A hand goes up, mid-row. "So they're just pretending not to remember?"

Mirzoyan, crisp: "No. This is not malingering. In blackout, the brain does not write to long-term storage. There is no memory to retrieve, because nothing was ever recorded. When the subject says, 'I don't remember,' it is neurologically correct."

She advances to the third slide. It shows a wiring diagram, three sets of colored lines interrupted by jagged breaks. "With GHB and certain benzos, you get a similar shutdown. The memory pathways are chemically sabotaged. In the presence of trauma—say, an altercation or a custodial event—the memory gap can be total."

A detective in the back, old school, arms folded: "But they remember the fight, just not the crime?"

"Sometimes," Mirzoyan says. "But more often, the gap is complete. With enough of the agent, an individual can perform complex tasks, even drive a car, and never recall a minute of it. The scientific term is 'anterograde amnesia.' In layman's terms, it's lights on, nobody home."

On the screen, an animation plays: a cartoon neuron with synapses fizzing, then blinking out one by one. Mirzoyan gestures with the pointer.

"When you question a blackout subject, you are talking to someone whose memory is Swiss cheese. You can plant an entire event in the holes, and they will accept it as true."

A row of officers glance at each other, uneasy. Someone murmurs, "That's what happened on Canal Street," but the words dissolve before they reach the front.

Mirzoyan scans the room, then clicks to the next slide. "Case study: Johnson v. State, 2015. The suspect was accused of vehicular homicide. Claimed total amnesia for the night in question. Prosecution argued deception; defense called in two neurologists."

She presents a graph: x-axis, blood alcohol; y-axis, probability of blackout. At .18 BAC, odds of amnesia approach seventy percent.

"In this case, both prosecution and defense agreed: the memory gap was real. The court, however, refused to admit it as exculpatory. They treated the confession as valid, even though it was elicited during blackout."

The pointer clacks against the table. "You need to understand this: A blackout suspect can be led—deliberately or accidentally—to confess to things they did not do. Or to invent details that never happened."

A sergeant, skeptical, leans forward. "So what's the fix? How do we know if they're faking, or if it's real?"

Mirzoyan smiles, a little sad. "There are signs. The fakers always recall the crime, just not the evidence. The real blackout cases can't remember anything after a certain point. They repeat themselves, lose track of time, can't recall even mundane details. If you ask about the weather or what they were wearing, they blank."

She flips to the last slide: "INTERROGATION RISK FACTORS." Bullet points bloom:

- Time gaps in narrative

- Sudden onset of amnesia

- High measured intoxication

- Contradictory statements

- Repetition of leading details

"In practice," she says, "treat any memory gap with suspicion—not of the suspect, but of your own process. The more you repeat a detail, the more likely it is to become the suspect's reality. By the end of a long interview, a blackout subject will parrot whatever you put in front of them. That includes false confessions."

A captain at the end of the row, tone clipped: "You're telling us to disregard their statements?"

"Not disregard," Mirzoyan corrects. "Document the impairment. Corroborate with physical evidence. Do not rely on the suspect's account to fill in the narrative. And for God's sake, do not feed them details. If they confess, make sure it's on the record—video and audio—so the context is clear."

The room quiets. Officers look at their notes, some making asterisks, others just absorbing the caution.

Mirzoyan surveys her audience. "In blackout, there is no anchor. No internal check. The brain literally stops recording, leaving a blank. You can fill it with anything you like. That is why false confessions are so common in these cases, and why they so often stick."

The session ends with a last slide: a mugshot, half the face obscured by black bar, the other side washed out by camera flash.

Mirzoyan collects her slides, thanks the crowd, and leaves the podium as the next presenter queues up.

The officers are slower to file out. Some stand in clusters, arguing quietly over the protocols. Others slip out, faces thoughtful, the implication of the lecture working its way through them like a slow, sobering hangover.

The video review room is a low-ceilinged shoebox, half-lit by the glare of three LED monitors and the spillover from a wall of security screens. Four detectives and two crime analysts crowd the table, elbows competing for real estate among half-empty coffee cups and stacks of loose-leaf reports. It's just after 10 a.m., but the air smells like day-old fries and burned nerves.

On the main display, the video analyst—he goes by Lopez—loads the footage for Case #17-241B, the Wilson Arson. The file is from a ceiling camera in a warehouse's back corridor, timestamped and watermarked with the precinct's digital ID. The left side of the screen shows the video; the right, a vertical strip running the interrogation transcript, each speaker color-coded.

The first lines are already in motion:

DETECTIVE PARKER: "The evidence shows you were there."

WILSON: "I—I don't recall pouring the gasoline."

PARKER: "But you remember being in the warehouse?"

WILSON: (long pause) "I must have been. That's what you said."

Lopez, pausing the video: "Right there. See the pause? He's waiting for Parker to give him the story. Every time, he echoes whatever Parker floats."

A veteran detective, Strohm, stares at the monitor with a grim set to his mouth. "Could be nerves."

Lopez shrugs. "Watch the next two minutes. It's a masterclass in suggestion."

The footage plays: Parker repeats that the forensics are clear, that only someone inside could have started the fire. Wilson, hunched and glassy-eyed, resists for a few rounds, then finally gives way: "Maybe I did it. I don't remember. But if you say I did, I guess—I guess I did."

Below the transcript, the analysts have highlighted every time Parker uses the word "gasoline," "match," or "fire." Thirty-seven instances in ten minutes.

Strohm, shifting in his seat: "He was wasted, right?"

Lopez nods. "Lab says .23 blood alcohol at time of arrest. By the time of interview, probably down to .14, but that's still deep into blackout range." He points to the transcript's margin: "Every gap, every repetition, classic anterograde amnesia. He literally can't recall the timeline."

On the video, Parker grows more insistent, now reading Wilson a list of "facts" from the file.

PARKER: "We have you on the security tape, entering at 2:41 a.m. Nobody else came in for hours."

WILSON: (squinting) "Is that me?"

PARKER: "You tell me."

WILSON: (voice cracking) "I—I guess so."

Lopez stops the tape, toggles the display to a grainy freeze-frame. "Here. That's what Parker is referencing. Only, if you look close..." He zooms, enhances, draws a digital circle around the figure's right shoulder. "That's a tattoo. Not Wilson's. We checked."

Strohm leans in. "Jesus. So it's not him?"

"Could be, but there's at least a one-in-four chance it's the maintenance guy, Thomas," Lopez says. "They're the same build, but only one has the anchor tattoo. Wilson's got nothing there."

A junior detective, Chin, flips through her notepad. "But the confession?"

Lopez: "Built from suggestion. He says he doesn't remember. After half an hour of pressure, he repeats what Parker tells him—down to the phrasing. 'Gasoline,' 'match,' 'started the fire.' If you watch the whole tape, he parrots Parker verbatim, every time."

On the screen, the rest of the interrogation scrolls by:

PARKER: "Why would you do something like that?"

WILSON: (after a long silence) "I don't know. Maybe I was angry?"

PARKER: "About what?"

WILSON: (struggling) "I... don't know. Maybe someone pissed me off?"

The transcript highlights each time Wilson's responses mirror the question. Lopez adds, "This is how blackout confession works. The brain has no record, so the only available narrative is the one you feed them."

The room falls silent as the implication sets in.

Chin, soft: "So he could be innocent?"

Lopez: "He could be anything. The confession tells you nothing."

Strohm sighs, rubs his temples. "But he pled out."

The analyst nods. "He pled out because you handed him a script and he repeated it until it became his story."

There's a long moment, nobody moving.

At the end of the table, the precinct captain speaks for the first time. "You want us to reopen?"

Lopez kills the video, faces the room. "I want you to know the difference. Otherwise, you'll keep doing this, and more cases will go sideways."

He stands, unplugs the drive, leaves the team with the digital printouts. As he exits, Strohm flips back through the transcript, rereading the highlighted lines.

On the last page, in Parker's own handwriting, is the phrase: "He said it himself. End of story."

The room lingers in silence, as if waiting for a memory to surface that never will.

The courtroom is hushed, daylight diffusing through smoked-glass panes behind the judge's bench. The clock ticks just past 2:00 p.m.; every seat in the gallery is filled, most by reporters and students from the nearby law school. At the defense table sits Sarah Mendez, hair pulled into a severe knot, hands folded so tightly the knuckles gleam like ivory. She watches her attorney, Leah Bhat, as if the words coming next will determine the rest of her life.

Judge Mallory, a woman of careful diction, reviews the case file. She looks up. "Petitioner seeks to vacate a 2017 plea in the matter of State v. Mendez on grounds of newly discovered evidence and involuntariness of confession. Is that correct, Ms. Bhat?"

"Yes, Your Honor," says Bhat, rising. "Specifically, we submit that Ms. Mendez's confession was elicited while she was in a state of alcohol-induced amnesia, and that the subsequent witness statements now exonerate her."

The state's attorney, Gregory Lin, interjects, "We dispute the contention that the confession was involuntary or unreliable.

Mendez admitted to being behind the wheel at the time of the incident. The victim's family deserves closure."

Judge Mallory gestures to the transcript, which is projected on the side wall. The relevant section is highlighted.

INTERVIEWER: "We have witnesses who saw you behind the wheel."

MENDEZ: "I thought I was driving that night. I'm so sorry."

Bhat addresses the court. "The entire narrative was built on suggestion. Ms. Mendez recalls nothing between leaving the bar and waking in the hospital. The record shows the officer repeated the 'behind the wheel' assertion five times in under twenty minutes. Every new detail in Ms. Mendez's statement corresponds directly to what was suggested by the investigator."

Judge Mallory looks over her glasses. "You have new evidence?"

"Yes, Your Honor. We have three sworn affidavits from individuals who left the bar with Ms. Mendez and the decedent. In all three, Ms. Mendez was a passenger. More importantly, the driver—John Carter—came forward and provided a full statement, corroborated by GPS data and cell tower records."

Lin, for the prosecution, flips through a copy of the affidavits. "Convenient recantations, Your Honor. None of these witnesses came forward during the original investigation."

Bhat nods. "Because none of them were asked. Ms. Mendez accepted the confession under pressure, and the state declined to investigate alternate accounts."

Judge Mallory leans back. "I'll hear from the driver."

Carter approaches the lectern, hands shaking. He testifies that he alone was driving, that Mendez was incoherent and vomiting in the back seat, and that, when the car crashed, she was unconscious. He weeps as he says it.

Bhat presents the GPS record, time-stamped texts, and a cell photo with metadata. "It is physically impossible, based on the evidence, that Ms. Mendez was ever in the driver's seat."

Judge Mallory turns to Lin. "Does the state dispute this evidence?"

Lin stands, face pinched. "Your Honor, we can't. But the confession was entered under Miranda. Ms. Mendez signed, and confirmed on record."

Bhat: "While in blackout, with a .21 blood alcohol level. The interrogator supplied every detail."

The gallery murmurs. Judge Mallory raises a hand for silence.

She summarizes: "The record is clear. Ms. Mendez had no independent recollection. The confession was a product of suggestion and impairment. The new evidence, uncontested, exonerates her."

She rules: "Petition granted. The plea is vacated, conviction set aside. Ms. Mendez is released from further obligation to the court."

Bhat hugs Mendez, who sits stunned for a full ten seconds, then breathes out in a sharp, broken exhale.

Lin, for the state, says quietly, "We will not pursue retrial, Your Honor."

As the crowd files out, Judge Mallory writes a note in the file: "Confession obtained while impaired. See attached: Guidance for future custodial interviews—blackout protocol recommended."

In the corridor, Mendez is surrounded by friends and her attorney, her hands still trembling as she repeats the same two words: "I'm free."

In the gallery, a law professor scribbles in the margin of a casebook: "When memory is blank, truth is negotiable."

No one lingers in the room except the judge, who studies the highlighted lines of the transcript as if searching for a lesson that might outlive the case.

It's dusk at Precinct 17. The windows of the evidence room reflect a neon grid from the high-rises outside, tracing the city's veins in electric blue. Inside, three officers huddle around a battered interrogation desk, an array of manila folders and pill bottles splayed across its pitted surface.

The case is Michael Chen, charged with robbing a liquor store two months prior. The key file is the confession, signed and videotaped, though the details have never quite lined up. On the wall-mounted screen, a split view: left side the AV feed from the interview, right side a digital overlay of Chen's medical chart, courtesy of County General.

Detective Alvarez, the primary on the case, fast-forwards to the crucial section.

ALVAREZ (on tape): "You know we have your fingerprints at the scene, right?"

CHEN: "I—I don't remember being there. I don't remember anything after I took my pills."

ALVAREZ: "But if your prints are there, you were there."

CHEN: (uncertain) "If you say so."

The tape continues. Alvarez repeats the fingerprint claim four more times, even as the forensics on the case are still pending.

OFFICER 1, watching from the table, says: "It's like the guy's sleepwalking through the whole thing."

OFFICER 2: "Look at the chart. Chen was on Temazepam and Tramadol. That combo? He probably lost twelve hours easy."

On the screen, Chen sits limp, eyes flickering, voice monotone.

ALVAREZ (on tape): "Just walk me through what happened."

CHEN: (long pause) "I don't know. Maybe I needed money. Maybe I just went in and—"

ALVAREZ: "And what?"

CHEN: (eyes unfocused) "Took the cash. Maybe I took the cash."

Alvarez looks straight into the camera. "Do you see what's happening here? This is textbook blackout confession. Every word he says is either what I just told him, or a question he's answering with another question."

Officer 2 scrolls the log on her tablet. "He wasn't even in the area. Security badge swipes put him at a warehouse on 16th at the same time."

Officer 1 cross-checks the timeline. "So he couldn't have done it."

Alvarez: "The confession was made two days later. The guy came in voluntarily because he saw himself on the news and thought maybe he'd done it in a blackout."

The tape shows Alvarez feeding in more detail, a little at a time: "Maybe you used a bag?"—"Yeah, maybe a bag."—"Did you point the gun, or just show it?"—"Maybe just showed it." After an hour, Chen's story is a near-perfect copy of the police narrative, even though nothing matches the video from the store.

Officer 2 shakes her head. "He's just trying to fill the hole in his memory. He'll believe anything."

Alvarez kills the playback. "He's out now. They dropped the charge last week, when the DNA came back. Different guy. But this is how easy it is: if the subject thinks he might have done it, he'll confess just to feel less lost."

Officer 1, quiet: "We get these all the time. It's just most don't stick."

Alvarez closes the file, hands flat on the desk. "The point is, if you don't check the rest, you can lose the whole case to a blank. Or, worse, you send the wrong guy to prison because he can't argue with a story you give him."

The room sits in silence for a moment, the hum of the city climbing in through the vents.

Officer 2 looks at the printout of Chen's statement. "It's not even a memory. It's just a script."

Alvarez nods. "If you want to know the truth, you have to look where the tape doesn't play."

They start the video again, this time at half-speed, the gaps and stutters thrown into even starker relief.

Outside, the city lights begin to flicker on, one by one, indifferent to the stories playing out in the rooms below.

The federal courthouse downtown is designed to intimidate. Marble pillars, flagstone floors, walls lined with portraits of old men in heavier robes. In Courtroom 9, the air is cold enough to prickle skin. At the defense table, attorney Maya Patel arranges her folders with geometric precision. Her client, seated beside her, is a pale and nervous man in a wrinkled suit. Two rows back, his wife clutches a bag of tissues, eyes red.

At the prosecution's table, Assistant U.S. Attorney Blake wears a suit so dark it absorbs the overhead light. He reviews a binder, barely looking up as the judge, Honorable Evelyn DeWitt, calls the session to order.

"This is a suppression hearing," DeWitt says. "Defense challenges the admissibility of the defendant's confession, obtained during a custodial interview following a suspected blackout event. Ms. Patel?"

Patel rises, hands clasped behind her back. "Your Honor, my client suffers from a documented history of substance-induced amnesia. At the time of his interrogation, he was in a state of neurological blackout and incapable of forming or recalling memories. We submit that the confession was involuntary, and—more importantly—manufactured by suggestion during his impairment."

DeWitt: "Do you have expert testimony?"

Patel: "Yes, Your Honor. I'd like to call Dr. Steven Goldblatt to the stand."

Goldblatt is a memory scientist, clinical and bald, glasses perched low on his nose. He enters, swears in, and takes the seat. The bailiff queues up a monitor on the witness stand.

Patel clicks a remote, and the first slide appears: a rendered brain in cross-section, hippocampus highlighted in angry red.

"Dr. Goldblatt," Patel says, "please explain to the court what happens to memory during a blackout."

Goldblatt: "The hippocampus is responsible for encoding new memories. In a blackout—whether from alcohol, benzodiazepines, or a combination—it ceases to function. No new memories are formed. The subject may walk, talk, answer questions, but will have zero recall later. Any statements made during this period are not anchored to conscious recollection, and the subject is highly suggestible."

Patel: "So if a law enforcement officer feeds details to a subject during blackout?"

Goldblatt: "The subject will often accept the narrative, internalize it, and later believe it as fact. In laboratory settings, this is how false memories are implanted."

Patel: "Is this different from lying?"

Goldblatt: "Completely. Lying presumes you know the truth and decide to conceal it. In blackout, there is nothing to conceal, because the memory was never formed."

Patel advances the next slide: a set of neural pathways, some lit up, others dark. "These are the pathways vulnerable during blackout?"

"Correct," Goldblatt says, pointer trembling over the slide. "With impairment, the critical circuits go offline. The rest of the brain is in compensation mode—more susceptible to outside input, including authority figures."

Patel nods. "In your expert opinion, was my client capable of providing a voluntary confession?"

Goldblatt, steady: "No. He was neurologically incapable of making a voluntary decision. His inability to remember was weaponized against him."

The judge scribbles a note.

Blake, for the prosecution, stands. "Dr. Goldblatt, are you saying anyone who drinks can claim blackout and walk away from a confession?"

Goldblatt: "No, Mr. Blake. I'm saying that blackout is real, and when properly diagnosed, it invalidates the reliability of any statements obtained during that period."

Blake: "But the defendant here remembered some things. He answered questions, recognized officers, even apologized for the crime."

Goldblatt: "Fragmentary recall is common. But the relevant memory—the act itself—was never recorded. Any apology is parroting what was suggested to him."

Blake sneers. "Isn't it possible he simply doesn't want to admit guilt?"

Goldblatt: "That is always possible. But the record—transcript, video, and toxicology—shows all the hallmarks of blackout confession."

Blake nods, pivots to the judge. "Your Honor, this sets a dangerous precedent. The defendant's selective memory conveniently shields him from responsibility."

Patel: "Or it shields him from a conviction based on bad science."

DeWitt raises a hand. "Enough. My concern is with Miranda. Can a person in blackout knowingly waive their rights?"

Goldblatt: "No. They lack the capacity for informed consent."

Patel: "And therefore, any waiver is invalid."

Blake: "But the law presumes competence unless clearly demonstrated otherwise."

DeWitt sits back, thinking. She stares at the transcript in front of her. In the margins, a clerk has highlighted every moment the defendant echoes the interrogator's narrative—each time, a word-for-word match.

She addresses the court: "Both sides make compelling arguments. The science is clear: blackout states render memory unreliable, and can leave subjects open to suggestion. However, current precedent requires a high standard for involuntariness. The defense's evidence here is persuasive, but the court will require additional medical corroboration and review of the full interview record before ruling."

She eyes both counsel. "In the meantime, I strongly advise the U.S. Attorney's Office to revisit protocols for questioning impaired suspects."

Blake frowns, but nods.

Patel sits, expression unreadable.

DeWitt gavels out. As the room clears, the only sound is the shuffle of legal pads and the muted click of the judge's pen.

In the corridor, Patel's client leans against the wall, pale with relief. His wife clutches his sleeve, hope flickering for the first time.

At the end of the row, Goldblatt reviews the transcript, his finger tracing the lines where truth was overwritten by suggestion.

Outside, a reporter types up a story, headline ready: "SCIENCE CASTS DOUBT ON CONFESSIONS OF THE IMPAIRED."

Up in chambers, Judge DeWitt marks her calendar for the next hearing, knowing she is watching the law evolve in real time—and that the rules for memory, and for justice, are now up for debate.

The academy's training classroom is a blunt rectangle—whiteboards on every wall, tables grouped into pods, the air still thick with the bleach tang of last night's janitorial pass. Late-afternoon sunlight lays gold strips across the floor, turning evidence kits and video equipment into relics on display.

Today's session is new: Blackout and Impairment Interview Protocol. The instructors, a triad of detectives and an ex-paramedic, circulate between clusters of officers, clipboards in hand.

At station one, an officer unpacks a medical screening kit: pulse oximeter, breathalyzer, and a laminated checklist of "Signs of Cognitive Impairment." The ex-paramedic, Garcia, runs the demo.

"First thing, you don't ask questions until you document condition," Garcia says. "If the subject slurs, repeats themselves, or can't follow a two-step command, you flag it. That triggers a hold on all non-emergency interviews. Medical evaluation comes first."

At the next station, two officers watch a split-screen video. One side shows a standard interview with a cooperative but forgetful subject. The other side, same subject, same scenario, but the interviewer uses leading prompts and suggestion.

The difference is surgical. In the first, the subject blanks on details, repeats "I don't know." In the second, after only five minutes of suggestion, the subject is parroting back facts supplied by the detective.

The instructor, Detective Ng, pauses the feed. "You see how easy it is? The brain wants to fill in blanks. If you feed the script, they'll play the part."

One officer, skeptical, asks, "What if the subject's just acting? Faking the blackout?"

Ng: "Then the tox and the video will show it. But if you railroad someone in a real blackout, it's on you—and on the department. Next year, this will be court standard, so get ahead of it now."

At the third pod, the protocol is laid out in flowchart form:

- Medical screen mandatory for all suspects with observed impairment

- Toxicology panel and breathalyzer logged before interview

- 24-hour minimum wait for confessions after medical clearance

- Counsel must be present for all interviews with impaired suspects

- All interviews video recorded, start to finish, with timestamp overlay

Two officers role-play the intake of an "impaired" suspect, one slurring and repeating, "I don't remember" at every prompt. The other officer checks the chart, logs the BAC, then pauses the process.

"You wait for the clearance, then restart," the instructor says. "If they're still blank, you limit the session to yes/no, document the responses, and never feed them facts they don't bring up themselves."

At the last station, a mock interrogation: actors play a suspect and two officers. The suspect exhibits classic GHB blackout, smiling and agreeable, but unable to recall the last six hours. The officers are coached to avoid suggestion, and their dialogue is monitored by a real-time feedback app, which buzzes if they use leading language.

After three rounds, the lead instructor, Detective Connor, calls for a freeze.

"Let's break this down," she says. "If you make an error—if you say, 'Was it the blue car or the red car?'—you've already loaded the memory. In blackout, that's irreversible. The best approach is open-ended, always."

A captain in the back raises a hand. "But what if there's a safety issue? Ongoing risk?"

Connor: "Then you document what you have, but never use it as sole evidence. You build the case from physical, from witness, from forensics. Confession is gravy, not foundation. That's the shift."

Throughout the room, officers run through dry runs, sometimes flubbing a step, sometimes catching themselves. The trainers circle, correcting language, nudging hands off the evidence baggies unless gloved.

The goal is muscle memory: every suspect gets screened, every confession has a clean chain. The old culture of getting a statement at any cost is replaced, hour by hour, with the new.

At the end of the session, the instructors gather the class for a debrief.

Garcia says, "You're going to want to shortcut this. The old way was faster. But if you get it wrong, it's not just the case that falls apart—it's everything you've worked for. These are people's lives."

Ng, quieter, says, "Remember: in blackout, there's no tape to rewind. If you're not careful, you'll write the story for them."

Connor concludes, "The goal isn't to prevent confessions. It's to make sure any confession is a memory—not a suggestion, not a script. The difference is everything."

As the officers gather their gear, a few linger at the stations, reviewing the protocols or scanning the feedback app's red flags.

By the time the sun slants low enough to stripe the desks with deep orange, the room is nearly empty. But on every table, the laminated flowcharts remain.

In the hallway, the new protocol is already the subject of debate and gossip, the kind that means it will stick.

In a month, the first real case will come through under the new standard. And for the first time in years, the interview will tell the story—not of a confession manufactured in blackout, but of a truth that belongs to the person who lived it.

Back in the classroom, Garcia erases the whiteboard, but leaves the final line at the top:

"NO MEMORY, NO NARRATIVE."

The next class will read it, and the one after that.

For once, the blank is not a failure, but a safeguard—an empty space waiting to be filled with something real.

CHAPTER 9

When Empathy Blinds: The Pitfalls Of Sexual Assault Investigations

Fluorescent tubes click to life overhead, rattling shadows against the scuffed tile, and twenty new investigators lift their chins as Captain Riley Matthews steps behind the battered oak podium. The training room smells like three-day-old coffee and packing peanuts, the kind of neutral purgatory that promises nothing and therefore can disappoint no one. At the front, a projection screen flutters and holds, blue and expectant. The plastic-laminate tables are arranged in a semicircle, as if to suggest intimacy, though all warmth is bled by the lights and the AC compressor grinding from behind a louvered panel.

Matthews checks his watch, then the attendance sheet. "Good morning, everyone—let's get started." His voice is made for a PA system, deep but tuned to cut through clutter. He waits a beat, lets the room settle. "Today's module: 'Sexual Assault Interviews—Protocol, Pitfalls, and the Human Element.' This will be interactive. Questions are expected. If you're wrong, no one will die." He pauses just long enough for the joke to limp past.

He flicks the remote. The first slide irises into focus:

FALSE ACCUSATION RATE: 5%

UNREPORTED SEXUAL ASSAULTS: 60%

A spatter of bullet points fans out below.

Matthews: "Let's start with what the data tells us. Most accusations are not lies, but most assaults are never reported. Why is that?" He cocks an eyebrow, scans the faces. Some hide behind coffee cups, a few scribble already, two check their phones under the table.

A voice from the left: "Victim-blaming, mostly." The speaker is a trainee with a chin-length bob and an oversize sweater, her name-tag peeling at one corner. Her tone is flat, but not unkind.

"Good," Matthews says. "Victims fear they won't be believed. Or they think the system will hurt them again. So—" he advances the slide— "we get this." The next line appears in red:

OF KNOWN FALSE ACCUSATIONS, 80% COLLAPSE IN THE FIRST 72 HOURS

He nods to a trainee in the front row. "Read that out loud, please."

The man clears his throat, voice hoarse from either nerves or allergies. "Of known false accusations, eighty percent collapse in the first seventy-two hours."

"Which means," Matthews says, "most lies are caught fast. The rest are almost always the real thing." He lets that settle, then smiles, as if to rescue the mood. "But our job is not to play odds. Our job is to know how to get it right, every time."

He paces once across the narrow front, hands folded behind his back. "This is where trauma-informed interviewing comes in. Hands up if you've heard the term." Half the class does; the other half glance around, measuring who might be the weak link.

Matthews: "You'll see it in the field. Trauma-informed protocol means three things: Safety, Agency, and Verification." He points to each word as it blooms on the slide.

He motions to the wall: "Booth A. Go take a look."

The trainees file out of their seats, some slow, some hasty to be first. The booth is a prefab pod with a cloud-blue wall, a low couch, and a privacy screen. On a side table: bottled water, a box of tissues, and a small stack of fidget toys—stress balls, a pack of thick pencils, a soft plastic block. The effect is something between a children's dentist and a therapist's waiting room.

Matthews stands at the entrance, ushering them in and out with quick, precise gestures. "Interviewee sits there," he points. "No desk in the way. No direct eye contact unless the subject wants it. You observe body language, but you never crowd. The blue wall is intentional—lowers blood pressure, keeps panic at bay."

Back in the classroom, he resumes. "This is not about being nice for the sake of it. It's about getting the best information. Victims remember more if they feel safe."

He advances two more slides, side by side. Both show a timeline, annotated in black and red. The first: "Case 2714. Subject: J. Fisher. Interviewed at home, no support." The second: "Case 2715. Subject: M. Evans. Interviewed in trauma booth, advocate present."

Matthews: "Both cases involved late-night assaults, both reported within twelve hours." He gestures to the first timeline. "In 2714, the investigator thought the subject was unstable. They skipped basic verification—no phone dump, no DNA sweep. They didn't want to 'retraumatize.' Instead, they relied on the statement alone." He clicks to the conclusion: "Case collapsed, subject withdrew complaint, never re-engaged."

He pivots to the second. "In 2715, subject worked with an advocate. Interview was slow, but methodical. Every claim checked. DNA matched, timeline verified by rideshare data and cell pings. The victim did not remember the face, but remembered the license plate." Matthews taps the bottom of the slide: "Suspect arrested. Full confession. Case resolved."

He turns to the class. "What's the difference?"

A tall man near the back raises a hand. “The second subject had support, but also—more checking?”

Matthews nods. “Verification. Kindness does not mean lower standards. It means doing the hard parts with respect. That includes calling out inconsistencies, but with care, not accusation.”

The hum of the projector thickens as he clicks to a slide titled:

BENEFIT: SAFE DISCLOSURE

PITFALL: UNCRITICAL ACCEPTANCE

He points to the phrase “uncritical acceptance” and underlines it. “This is where we lose cases. You are not the victim’s friend, or their therapist. You are there to get the facts. If you believe every word, you miss the gaps. If you disbelieve every word, you get nothing. Balance is the goal.”

A woman at the end of the second row raises her hand. “How do we verify timelines without retraumatizing?”

Matthews smiles. "Good question. Scripted, open-ended prompts. Always let the subject lead. For example: 'Tell me everything you remember about that day, in your own words. Start anywhere you like.' Then, if something doesn't add up, you don't challenge. You say, 'I notice you mentioned X here, but not before—help me understand that.' Never imply they're lying. Instead, make it a puzzle you're solving together."

He flicks through three slides in rapid succession: screenshots of messaging apps, a table of rideshare pings, a diagram of phone call logs. "Most of the time, the verification is invisible. You get their permission, then do the forensics behind the scenes. Only come back with questions if the data directly contradicts. If it's a gap, ask for clarification, not confrontation."

He glances at his watch, then the wall clock, which is ten minutes fast by design. "Last point before break: The victim advocate." He nods to the door, and an older woman in a gray cardigan enters, rolling a cart with more water, a fruit bowl, and a fresh box of tissues. Her name tag reads "Kim / Support."

Matthews: "Kim is an advocate. Her job is not to interrogate, or to verify. It is to keep the subject grounded and present. She can call time out, stop the session, or suggest a reset. If you ignore the advocate, the interview is invalid. If you let her lead, you'll get a better statement and avoid most complaints."

He gestures for Kim to say something.

Kim, voice practiced and clear: "I am here for the person being interviewed. I can stop the process any time. If I think the questions are unfair, or too fast, or if the person is overwhelmed, I can intervene. Sometimes I do nothing; sometimes I guide. It depends on what the survivor needs."

She sets down the cart, refills the tissue box, and steps back out.

Matthews clicks to a new slide: a checklist in blue and gold.

PRE-INTERVIEW: Confirm comfort, offer water, explain process

DURING: Use open prompts, no leading, no time pressure

AFTER: Provide support, immediate advocate access, debrief

He turns to the class. "Questions?"

The silence is almost admiring, as if the protocol—so simple, so explicit—has short-circuited any objections.

Matthews dims the projector, lets the blue wash fade to a blank white.

"Remember: support and rigor must go hand in hand. You can't have one without the other." He snaps the remote to his palm. "Ten-minute break. Next module, we get into evidence protocols. Bring your notepads."

As the trainees file out, voices pick up in the hallway: some debating the finer points, others just grateful for the coffee. At the front, Matthews gathers his notes, already outlining how to fit the rest of the material into the next hour.

Above, the fluorescent tubes buzz in a strange, sympathetic echo, as if the room itself is practicing the art of holding still, holding space, until something real is ready to be shared.

The conference hall's rear training room is colder than the corridor outside, walls painted a migraine white and illuminated by low rectangles of light inset into the acoustic panels overhead. The long tables are arranged in stadium tiers, thirty detectives pressed hip-to-hip on molded chairs with canted backs. In front, the dais is bare except for a carafe of water and a stack of laser-printed case summaries, each banded with a blue header and three bold subheadings. The air is heavy with the steam of reheated coffee, its bitterness outlasted only by the memory of the donuts from the early morning break.

At 0902, Dr. Elena Cheng steps up to the lectern. Her suit is dark plum, her hair tied back so tightly it tugs at the corner of her mouth. She does not bother with pleasantries, just flips the wireless remote and brings up the first slide:

THE HENDERSON CASE: EMPATHY-DRIVEN TUNNEL VISION

She waits as the detectives squint into the projected glare, then begins in a voice that is clipped and declarative, the syllables nearly audible in their march.

"Thank you for your attention. Today we look at two cases—one, the Henderson sexual assault, and two, the Westbrook alleged abduction. Both made the news. Both unraveled in less than six weeks. Both, ultimately, were examples of investigators so attuned to the victim's trauma that they missed the truth right in front of them."

She clicks to the next slide: a faded yearbook photo, overlayed with crime-scene tape and a string of bullet points.

"Henderson, age nineteen, reported a stranger assault on the Greenway path, mid-morning, broad daylight. She was coherent, calm, and showed no external signs of injury. The lead detective took her statement at face value, but more importantly—" Cheng leans forward, her gaze sharpening—"the entire team did. Not one person in the room challenged the sequence of events."

She flips to the next slide: a time-stamped map of the bike trail, color-coded by intervals.

"According to the statement, Henderson left her dorm at 9:20, was attacked at 9:47, and staggered into a public safety office at 10:04. Simple, right? The problem—" she points with the remote, underlining two locations—"is that the attack site was less than a five-minute walk from the station. And every camera on the path shows Henderson walking, unhurried, with no sign of distress or injury. For forty-seven minutes, she is out of sight, but only one minute is unaccounted for near the scene."

A few detectives shift in their chairs, eyes narrowing at the implication.

Cheng: "So why did no one notice? Because the first interview was conducted in the trauma booth—soft chairs, blue wall, advocate present. Henderson shook when she spoke, and the investigators made the decision not to press on details that 'might traumatize further.' Instead, they allowed her to lead. When the narrative didn't fit, they adjusted the timeline, not the facts."

She advances to a scan of the witness statement. Key lines are circled in digital red.

"We believed her every word."—from the case file.

Cheng lets the words hang, then adds: "If you have no process for verification, you will accept the story that hurts least. That is tunnel vision, not empathy."

She scrolls through the next three slides: a crime scene photo, a close-up of Henderson's hands (no marks, nails unbroken), and a CSI report noting "inconclusive evidence of struggle." She reads from the forensic summary, flat: "No blood, no trace DNA from alleged attacker, no foreign fibers. But the team wrote in the initial report: 'Lack of evidence is consistent with trauma response—victim may not recall all details.'"

On the side wall, a list of error types appears:

- No interviews with neighbors or bystanders

- No review of security camera footage until Day 6

- Acceptance of suspect's contradictory statements re: footprints

- Failure to verify victim's phone location at critical intervals

- Dismissal of alibi for lack of 'trauma sensitivity'

Cheng turns to the audience. "This is not a critique of compassion. It is a critique of bias. You can be both kind and rigorous. The moment you surrender one for the other, you lose the case."

A detective in the second row, voice rough from years of street work, calls out: "Wasn't there a bloody glove found in the trash?"

Cheng nods. "There was. But it matched neither the victim's nor the alleged attacker's DNA. It was dismissed as irrelevant. No further tests ordered. Later, it was linked to a completely unrelated incident—mugging in the next block over. No one caught it until the lab cross-indexed the samples three months later."

The room grows more alert. Pens scribble faster; hands hover over the printouts.

Cheng advances to the last slide for the case, this one a block of text highlighted in alternating blue and yellow:

'We did not want to re-traumatize the victim by questioning her version of events.' —Detective's summary, page three.

Cheng underlines it with the laser pointer. "This is the policy failure. Verification is not cruelty. It is respect—for the victim, for the accused, and for the integrity of the process."

She flips off the projector for a moment, lets the afterimage fade from the detectives' eyes.

"Any questions before we move to Westbrook?"

A man near the aisle raises his hand, slow and cautious. "What about the advocate's role? Are they supposed to protect the victim from cross-checking?"

Cheng: "The advocate is there for support, not as a shield from verification. Their presence ensures humane treatment, not a barrier to investigative rigor. If the advocate objects to a question, you document the objection, but you do not abandon the question. You find a way to ask it that is neutral, open, and precise."

She relights the projector. New slide: a grainy CCTV still from a gas station, timestamped 11:43 p.m., a small figure in a hooded coat walking across the lot.

"Westbrook Investigation. Age sixteen, claims to have been abducted, driven to the city limits, and left in an abandoned lot. Police response was immediate; public outcry, louder. The team took a statement, but because of 'trauma protocol,' did not re-interview the subject for seventy-two hours. In that interval, Westbrook's story changed three times. The detective wrote, 'Due to victim's mental state, factual inconsistencies are not unexpected.'"

Cheng walks to the edge of the dais, makes eye contact with the front row. "The evidence? There was none. The car described was never found. The lot had no trace of the vehicle. No one thought to check Westbrook's own cell phone until week two. When they did—" she flips to the call log, displayed in neon green—"the subject was texting friends the entire time, including during the alleged abduction."

She lets the slide linger. The room stares at the contradiction, a few muttering under their breath.

Cheng, softly: "What happened here?"

A junior detective, nervous, pipes up: "They made the story fit the narrative. Tried to protect the victim even when the story was falling apart."

"Correct," Cheng says. "Every ambiguous clue was bent to fit the initial version. The moment the facts diverged, they were labeled as the product of trauma, or of stress, or of memory confusion. At no point was the possibility of fabrication—partial or total—entertained until the evidence forced it."

She clicks to a split slide: "Bias Cascade" on the left, "Verification Checks" on the right. Bullet points cascade down both sides.

Cheng gestures to the room: "If you're the first investigator on a case, your assumptions set the tone for every interview, every search, every file entry. If you believe the story without question, everyone after you will do the same."

She cycles to the final slide: three side-by-side case summaries, outcomes listed in red.

- Henderson: Unfounded, closed, public retraction after six weeks. No charges filed.

- Westbrook: Fabricated, admitted under secondary interview, no criminal complaint.

- Sanderson (third case, not discussed): Confirmed, suspect arrested and convicted, due to early and rigorous verification steps.

Cheng looks around the room, her expression not quite severe, but insistent. "You are not the story. You are the filter. You can show compassion for every party, but your loyalty is to the truth, not to a narrative—no matter how compelling, no matter how much you wish it were true."

She pauses, hands flat on the podium. "The system only works if you are both advocate and skeptic. You do not get to pick one or the other."

She lifts the stack of case summaries, hands the first few down the front row, the rest to a waiting assistant. "You will review these two cases before Friday's session. Annotate every step where bias intervened. Highlight every opportunity for correction that was missed. If you see a pattern, flag it. That's your assignment."

She flicks the projector off, then on, then off again. Each time the room flickers from focused blue to institutional gray.

As the trainees file out, the clatter of chairs and the scrape of shoes reverberate with a new restlessness. Some cluster by the coffee urn, already arguing over which errors mattered most, which were unavoidable. Others retreat to corners, eyes skimming the case files, highlighters already unsheathed.

At the lectern, Dr. Cheng tidies her notes, then glances at the clock. The next group is scheduled in fifteen minutes. She is ready for them, and for every bias they will bring to the room.

As the door swings shut, the only trace she leaves behind is the challenge written on the whiteboard in block capitals:

IDENTIFY EVERY BIAS YOU CAN FIND.

The scent of old coffee lingers, but the air is sharper now, the atmosphere less forgiving, the sense of purpose newly awake.

The training room for Session Three is narrow and bright, walls painted a shade of institutional beige that promises nothing and erases all memory of what color was before. The tables are pulled into a single oblong horseshoe, with twenty investigators—names stenciled in block letters on front-facing placards—ringed around Agent Marcus Lee, who stands before a rolling whiteboard tattooed in four shades of dry-erase. Overhead, two projectors throw twin rectangles of light onto the far wall, one a live-scroll of annotated transcript, the other a color-coded checklist that grows and subdivides as the hour proceeds.

The room is sharp with the chemical sting of fresh marker and the slow exhale of recycled air.

Lee starts by greeting each table. "Team A—good to see you again. Team B, you survived the last module? Team C, you look better caffeinated this time." There is a low ripple of laughter, genuine, a relief after the grimness of the last session.

He picks up a blue marker, caps it with a click, and writes at the top of the board: "OBJECTIVITY—PROTOCOLS."

"Today," he says, "we do two things: first, learn how to interrogate the facts, not just the people; second, get our hands dirty with real case files." He gestures to the stack of folders at the end of the table—each labeled with a case number, sealed with a fat blue rubber band.

He paces once, then flicks a remote. The left-side projector fills with a chunk of transcript:

INVESTIGATOR: Did he force you into the apartment?

VICTIM: I think so, yes.

INVESTIGATOR: And then he closed the door, right?

VICTIM: Yes.

INVESTIGATOR: Did he say anything threatening?

VICTIM: I… I don't remember.

Lee taps the board. "What's the problem here?"

A woman from Team C raises her hand. "All leading questions."

Lee: "Yes. Everything is a yes/no, with the answer already embedded in the question. We might as well write the statement for her."

He points to a second excerpt, in red:

INTERVIEWER: Can you tell me, in your own words, what happened when you entered the apartment?

VICTIM: He pulled me inside. He was angry, but I don't know what he wanted. He kept saying I had to sit down.

Lee: "Better, right? Open prompt, zero leading. The narrative is hers, not ours."

He uncaps a black marker and writes: "RULE ONE: LET THE NARRATIVE LEAD."

He scrolls to the next transcript:

INVESTIGATOR: You said it happened at eight p.m., but your phone shows texts from the suspect at 8:23. Can you explain that?

VICTIM: I thought it was earlier.

INVESTIGATOR: Did you get the time wrong, or did the texts happen after?

VICTIM: I'm not sure. Maybe I misremembered.

Lee circles the lines in blue. "What's the move here?"

A man from Team A: "Don't accuse—ask for clarification. Say something like, 'Help me understand this gap.'"

Lee grins. "Yes. The moment you frame it as a contradiction, you plant the idea that she's lying. Instead, it's a puzzle—one you're solving together."

He writes: "RULE TWO: PUZZLE, NOT PROSECUTION."

He steps to the side, clicks to the right-hand screen. It fills with a downloadable checklist:

PHYSICAL SAMPLES (DNA, swabs, clothing)

ELECTRONIC COMMUNICATIONS (texts, calls, social)

SURVEILLANCE (CCTV, traffic cams)

WITNESS STATEMENTS

INDEPENDENT CORROBORATION (timelines, receipts, third parties)

Lee holds up a thick sheaf of printed checklists. "Pass these down. Your job: annotate as we go. If you see a gap, flag it. If you see a leap of logic, highlight it."

Pages are distributed, pens uncapped. The ceiling fan ticks on, a soft background percussion.

Lee taps the first item: "Physical samples." He brings up a case file—photograph of a ripped shirt, a close-up of a torn button, a swab kit lined in evidence tape.

"Take Case 2228. Victim reports assault, claims shirt was torn in struggle. First investigator never logged the shirt, just took a photo. When the evidence was finally collected, it had been laundered. DNA lost. Case fell apart in court."

He underlines "CHAIN OF CUSTODY" in red. "If it's not documented, it didn't happen. If you're squeamish about collecting evidence, the defense will make you pay for it."

He moves to the next: "Electronic communications." A slide pops up, showing a log of texts, half of them deleted, the rest full of vague statements and timestamps that contradict the interview narrative.

"Case 2228 again. Suspect and victim exchanged 47 texts before the incident, many deleted. Digital forensics pulled them back. Turns out, the two had been arguing all week—context the initial team missed. If you don't pull the phone records, you're blind to motive, escalation, and possible consent issues."

Lee turns, inviting the room: "What's the risk here?"

A woman from Team B: "Cherry-picking the messages. Only reading what supports your theory."

Lee: "Exactly. You read the whole thread, not just the three texts that look damning."

He scrolls to "Surveillance." A pixelated still from a gas station camera appears: two figures, one in a red jacket, the other indistinct, timestamped.

"Never rely on victim or suspect to identify clothing colors, make or model of car, or sequence of movement. Camera lies less than memory. But—" he points— "interpretation still matters. This video shows the suspect with the victim, but only for fifteen seconds, nowhere near the claimed location. You have to check every frame, not just the highlights."

He flicks to "Witness Statements." A side-by-side appears: three witnesses, each giving a different description of the suspect's height, clothing, even gender.

"Memory is trash," Lee says, half-joking. "The more you press, the more likely you'll get a story that fits the last thing you said. Compare all three at once. Look for overlap, not perfection."

He writes: "RULE THREE: VERIFY VIA VARIANCE."

The final bullet: "Independent corroboration." Lee draws a box around it. "This is your ace. If everything else falls apart, third-party evidence will save the case. Credit card receipts, bus pass logs, Uber data, even weather reports. Anything that can't be gamed by the people involved."

He slides to a summary checklist, then hands out the first case folder to each group. "Here's your practical: go through the file, and annotate every time the process failed, or could fail. Flag the leading questions, missing verification, or blind acceptance of a single narrative."

The groups fall silent, heads bowed over the printouts. Some flip straight to the transcripts, others to the forensics. A low buzz of discussion starts, first tentative, then growing as investigators find the gaps, the contradictions, the moments where protocol could have changed the outcome.

Lee paces, listening, interjecting only to steer or clarify.

At the half-hour mark, he brings the room back with a snap of the marker.

"Pop quiz. Who can recite our three rules of objectivity?"

Team C's lead: "Let the narrative lead. Puzzle, not prosecution. Verify via variance."

Lee nods. "If you do those three things, you're better than ninety percent of field investigators. If you slip, the case may not survive review. Or worse—you'll put the wrong person away, or let the right one walk."

He checks the clock, then clicks the projector to a blue screen.

"Next session: field application. You'll test these protocols in a mock interview, live camera, and you will be graded—by me, by each other, and by the protocols themselves. No pressure." He smiles, and the room gives a collective exhale, part dread, part anticipation.

"Break for lunch. Practice on your own, or partner up. If you need extra checklists, grab them on the way out. See you back at 1400."

The investigators gather their materials, some already debating points, others copying annotations, a few just sitting with the weight of the morning.

Agent Lee wipes the board clean, blue marker smearing to a pale echo, then lines up the pens at the base.

The training room is quiet for a moment, the fans making small cyclones of air, the checklists fanned out on every desk like cards waiting to be dealt.

And in the stillness, you can almost hear the shift: the narrative is now theirs to build, or to break, as the evidence requires.

The final training session is held in a wedge of a room tucked into the northeast corner of headquarters, where polished wooden floors trap the late-afternoon sun and the dust motes circle like pale gold spores. Twelve investigators sit at three round tables, the surfaces crowded with notepads, highlighters, and half-drained mugs of tea. At the front stands Sergeant Priya Kapoor, sleeves rolled to the elbow, her hair clipped back in a bun as neat as a punctuation mark. She holds a stack of glossy protocol packets, their covers a reflective navy that mirrors the windows behind her.

"Let's bring it in," Kapoor says, her voice low but insistent. She hands a packet to each table, then waits for the rustle of pages to subside.

The protocol is brand new—most in the room have only heard rumor of it, and now the legend is flattened out into 54 pages of stepwise instruction.

"Today we integrate victim support with verification," Kapoor begins. She clicks a wall-mounted remote, and the screen behind her flickers to life. The first slide is a flowchart in color: blue, yellow, red. At each node, a crisp font shouts the stages of the new process:

- INITIAL INTAKE—dual investigator presence

- ADVOCATE BRIEF—mandatory, before any substantive questioning

- AUDIO-VISUAL RECORD—continuous, no exceptions

- FORENSIC COLLECTION—standardized, chain of custody logged in real time

- SUPERVISORY REVIEW—every case, every time

Kapoor walks through the sequence, stopping at each step to elaborate. "The intake is always done in pairs, to minimize pressure and reduce the risk of one officer guiding the narrative. The victim advocate is brought in first, before any facts are established. No deviation. The interview is recorded, beginning to end. If there's a break, it's logged and explained. Forensics are not an afterthought—they happen as early as possible, and everything is photographed, bagged, and entered into the database before the next step."

She clicks to the next slide, which zooms in on the role of the advocate. "Some of you haven't worked with a dedicated victim specialist. That changes as of this month. Sarah Cole is in the back—" Kapoor gestures, and a woman in a pale gray sweater stands. She is in her late forties, hair streaked with silver, her smile practiced but genuine.

Kapoor: "Sarah, would you run the protocol?"

Cole steps up, hands folded at her waist. "My job is simple. I'm here to listen and explain each step as it happens. I don't argue, I don't coach, I just make sure the subject knows exactly what to expect. If they need a break, I ask for one. If they feel overwhelmed, I help them name it. The goal is not to 'protect' the subject from the process—it's to keep them functional, so their statement is real, not an artifact of stress."

She turns to the group. "If you're worried about losing control, don't be. The protocol is designed so that no one person can tilt it in one direction. If there's disagreement, it's logged, and reviewed by a supervisor before it goes into the final file."

Kapoor nods her thanks, then pulls a flip chart onto the easel next to the screen. She flips to the first page: "SUPPORTIVE MEASURES."

She lists them off: "Separate rooms for advocate and subject, so the advocate can prep and debrief. Step-by-step explanation of process, written out for the subject to review and keep. Lighting is soft but not homey—think neutral, not nurturing. Chairs are ergonomic, but there's no couch, no blankets, no pillows. The point is to make the space safe, not to create a false sense of family."

She runs through a quick role-play, with Cole as advocate and a trainee as the victim. The dialogue is neutral, but every word is monitored for tone. When the investigator slips into a leading question, Cole interrupts: "Let's let them finish their thought." Kapoor nods, logs the intervention on a legal pad, and resumes.

As the sun lowers, the window's grid pattern climbs the far wall, breaking the institutional palette with diagonal bars of gold. The room's energy softens—not in fatigue, but in a kind of collective awareness that the protocols are now theirs to use, to live inside.

Kapoor brings up the final slide: "BEST PRACTICES—FIELD APPLICATION." It is a list, nothing more:

- Document everything, even breaks and mistakes

- Never rely on a single narrative

- Always explain the process, every step

- Use the advocate; never bypass

- Debrief as a team, not solo

She closes the session with a single line, read from the bottom of the protocol packet: "Balance is our safeguard."

The class is dismissed. Chairs scrape back, packets are gathered, and for a long minute no one leaves, as if the sunlight itself has made the room sticky with intent.

Kapoor collects the camcorder, scans the tables for stray handouts, then turns off the screen. "Maintain these protocols in every case," she says, quiet but final.

Outside the blinds, the day is nearly gone, but the learning is still etched into the room—the way the shadows fell, the way the words landed, the way every investigator left with the same packet, and the same weight of responsibility.

In the corridor, the twelve pause before splitting off, each already replaying the steps in their minds.

For the first time, the process feels less like a wall and more like a guardrail, something that keeps you from falling off the edge and into the story you wanted to believe.

CHAPTER 10

Dominant Witness Theory: How Strong Personalities Shape Investigations

Dominant Witness Theory: A Definition and Primer

The term "Dominant Witness Theory" is not new to law enforcement or to the cognitive sciences, though its importance in criminal investigations is only recently catching up to the scale of its effects. The theory, simply stated, posits that within any group of eyewitnesses, the recollection of events will, over time and exposure, align with the version articulated most forcefully by the most assertive member present. This effect occurs regardless of the initial accuracy of the dominant account. Once a narrative is established and repeated, the remaining witnesses—whether consciously or not—adjust their memories to fit the mold. The implications for investigators, attorneys, and fact-finders are profound.

Memory, as covered in the previous chapters, is not a video playback. It is a living process, inherently plastic, shaped by internal and external factors alike. Suggestive questioning, leading prompts, and narrative cues all create room for distortion, whether by accident or intent. Dominant Witness Theory (DWT) addresses a related, often-overlooked source of error: not the language of the interrogator, but the influence of other witnesses.

What is a "dominant" witness? In the context of DWT, it refers to the individual who, by force of personality, social status, or simply verbal fluency, sets the narrative agenda. This is not always the loudest person in the room—sometimes it is the most certain, the one least hesitant to fill a silence with a detailed account. Over repeated interviews or group debriefs, the dominant narrative takes root and, through a process akin to social osmosis, becomes the "official" version, often at the expense of other, potentially more accurate memories.

Empirical Evidence: How Group Memory Bends

A 2017 meta-analysis by Wexler & Jameson, reviewing over 1,200 group eyewitness studies, found that when witnesses were permitted to discuss an event among themselves prior to providing formal statements, 61% of all witness pairs exhibited significant convergence in their recollections, even when their initial statements were starkly divergent. In groups of four or more, this convergence rate rose to 78%. The final account almost always favored the most confident or detailed retelling, regardless of whether it matched physical or forensic evidence.

To see this effect in action, consider the following scenario—a composite case, assembled from actual fieldwork and laboratory studies:

At 9:45 p.m., a street robbery occurs at a crowded intersection. Five bystanders witness the incident. In the immediate aftermath, all five are held on site by police for questioning. The officer, understaffed and eager to speed the process, allows the witnesses to wait together before formal interviews. Over the next hour, the group discusses the event multiple times, attempting to "help each other remember." By the time individual statements are collected, four of five witnesses describe the perpetrator as wearing a red jacket and a baseball cap.

The fifth, initially insistent that the suspect wore blue, now adds, "I think it was blue, but maybe it looked red in the light, like they said."

Surveillance footage later reveals the perpetrator wore a blue hoodie, no hat. The group's error is not simply additive; it is multiplicative, with each discussion making the false memory more entrenched.

This pattern, replicated in hundreds of studies, reveals two key points: (1) the presence of a dominant witness increases convergence; (2) the accuracy of the dominant narrative is not predictive of its success in "overwriting" other accounts.

Dominant Witness Mechanisms: How the Influence Works

The mechanism by which dominant witnesses assert control over the group narrative is both psychological and sociological. Three interlocking forces drive the process:

1. Social Conformity

The desire to belong, to avoid conflict, or to be perceived as credible pushes individuals toward consensus. Solomon Asch's classic line-length experiments, in which subjects consistently reported a false answer in the face of group consensus, are frequently cited in law enforcement circles—but rarely extended to the domain of memory. The principle holds: witnesses, even when certain, will often defer to a confident peer rather than risk appearing "off" or uncooperative.

2. Authority Bias

In mixed-age, mixed-status groups, the recollection of an older, higher-status, or otherwise authoritative figure is adopted more readily. In field studies, a teacher's memory of a school incident is repeated and magnified by students, even when it is directly contradicted by security footage. In family groups, the patriarch or matriarch's recollection dominates, regardless of factual error.

3. The Erosion of Self-Doubt

Perhaps the most insidious effect: the gradual undermining of personal memory through exposure to group "truth." Over time, the passive witness begins to question not only the specifics, but the existence of their own memory. The internal dialogue shifts from "I know what I saw" to "Maybe I saw it wrong." In practice, this means that even when forensic evidence supports an outlier's version, their confidence is so eroded by repeated contradiction that they are less likely to defend it—or to mention it at all.

Sidebar: Experimental Data on Witness Influence

- In a 2019 controlled trial, participants viewed a simulated crime and were then divided into groups. In each group, one "seeded" member was trained to offer a detailed but slightly incorrect description (e.g., "The thief had a beard" when none was present). In over 70% of group interviews, the beard detail was adopted by at least one other member.

- When initial interviews were conducted in isolation, accuracy rates remained at or above 85%. When witnesses were allowed to converse before statements, accuracy dropped to 53%, with dominant details overwriting the rest.

- The duration of group exposure mattered: every five minutes of additional discussion increased the chance of convergence by 10%.

Applications and Warnings

For investigators, the lesson is clear: any delay in separating witnesses after an incident is an invitation for narrative drift. Allowing group discussion—whether by design or neglect—results in a flattening of perspective, often to the detriment of accuracy. The dominant witness effect is not an anomaly, but the rule.

This does not mean that all dominant witnesses are unreliable, or that the consensus version is always incorrect. It does mean, however, that group dynamics create a powerful filter, one that may erase outliers or "weird" facts that are in fact crucial. The quietest, least certain voice in the room may possess the only correct detail—until it is talked out of them by social gravity.

Summary Points

- Dominant Witness Theory explains the tendency of group memory to align with the account of the most assertive member, regardless of initial accuracy.

- The mechanism relies on social conformity, authority bias, and the gradual erosion of self-doubt among passive witnesses.

- Group discussion prior to formal interviews significantly reduces accuracy, and the dominant account is often the least challenged, most repeated, and best remembered.

- Investigators must take care to minimize group interaction, document initial memories before discussion, and remain alert to the dynamics of dominance and submission within witness pools.

The chapter ahead presents a real-world case study in which these forces played out with high stakes. But the lesson here is the same as it was for neutral questioning: the process shapes the outcome. The structure of the interview, the sequence of events, and the personalities in play are not just background—they are the battlefield on which the truth is contested.

Case Study: The Riverfront Robbery and the Collapse of Witness Independence

On July 14, 2018, just past 10:30 p.m., a robbery occurred outside the Riverside Bistro, a restaurant at the edge of a mid-sized city's historic district. The incident itself was brief—a man approached a couple leaving the restaurant, displayed a weapon, and demanded the woman's handbag. The suspect fled toward the river, vanishing before police could respond. In the aftermath, five witnesses gave statements: the victim, her companion, and three bystanders seated on the patio.

Within seventy-two hours, a suspect was arrested and charged. Six weeks later, DNA evidence exonerated him. The error was not in the evidence collection, nor in the analysis. The failure was in the handling of the witnesses, and the fatal flaw was the unchecked dominance of a single, confident voice.

Phase 1: The Scene and the Separation Protocol

The responding officer, per department protocol, separated the witnesses immediately. The couple was interviewed together in a patrol car, while the three bystanders—two college students and a bartender on a smoke break—were each interviewed in situ, at different tables. All five statements were taken within an hour of the event.

The raw statements, redacted for privacy, are excerpted below.

Witness A (Victim):

"He was tall, maybe six foot or a little over. Thin face, light eyes, brownish hair. He said not to scream. I saw a gun, small, silver, like a toy almost. He wore a black hoodie, sleeves pulled over his hands."

Witness B (Companion):

"Average height. Maybe my height? Five-ten? White male, maybe late 20s. Hair was... dark, not sure if black or brown. I don't remember a beard. Hoodie and jeans, I think. He kept one hand in the pocket."

Witness C (Student 1):

"He came fast, from the side. Hoodie up, couldn't see the face. Pretty sure he was Black, maybe mixed? Not super tall, normal size. He grabbed her, took the purse, ran toward the river. Didn't see a gun."

Witness D (Student 2):

"Black male, hoodie. I didn't see a gun, but he acted like he had one. He was in and out, maybe ten seconds. Height? Couldn't say. Seemed quick, not big."

Witness E (Bartender):

"Looked white to me, but it was dark. He had a hood up, but I thought I saw stubble. Didn't see a weapon. He mumbled something to the woman, not sure what. Maybe five-nine? He ran toward the river path."

Immediately, the variations stand out: disagreement on race, height, weapon, facial hair, and even the presence of a gun.

Phase 2: The Debrief and the Drift

Standard procedure calls for independent statements before any contact between witnesses. However, the detective assigned to the case, overwhelmed by the simultaneous interviews, permitted the three bystanders to sit together in the restaurant lobby after their statements were taken, "for comfort." The two students began rehashing the incident with the bartender present. The conversation was not monitored or recorded.

Within a day, all witnesses were recalled for follow-up interviews. This time, the statements were nearly identical, adopting language and details from Witness C—who, as it turned out, was the most confident and socially dominant of the group.

Compare the first round of statements to the second:

Round 2 Excerpts:

Witness C (Student 1):

"Definitely a Black male, maybe 5'11", had a gun in his hand but kept it pointed down. Hoodie and dark jeans. He pushed the woman, grabbed the purse, and ran."

Witness D (Student 2):

"Black guy, maybe six feet. Hoodie up. I saw the gun, looked black, not silver. He pushed her and took the bag. He ran east toward the river."

Witness E (Bartender):

"I remember now, he was Black. The hood was up, but I saw his chin. He had a gun, I think. He pushed the lady, then took off."

Even the victim and her companion's accounts, in round two, shifted toward the dominant group memory:

Victim (A):

"Maybe he was mixed? His skin looked light, but not totally white. The gun was black, not silver, maybe I remembered wrong. He said, 'Don't scream, or I'll use it.'"

Companion (B):

"Now that I think about it, he could have been mixed. The lighting was bad, but I don't know why I said white. He had a black hoodie, and the gun was dark, not shiny."

Phase 3: The Language Convergence

A forensic linguist later reviewed the interview transcripts. What emerged was textbook dominant witness influence: the specific phrasing used by Student 1—"Black male," "gun in hand but pointed down," "grabbed the purse, ran toward the river"—was echoed, often verbatim, in every subsequent statement.

Key terms from the dominant witness, as they spread through the group:

- "Black male," initially used only by Witnesses C and D, appears in all five statements by round two.

- "Grabbed the purse, ran toward the river," unique to C in round one, becomes universal by round two.

- "He pushed her," mentioned only by D in round one, is adopted by all but one witness in round two.

- The color and type of gun, initially variable (silver, black, "like a toy," "maybe just his hand"), converge to "black gun" in four of five second-round interviews.

The victim's initial description—a tall, thin-faced, light-eyed, brown-haired man—gave way to the dominant group memory: a Black male, average height, black hoodie, dark gun.

Phase 4: The Investigative Consequences

Detectives, relying on the converged witness accounts, issued a BOLO ("be on the lookout") for a Black male, approximately 5'11", late twenties, black hoodie, armed with a handgun. Surveillance review focused on this profile, and within two days, a suspect—Demetrius Rowe, 27, matching the group composite—was identified by patrol as "a known local with history." He was arrested while walking home from his job at a nearby construction site.

Despite Rowe's protestations of innocence, and an alibi supported by co-workers, the case built around the witness statements. At lineup, all three bystanders identified him as the robber. The victim and companion, when pressed, "thought" he "could be the guy."

Two weeks later, DNA from the purse strap and clothing fibers collected at the scene excluded Rowe as the perpetrator. A subsequent review of security camera footage, previously overlooked due to the focus on the "Black male suspect," revealed a different man—taller, thinner, white, wearing a black hoodie and dark pants—committing the robbery. He was later arrested and confessed.

Phase 5: Forensic Analysis of the Collapse

A post-mortem of the case, conducted by the department's Internal Review Board, identified the dominant witness effect as the principal failure point. The convergence of language, the erosion of diversity in witness accounts, and the overconfidence of the investigators in the "group truth" created a classic feedback loop: initial divergence ignored, subsequent convergence celebrated as confirmation, and critical evidence filtered through the lens of the dominant narrative.

From the Review Board's summary:

"In this case, the earliest, most independent recollections were the most accurate. All subsequent convergence was a function of social conformity, not improved memory. The failure to maintain separation and document initial variance led directly to the wrongful arrest."

Practical Lessons

1. First statements are gold. The further from the event, or the more exposure witnesses have to each other, the less reliable the recollection becomes.

2. Never treat group consensus as validation. Instead, flag it as a potential warning sign for narrative drift.

3. Language matters. The specific words, phrases, and "facts" introduced by a dominant witness are likely to be repeated—and amplified—by others.

4. Physical and forensic evidence must remain independent of witness composites. If initial evidence does not match the dominant story, the discrepancy is a clue, not a nuisance.

The case of the Riverfront Robbery is not an outlier. In the national exoneration database, a majority of overturned convictions involving multiple witnesses featured some degree of narrative convergence post-incident. In nearly every case, a single assertive witness—sometimes right, sometimes wrong—rewrote the memory of the group.

Dominant Witness Theory is not just a laboratory construct. It is the engine behind the silent flattening of perspective that plagues real investigations. The best safeguard is vigilance in the earliest moments—when the noise is still loud, the contradictions still raw, and the truth has not yet been rendered down to a single, confident voice.

Protocol: Neutralizing Dominant Witness Effects in Criminal Investigations

The risk of witness contamination by dominant personalities is not theoretical—it is a statistically robust, field-validated reality. The previous case study made clear the stakes: a misdirected investigation, a wrongful arrest, and a near-miss with wrongful conviction, all stemming from the unchecked narrative gravity of a single confident voice. To translate the lesson into operational practice, law enforcement must employ specific protocols that identify, disrupt, and document dominant witness effects from the very first contact.

I. Detecting Dominant-Passive Dynamics

The first line of defense is awareness. Investigators must be trained to spot the telltale signs of dominance and deference in witness pools.

Key indicators of dominance:

- Body language: Dominant witnesses tend to make direct eye contact, use broad gestures, and physically orient themselves toward both the investigator and other witnesses.

- Speaking order: In group contexts, dominant witnesses speak first and often, interrupt others, and restate their version repeatedly.

- Language markers: Use of certainty ("I know for a fact..."), declarative statements, and detailed narratives, as opposed to tentative or hedged recollections.

- Deference cues: Passive witnesses often preface statements with qualifiers ("I'm not sure, but..."), look to the dominant for approval, or echo phrases used by them.

Operational Tip: During group debriefs (e.g., emergency scenes, preliminary holding), a brief period of silent observation before interviews can reveal who holds social sway. Note these dynamics for the case file and for later review.

II. Structured Interview Protocol

A. Immediate Separation

Upon securing a scene, witnesses should be separated physically and, if possible, spatially so that sightlines and overheard conversation are eliminated. Even brief exposure to a dominant narrative can alter recall. The separation must be documented—time, location, and duration for each witness.

B. Staggered Interviews

Conduct initial interviews as close to the event as feasible, and always before witnesses have opportunity for discussion. Prioritize those most at risk for influence (e.g., children, individuals of lower social status, those already exhibiting deference) for earliest interview slots.

C. Individualized Questioning

The opening prompt should always be open-ended and free of context:

- "Tell me everything you remember, starting from the beginning."

- "Use your own words; I want to hear exactly what you saw."

Follow-up questions must avoid leading language and avoid cross-referencing details from other witnesses.

D. Reassurance for Passive Witnesses

Passive witnesses often lose confidence in their memory when confronted with ambiguity or lack of consensus. The investigator should explicitly normalize memory gaps and variance:

- “It’s common for people to remember different parts.”

- “Even if you’re unsure, I want you to include it.”

This approach increases the chance that unique but crucial details are preserved, rather than self-edited away.

III. Documentation and Independence

A. Independent Statements

Each witness’s statement must be documented separately, with no cross-contamination of notes or prompts. Where possible, use audio or video recording to preserve not just the content, but the confidence and manner in which details are expressed.

B. Statement Timestamping

All witness statements should be timestamped—down to the minute. Any group interactions that occur between statement collection and follow-up interviews must be documented.

C. Cross-Statement Analysis

As part of the post-interview review, investigators should actively look for language convergence and drift over time. If a witness's phrasing or certainty changes after group exposure, flag this in the report and consider weighting the initial, independent account more heavily in analysis.

D. Influence Logging

If it is discovered that witnesses have discussed the event (whether intentionally or by accident), log the nature of the contact, duration, and any observable outcome on subsequent statements.

IV. Interviewing Techniques to Mitigate Dominant Effects

- Use closed, private spaces for interviews, especially with children or those likely to be influenced.

- Avoid any mention of "what others said," even in casual or rapport-building conversation.

- For follow-up interviews, prompt witnesses to recall their original memory, not their current "shared" version: "When you first thought about it, how did you remember it then?"

- Consider using alternate interviewers for repeat statements to reduce subconscious cueing.

V. Training and Institutionalization

A. Investigator Training

All personnel involved in witness handling must receive formal instruction on Dominant Witness Theory and its operational consequences. The curriculum should include:

- Recognition of dominance and deference cues.

- Practice with open-ended, neutral questioning.

- Case studies illustrating narrative drift and wrongful consensus.

B. Scenario-Based Exercises

Use mock investigations with seeded dominant witnesses to train teams in preserving initial diversity and catching convergence in real time.

C. Ongoing Review

Supervisors must review major case statements for signs of convergence or contamination, and provide feedback to field investigators. Whenever possible, integrate witness independence checks into internal audits and quality control.

VI. Checklists and Red Flags

For convenience, a field-ready checklist:

- [ ] Witnesses physically separated on scene.

- [ ] Each interview conducted in isolation.

- [ ] No leading prompts; open-ended start.

- [ ] Variances between accounts logged, not "corrected."

- [ ] Initial statements prioritized in case file.

- [ ] Group interactions (if any) logged with details.

- [ ] Follow-ups flagged for drift or convergence.

- [ ] Supervisor review of narrative changes.

Red Flags:

- Witnesses repeating identical phrases or descriptions.

- Sudden changes in a witness's certainty after group exposure.

- Reluctance by witnesses to assert original memory in later interviews.

- Investigators unconsciously pressuring outlier witnesses to conform.

VII. Impact on Wrongful Identifications and Case Accuracy

Empirical research (see previous chapter) demonstrates that cases following structured witness independence protocols have a 34% lower rate of false suspect identification, and an 18% higher rate of later corroboration by physical evidence. Agencies that institutionalize these methods see improved case resolution rates and fewer reversals on appeal.

Most importantly, the dignity and integrity of each witness's experience is preserved. The story of the event remains plural, not flattened. The truth emerges from careful comparison, not from social pressure.

Conclusion: The Human Factor is the Wildcard

All the science and procedure in the world cannot eliminate the basic human tendency to defer to the most confident person in the room. But law enforcement can, and must, design systems that keep that tendency from distorting the investigative record.

The dominant witness is not the enemy. Nor is the passive witness a liability. Both are essential data points, and the job of the investigator is to keep each account as clean and distinct as possible—until the full picture can be assembled, with all its contradictions intact.

It is not consensus, but the preservation of difference, that gives the investigative process its power.

In every case, the first and final responsibility is the same: trust the process, not the loudest voice. Build protocols that shield memory from the warp of confidence. And never forget that the truth, like memory, is a conversation—a space where what is known and what is unknown can both exist, side by side, until the evidence settles the matter.

CHAPTER 11

Under Pressure: Public Demand And Investigative Integrity

The plaza outside the city's police headquarters is a shallow amphitheater, one flat concrete apron sloped imperceptibly toward the street, ringed by a phalanx of battered municipal planters and the low hum of security bollards. At 11:00 sharp, the plaza is not empty. It is packed—three rows deep in local media, a flock of city reporters bristling with tripod legs, phones, shoulder rigs, every lens drawn up and out, pointed like artillery toward a three-step riser and the empty podium at its center.

It is July, but a wind off the river makes the air brittle, and every time a camera flash detonates, the crowd blinks, a living nervous system. Above, the news vans stack like food trucks at the perimeter: Channel 4, Eyewitness 7, two streaming startups, all their gear hissing to life. On the lead van, a digital ticker glows in red: HOURS SINCE MURDER: 52.

The story, for anyone not living inside a screen, is "The Parkside Killing." Three nights prior, a tech entrepreneur named Lyle Shein was found dead in a city park, neck fractured, face caved in with a landscaping brick. The body was discovered by a dog-walker at 6:17 a.m. and, by 7:00, the news was everywhere. The papers ran it above the fold. The networks played it on loop: a mugshot, then a photo of the scene, yellow tape fluttering in the morning's blue. By noon, the mayor had issued a statement calling it "senseless." By sundown, someone on Reddit had named it, and the name stuck.

At 11:03, the doors of the headquarters roll wide, and the assembled crowd stiffens. Out comes the chief—impeccable in midnight blue, chest straining with medals—and next to him, the lead detective, face weathered and mask-still, hairline drawing a severe parenthesis around the skull. They walk slow, as if savoring the seconds before the feeding. The microphones are alive before the podium is reached.

"Chief!—has the suspect been identified?"

"Detective!—can you confirm the reports of a witness?"

"Is it true there were no cameras in the park?—"

"—sources say the scene was contaminated, can you comment—"

Every question overlaps the next, some shouted for soundbite, some for genuine desperation. The chief lifts a hand—ceremonial—and the wave of noise backs up one syllable, then two, before resuming as a new species of din: the indignant murmur.

At the lip of the riser, the detective's jaw tightens. He does not look at the cameras, only at the printouts clutched in his left hand, marked in blue pen. The chief waits for the right moment, then steps to the podium, lips pressed tight.

"Thank you all for coming. We have an update in the investigation of the tragic homicide that occurred early Sunday morning at Parkside.

Detective Voss will brief you on the progress of the case. We appreciate your cooperation as we continue to gather facts—"

A hand shoots up from the front row, the reporter's shirt so white it stings the eyes. "Chief—there's still no suspect in custody, correct? It's been 48 hours already—when can the public expect an arrest?"

The chief's composure cracks at the edges; he glances at his watch, as if calculating time not just since the murder, but since the last attack from this same journalist. "The investigation is proceeding as swiftly as possible," he says. "We will not jeopardize its integrity by rushing. Detective Voss will answer further."

The transfer is seamless, but Voss's movement is not. He grips the podium hard enough to bleach the knuckles. The camera flashes set off in new rhythm, each one a strobe; the effect is to freeze Voss, again and again, in a posture of braced endurance.

Voss speaks in the flat register of the exhausted: "As of this morning, the department has processed over two hundred tips. The forensics team is continuing to evaluate evidence from the scene. We have not made any arrests at this time. The park remains closed to the public."

A different reporter calls out, this one's badge clipped sideways to the lanyard: "Are you investigating the reports that the victim had received threats?"

Voss: "We are looking at all angles. At this stage, we are not releasing specifics regarding the victim's private communications."

A voice from the rear—Channel 4, veteran, first to every fire—"Is it true a city worker entered the scene before police arrived?"

Voss pauses, just a second too long. "At the time the body was discovered, the area was not yet secured. This is not unusual in public spaces. The scene has since been thoroughly documented by forensics."

"Was the worker questioned?"

"All witnesses present at the scene have been interviewed. None are suspects at this time."

A third voice, not shouting but with more bite, cuts in: "Detective—statistically, most murders are solved within 72 hours. Are you confident this case will be closed by Friday?"

The countdown ticker, impossible to ignore, blares "52" in red even as the question lands. Voss looks at the display, then at the chief, then back at his notes. He answers, careful and deliberate: "We are committed to solving this case, no matter how long it takes. But yes, we are optimistic based on the evidence gathered so far."

The press conference pivots, then accelerates. Every reporter has a version of the same question—How soon? How close?—and the answers circle, careful not to reveal what isn't yet solid. A cluster of photojournalists breaks off to capture reaction shots: the detective's hard-set face, the chief's forced calm, the restless shifting of uniformed officers in the lobby behind the glass. The chief, no longer answering, stares into the crowd as if searching for the next landmine.

At 11:28, the questions turn more aggressive.

"Why is the city so slow to release footage from nearby traffic cams?"

"Are you afraid publicizing a suspect description will spook the killer?"

"Has the mayor's office interfered with the flow of information?"

The last question is a live wire. The chief cuts in, voice up half a decibel. "The mayor's office has been supportive. The only priority here is bringing justice to the victim and his family."

The lead detective's jaw clamps so tight the muscle chords stand out. He does not look at the mayor's liaison, who is standing just out of frame, phone held out like a Geiger counter.

By noon, the conference has devolved into sound bites and flashbacks, each journalist chasing the angle that will land first on social. In the lull, a Channel 7 tech adjusts the focus on the news van's countdown clock, now at "53," and the number glows over the entire scene, burning into the retina of every person on the plaza.

In a side conversation, two rival journalists compare notes.

"He looks like he hasn't slept in days."

"They're getting hammered at city hall. I heard someone's leaking the next-of-kin interview already."

"You think he's got a real lead?"

"No. But they're going to arrest someone, anyone, by tomorrow. Watch."

The cameras, still hungry, follow the chief and Voss as they retreat to the glass doors, where a uniformed officer waves them through with practiced formality. Once inside, the lobby returns to normal, the hum of HVAC and the undertone of phones ringing behind the partition. Outside, the media pack lingers, hoping for a slip-up, an after-action, or the smallest scrap of new data.

On the street, the red countdown stares back, patient as a bomb.

A block away, the city's digital billboards rotate between a public safety warning—SEE SOMETHING, SAY SOMETHING—and the familiar face of the murder victim, frozen forever in a toothy smile. The tagline: "Help us bring Lyle's killer to justice."

In the headquarters, the chief checks his watch again. Fifty-three hours down, not even halfway to the next press cycle. The clock is the story now. The case has become a timer, and the world expects it to go off on cue.

If every investigation is a race against time, the "72-Hour Rule" is the gun at the starting line, the official and unofficial mark against which all efforts are measured. In homicide, the myth is now codified: solve it in three days, or watch the case calcify and drift toward the cold file shelf. The media abets this story, amplifies it. Every cop show, every local news segment, every city-desk story about a murder that "broke wide open in the first forty-eight" is a nail hammered into public expectation. What no one says, not out loud, is how the pressure of that clock warps the work itself.

Across the country, in precincts with populations over 100,000, a quick survey of case logs tells the tale: in media-saturated murders—those with more than one front-page headline or three network segments in the first week—over 70% of initial suspect IDs occur within three days of the crime. Compare that to routine, untelevised killings, where the rate is closer to 22% in the same window. At first, it looks like a triumph of urgency. But look closer, and the picture inverts.

Internal audits from departments in six major cities, anonymized for politics, show the corollary: The more eyes on the case, the more corners cut to feed the narrative of "swift justice." In the years 2016–2021, media-profiled murders reached the indictment stage three times faster than their less-visible twins, but produced, on average, double the rate of suppression motions, chain-of-custody disputes, and post-conviction challenges. The cases that moved the fastest also stumbled the hardest when subjected to review.

The pressure is felt everywhere, but it is most visible in three distinct phases: lab work, witness statements, and suspect focus.

First, the labs. In the week after a high-profile homicide, the forensic evidence pipeline is rerouted—triaged for "priority status," according to chain-of-command memos. That means samples from the media murder jump the queue, often at the expense of other open cases. But priority means only speed, not thoroughness. In a 2020 review of state forensic labs, 43% of "urgent" samples were processed without full confirmatory runs, and 17% were later found to contain cross-contamination or incomplete DNA profiles. One audit noted, dryly, that "speed is inversely correlated with methodological completeness."

Second, witness work. In the first 72 hours, patrol officers and detectives fan out to interview every possible witness, from family to strangers who happened to be in the park or the alley or the transit line. The goal is coverage, not depth. Witnesses are logged, statements taken in rushed succession, and—most crucially—rarely re-interviewed. The first version stands, even when later inconsistencies emerge. In media cases, follow-ups drop by 65% after Day 4, as attention turns from information-gathering to building a presentable narrative.

A case from the Eastern Seaboard: two teens killed in a late-night shooting. The department, under relentless cable news glare, compiles witness statements from 11 separate sources. Seven of those are in direct contradiction to physical evidence or to each other. Three admit to confusion about the timeline. All 11 are quoted in the indictment. When the case unravels on appeal—key witnesses recanting, others revealed to have overheard speculation before their own interviews—the internal review blames "over-reliance on initial statements" and "failure to conduct iterative interviews." The gap is not in the witnesses' memory, but in the system's refusal to let the story evolve past its debut.

Third, suspect narrowing. This is where the "72-Hour Rule" bites hardest. With the demand for resolution—by city hall, by family, by the press—a short list is made on day one, and every fact after is sorted accordingly. Confirmation bias, usually checked by protocol, is allowed to run its course, bending the case toward a theory before the facts are all in. "Deductive" investigation, in the classic sense, takes over: start with the likeliest suspect, and make the puzzle fit. In high-pressure environments, deductive logic trumps inductive patience.

A classic comparison: Two murders, similar MOs, occur in different parts of the same city two months apart. The first, a robbery-turned-homicide in a liquor store at closing; the second, a nearly identical robbery at a gas station. The first case makes the news; the second, not. In the first, detectives move fast, assemble a suspect list by the end of Day 2, arrest a likely candidate by Day 5. In the second, with no media, the investigation proceeds methodically—witnesses are re-interviewed, video is pulled from adjacent properties, suspects are sifted slowly.

The numbers:

Case 1: Suspect arrested on Day 5. Forensics matched to the suspect, but with two tests inconclusive. Eyewitnesses provide "strong" IDs, but later, on cross, admit to having seen the suspect's face in the news before lineup. Post-conviction, new DNA analysis excludes the suspect. Case is vacated, then retried a year later with a different perpetrator.

Case 2: No suspect for ten days. But in that time, surveillance from three blocks is stitched together, a pattern of movement is logged, and a new suspect is identified based on the combined evidence—never mentioned in the initial wave of interviews. Arrest occurs on Day 19. Forensics are conclusive. No appeals, no suppression.

In a departmental review, the conclusion is succinct: "Media attention accelerates closure, but at the expense of completeness. Premature narrowing of suspect pools increases error rates by a factor of two."

Quantified panic is a self-replicating virus. Every time a department is burned in the press for "inaction," the next case moves faster, and the risk of misfire climbs. In some cities, the brass keeps a live dashboard of "hours to arrest" for every active case. The average for non-media homicides is 18.7 days. For media-cases, it is 4.6. The implied message: slow is failure, speed is virtue.

But the math never tells the whole story. In a closed-door panel at a national homicide conference, a veteran detective puts it this way: "Every cop who's done this knows the first three days are critical. You work the leads hard, you get the physicals and the witnesses before the memory fades. But the dirty secret is, the more the public watches, the more we feel compelled to give them a name—even if we haven't nailed the evidence down yet. It's not just about catching the right guy. Sometimes it's about keeping the city from melting down."

Anecdotes, but they multiply fast:

- In Baltimore, the "Riverbank Stabbing" reaches a breakneck closure with a suspect held before the autopsy is finished. The actual killer is found six months later in county lockup, after a jailhouse confession. The first suspect's charges are dropped, but not before he spends the better part of a year in pre-trial detention.

- In Los Angeles, a double homicide in a grocery parking lot is "solved" in 30 hours—after one shaky eyewitness and two pieces of circumstantial evidence. Media interviews celebrate the rapid work. DNA results, returned a week later, point to a different suspect entirely, but the momentum of the press makes it almost impossible to walk the case back. It takes three months, two press conferences, and a mayoral apology to put the error to rest.

- In Chicago, an internal audit finds that "high-profile" murders are five times more likely to result in civil litigation, usually over wrongful arrest or due process violations. The financial cost is staggering—over $11 million in settlements in a five-year span.

All of which leads to the most important, and least discussed, effect: the story becomes the theory, not the evidence. In the heat of scrutiny, "deductive" policing—start with a thesis, then collect the supporting data—overtakes the slower, more laborious "inductive" model, which lets the facts dictate the theory. The culture, under siege, tilts toward confirmation, and the error is not just in the outcome, but in the process.

Back at the press conference, the chief and the detective feel this logic in the bones. The chief's eyes on the countdown clock, the detective's hand gripping the podium: these are not just tells of stress, but signals of a deeper algorithm at work. The city wants a name, and soon. Every minute after 72 is a minute closer to failure—media, political, reputational, and, most insidious of all, internal.

The 72-Hour Rule is not a law, but it might as well be. It is the expectation that governs the cadence of every investigation, and it is the vector along which every flaw propagates. The lessons of science—control for bias, delay theory until the facts are set—are lost in the blast radius of the clock.

The detective who solves the case in 72 hours is a hero. The one who waits for the right answer, and takes a week, is an afterthought. In the end, the ledger balances: some cases are closed fast and clean. Others, closed fast, but only on paper.

What happens in the next 72 hours determines which side of the ledger the Parkside Killing will land on. The clock, impartial and implacable, ticks forward, waiting to see if this time will be any different.

Day 1: 08:11 a.m. The call comes in from a morning dog-walker, a block off Westlake Avenue, just past the liquor store and the boarded-up pharmacy. The dispatcher doesn't flinch—bodies are not rare in this part of town—but as soon as the first patrol arrives, the perimeter goes up. The victim, a woman in her thirties, is found posed: arms crossed, one shoe removed and set precisely by the curb. Uniforms work the scene with efficient, muted choreography. Before the coroner arrives, the first cameras are already rolling.

At 09:32, the local affiliate cuts to the parking lot, where a station wagon bristles with the gear of an amateur news crew. The segment goes live: "Another possible victim of the so-called Westlake Strangler found this morning—" and in that instant, the case is rebranded. There had been no official linkage of the three prior bodies to any serial pattern, but as of now, the story is national.

By noon, a dozen reporters have set up on the sidewalk, microphones in gloved hands, eyes narrowed against the frost and the lens flare. Inside the precinct, a detective sips coffee, scrolls the headlines, and shakes his head. "They're gonna crucify us," he mutters. "Unless we wrap this one fast."

Day 1: 15:47. The press conference is a formality—no new information, no suspect, no official cause of death. Still, the room is standing room only. The department's media officer, uniform starched and voice steady, reads from a single sheet: "We are treating this incident with the highest priority. Investigative teams are on site. We urge the public to remain calm and to report any suspicious activity." No one buys it, least of all the officer himself.

By sundown, the mayor is quoted in every local outlet: "This city will not tolerate a monster preying on our citizens. I have demanded answers by week's end." In the background, the chief of detectives stares into the middle distance, his mouth set in a line that will, by the next morning, become a meme: "Resting Regret Face."

Day 2: 06:25. The detectives convene for the shift handoff, and already the room is wired. Overnights have produced nothing: no new witnesses, no surveillance, nothing from the forensics. Still, the day watch is told, in explicit language, to "show progress" before noon. A memo, stamped URGENT in blue, is distributed: "All inquiries regarding suspect identity to be routed through PIO. Do not speculate. Report all tips immediately."

The lead investigator, a decade in homicide, knows the drill. She also knows that the forensics backlog means nothing will come back before Thursday, and that witnesses, if there are any, will have been thoroughly coached by news coverage before they speak to detectives.

The first break is a neighbor, woken by police, who reports seeing a man in a gray hoodie near the scene just before dawn. "Looked homeless," she says. "Kind of limped. Maybe forty?" The description is almost useless, but the newsrooms seize it—by 10:00, every broadcast features a rendering of "the suspect," despite the fact that the neighbor never saw a face.

Day 2: 13:09. The city's largest tabloid prints an extra: "WESTLAKE STALKER STRIKES AGAIN!" The font is large enough to read from a block away. The mayor's office, besieged by calls, emails the chief at 13:37: "Need to show movement. Public needs a face. Consider releasing the suspect sketch ASAP."

Internally, the investigators exchange texts: "No evidence yet. This is gonna bite us."

"It's all about the show, man. Don't get caught behind."

Day 3: 09:16. The first solid lead, or what passes for one, is a sighting at a bus stop—another "homeless" man, also in a gray hoodie, also limping. Patrol brings him in. He is groggy, coming off a bender, and cannot account for his whereabouts. He matches the neighbor's description, if only in the broadest sense.

The detective asks for a few hours to interview him. Instead, the PIO, now acting under the direct orders of city hall, schedules a press update for 10:30. The arrestee is paraded as a "person of interest." In the background, two detectives confer with a lab tech: preliminary DNA swabs show no match to the first three victims, but the data is still incomplete.

That afternoon, the media officer issues a statement: "We believe we have the perpetrator in custody. Investigation is ongoing."

Day 3: 21:00. The precinct's group chat lights up. "We have nothing," writes one detective. "Guy couldn't tie his own shoes last night. Alibi might hold." Another responds: "Doesn't matter. We'll close it anyway. City needs a win."

Day 4: The "suspect" is interrogated, processed, and—when no evidence links him to the crime—held on an unrelated bench warrant. The press, sensing the lack of substance, begins to pivot: "Is the Westlake Strangler Still Out There?"

Inside the precinct, morale collapses. "It's a PR job now," says one detective. "Nobody cares about the evidence." The shift commander's daily briefing is explicit: "If you have a lead, you follow it. If you have a suspect, you stick to him like glue. That's the priority."

Day 5: 07:45. Under pressure, the detectives run the suspect's DNA against the state database. Nothing. But on the logic that "something is better than nothing," they move ahead. The neighbor is asked to view a lineup, where she picks out the man in the gray hoodie, though hesitantly. "It could be him, I guess." The lead detective notes the equivocation in the file, but it never makes the next day's briefing.

At 13:30, the chief stands before the cameras and announces the arrest. "We are confident in our investigation. We believe the community is now safe." The mayor is not present, but her chief of staff provides a quote for the evening news: "Thanks to the tireless efforts of our police, the people of Westlake can rest easy tonight."

The cameras pan the scene. The suspect, handcuffed and squinting, is led into a cruiser. In the crowd, a woman whispers to her friend: "I hope they got the right guy."

Day 8: The forensic results return, incomplete but suggestive—some partial fibers, no fingerprints, and, crucially, no DNA match to the man in custody. Internally, the lead detective requests a review. Her request is logged, and ignored.

The DA's office, meanwhile, charges the suspect with first-degree murder. The media goes wild. Op-eds call it "the fastest serial-killer capture in recent memory." Talk radio spends a whole day dissecting the suspect's life, linking unrelated priors and drawing a chain from childhood trauma to present violence.

Year 1, Month 8: The trial is brief. The defense points out the lack of evidence, but the neighbor's equivocal ID, the circumstantial similarity to prior murders, and the relentless echo of the press carry the day. The jury convicts. The judge, facing re-election, sentences the man to life without parole. In the city, the mayor wins a second term, in part on a campaign of "public safety restored."

Year 2: The exoneration comes from an unlikely place. A murder in a neighboring county, identical in MO, is solved when the real killer is caught fleeing a traffic stop. His DNA matches all the Westlake victims, including the most recent. The state lab emails the city detective's office at 14:43 on a Tuesday: "High-confidence match. Recommend immediate review."

The chief is on vacation. The mayor is in D.C. for a policy summit. For forty-eight hours, no one in authority is available to respond.

By Friday, the news has broken. "Westlake Strangler Still on the Loose—City Blundered." The city attorney's office is flooded with calls. The public defender, who handled the original case, files a motion for immediate release and—once the dust clears—a $4.2 million civil suit. The payout is a record, at least for this jurisdiction.

But the cost is more than monetary. In the twenty months while the wrong man was behind bars, the real killer claims three more victims. The media, which had been eager to close the story, reopens it with the same tenacity. This time, the coverage is less triumph, more reckoning. A panel of experts, called to testify before a city commission, labels the whole affair "a classic cascade of confirmation bias, fueled by media and political pressure." The phrase becomes a hashtag within the hour.

From the internal review:

"The investigation was compromised from the outset by the insistence on rapid closure and a relentless focus on the first plausible suspect. Contrary evidence was sidelined. Forensic results were ignored. The press cycle dictated investigative choices at every turn. The result: a wrongful conviction, the destruction of one life, and the loss of three more."

A memo from the mayor's office, leaked six months later, is even more blunt:

"We needed a win. We gambled on a quick resolution, and it backfired. The only move is to own the error and rebuild trust. Suggest the chief step down. Prepare for the lawsuits."

The detective who led the case resigns. The neighbor who identified the wrong man moves out of state. The real killer, when finally tried, pleads guilty and receives a second life sentence.

But the story lingers. Every homicide in the city is now viewed through the lens of the Westlake debacle. The media, chastened, covers each new case with an undercurrent of skepticism. The public, weary, grows cynical about every press release and promise.

The "72-Hour Rule" survives, but now as a warning, not a goal.

In the final report, the last line is left unredacted:

"We will not let the need for speed override the need for truth. Not again."

But even as the ink dries, the clock resets, and somewhere a new case starts. The cycle will repeat, because the world, and the watchers, have not changed.

The "Cold Lake Disappearance" was, in the opening week, a local tragedy—a teenage girl not home for dinner, her mother frantic, her stepfather searching the brush around their house with a neighbor's borrowed flashlight. But by the end of Day 2, it is something else entirely: a superheated feedback loop of suspicion, accusation, and digital outrage.

The first viral post comes from the missing girl's aunt, a screenshot of a text she claims was sent at 11:24 p.m. the night before. The words—"I don't feel safe"—are overlaid in bold red letters, and within an hour the image has 10,000 shares, each one tagged #ColdLakeJustice. The family's GoFundMe, meant to cover "search expenses," passes its initial goal before midnight.

At 06:17 the next morning, the local precinct's social inbox is flooded. By 09:00, the case has its own Wikipedia entry, complete with a running tab of "person-of-interest" rumors, updated in real time. One entry, three days in: "Neighbors report hearing loud argument at 2200 hrs. Police have yet to question the stepfather."

Screenshots and web captures fill the digital record:

- A Change.org petition—DEMAND COLD LAKE POLICE DO THEIR JOB—breaks 50,000 signatures in 36 hours. The petition's main evidence: a cluster of Facebook comments, many by people who have never set foot in the county.

- A Twitter thread, purporting to "follow the money," posts five-year-old bankruptcy records for the stepfather, insinuating motive. A subsequent tweet, widely liked, features an unflattering photo of the man at a backyard barbecue, red-cupped and scowling.

- Instagram stories from classmates, none of whom were with the victim the day she vanished, fill in the gaps with speculation and, in some cases, open fantasy: "I heard she was running away to Florida." "No, she's in Canada with a secret boyfriend." "My cousin said her mom was controlling as fuck."

By the end of Week 1, the Cold Lake PD has received over 200 direct messages, half of them hostile, many explicitly threatening. One, to the department's public account: "If you don't charge the guy, we will." Another, to a detective's personal email: "Your family will regret this if you keep protecting the killer."

Within the department, the pressure is immediate and disorienting. The lead investigator, accustomed to three homicides a year and a dozen bar fights, is now the subject of a Reddit "Ask Me Anything," his face photo-shopped onto a clown suit by the end of Day 2. His family receives a pizza delivery every night for a week, each box labeled "DO YOUR JOB."

In the shift office, the whiteboard tracks not only tips, but "media events." Monday: 3 local news spots, 1 national. Tuesday: 2 local, 3 national, 1 cable. Wednesday: "48 Hours" sends a producer, who waits in the lobby, live-tweeting the lack of updates.

The detective, in an after-action interview:

Q: When did you know the case was out of control?

A: By Thursday. We hadn't processed all the phone dumps yet, and already there were podcasts calling us incompetent, or worse. By Friday, we were told the mayor wanted a suspect in hand. "For public peace of mind," was the phrase.

Q: Did that change your approach?

A: Everything changed. We had a possible sighting in a strip mall, two counties over, but it didn't fit the narrative online. People wanted the stepfather. Nothing else would do.

The next phase is a script, more rehearsed than written:

- Day 10: The stepfather is brought in for formal questioning, and the station lot is ringed by local and regional news vans. The man's lawyer, a cousin, is jeered as he enters.

- Day 11: The interview is conducted. The transcript shows no confession, no admission. But at 17:43, a leak goes out: "Stepfather detained in connection to Cold Lake case." It is not true, but by the time it's corrected, every major outlet has run it.

- Day 13: The stepfather is arrested, based on what the prosecutor calls "a compelling sequence of circumstantial evidence." The actual file, produced later under FOIA, lists only a neighbor's "vague recollection" of seeing him near the woods and an unreturned phone call to the victim's cell.

- Day 15: A candlelight vigil, covered by five TV stations, features the missing girl's mother, who pleads for closure and "justice for my baby." The crowd holds up signs with the hashtag, and the stepfather's mugshot is pasted to a sandwich board at the park entrance.

- Day 19: A local politician, running for re-election, tweets: "Cold Lake demands accountability. Our children must be safe. Thank you to law enforcement for their efforts." The tweet is copied, word for word, by three rival campaigns.

Inside the station, morale tanks. The detective's team is split—half convinced the arrest is a rush job, the other half too battered by the public to resist. The case file grows by the hour, but not with new evidence. Instead, it is padded with screen captures of posts, emails, threats.

Six weeks later, the missing girl is found alive in a suburb three states away, living under an assumed name with a boyfriend. She had staged her own disappearance, inspired in part by "runaway" videos on YouTube. When police recover her, she is unrepentant. "I didn't mean to hurt anyone," she says. "I just wanted out."

The charges against the stepfather are dropped, but not before he has spent 51 days in county lockup. He loses his job. The family breaks apart. The detective is reassigned, and his house, once a quiet split-level on a cul-de-sac, is the subject of a nighttime egging, captured on Ring camera and shared widely.

In the aftermath, the city conducts a survey to measure the impact:

- Public trust in Cold Lake PD, already low, drops 34% in three months.

- 67% of residents polled say they "believe police should respond faster, even if it means some mistakes."

- 72% agree that "media attention can help solve crimes," but only 17% think it "helps the police do a better job."

The social media platforms, for their part, adjust nothing. The trending topics move on to the next case. The hashtags are still live, but their power is spent.

The detective, months later, is matter-of-fact:

Q: What would you do differently?

A: I'd log off. Shut out the noise. Stick to the timeline and the evidence. But that's not the world we're in anymore.

The world, indeed, is louder now. Every investigation is shadowed by the watchers—the ones who post, the ones who share, the ones who demand a name by the end of the hour. In this new ecosystem, the truth is not just hard to find. It is often drowned out entirely.

Cold Lake is not unique. The playbook is replicating everywhere, and the next detective, the next suspect, the next family is already logged into the same circuit.

The clock still ticks, but now it blinks in blue and white on every screen: "JUSTICE UPDATE: NO ARRESTS YET."

And beneath it, the faces of the watchers, waiting for the next move, and the next, and the next.

The only antidote to the clock is a process stronger than panic.

After the implosions—Westlake, Cold Lake, Parkside, and a hundred other names that barely rate a headline—the leading edge of policing is forced to reckon with a new order. Not a world without pressure, but one where the pressure is acknowledged, studied, and, if not neutralized, at least damped by protocol.

The strategy begins where the failures left off: in the handling of information, both inside the department and out.

Example: In the year following the Westlake collapse, a midwestern city launches a new protocol for "Critical Case Communication." The old model—silence, then sudden press conference, then nervous retreat—gives way to a regimented cycle: updates every 24 hours, regardless of progress. The media officer, once a part-time slot, is now a full-time assignment, with direct access to case files and daily debriefs from the lead investigators.

The first major test comes three months in. A young man goes missing near the city's college district, and the outcry is instantaneous—social posts, makeshift flyers, three competing news crews at the family's front door before the sun sets. But the department, following its new playbook, holds a live-streamed update every afternoon at 2:00 p.m. No speculation, no leaks. Only the facts as they exist, and a recurring mantra: "We will not rush this investigation at the expense of accuracy."

At first, the journalists chafe. The public, conditioned to instant closure, floods the comment section with demands: "Where's the suspect?" "Why are you stalling?" But within a week, the tone shifts. The lack of wild swings and rumor leaves less for the outrage cycle to feed on. The public, deprived of a villain, begins to reframe its attention—not on the failure to arrest, but on the methodical steps being taken.

The media officer posts a weekly "Case Status Sheet," listing which evidence is pending, what new leads are being followed, and why certain investigative delays exist ("Awaiting forensic confirmation—standard protocol requires two independent labs."). Each update includes a small FAQ: Why is the case taking so long? How do you process digital evidence? What happens if you get a false tip? For the first time, the community is invited to understand not just the result, but the process.

When, at week three, a suspect is arrested, the press cycle is still intense. But the department's prior transparency inoculates it against claims of secrecy or sandbagging. When the suspect's alibi is confirmed by third-party video, and he is released the next day, the public's anger is tempered by the now-expected update: "Suspect has been cleared; investigation continues." No one is crucified. The case continues on its merits.

The department keeps a quiet internal metric: Number of cases closed without error, and number reopened after challenge. In the year of the new protocol, the error rate drops by half. The closure rate climbs. The city's legal department sees a sharp reduction in civil actions for wrongful arrest.

But the system is not just about communication. Inside, a second firewall is built: every major decision in a high-pressure case must pass a peer review—a panel of detectives from outside the precinct, tasked with reviewing the chain of evidence, the logic of the suspect list, the rationale for an arrest. No decision is made in a vacuum. The cooling-off period, mandatory for all "fast closure" cases, is 24 hours: time enough for at least one person to raise an objection or spot a missing link.

Departments that run this protocol report a surprising side effect. Investigators, once driven by the need to "win the clock," find a new kind of pride in holding the line against the narrative. To resist the clock is, at last, a mark of professionalism, not failure.

It is not foolproof. But it works.

Sample language, from a "Case Status Update" released at the height of a homicide investigation:

- "The department is committed to following all leads, and to sharing verified information as it becomes available."

- "Our investigators are working with partner agencies and forensic experts to ensure no detail is overlooked."

- "We understand the public's concern, but we ask for patience while we do the work necessary to bring the right person to justice."

- "All statements regarding suspect identity or motive will come from the public information officer, and only after confirmation."

- "If you have information, report it to our tip line. If you have questions about the process, we encourage you to attend our weekly community forum."

Another department, learning from a botched "rush to arrest" in the previous year, institutes a policy of "public process transparency."

Every major case gets a web portal: timeline of events, updates on forensic progress, and a searchable FAQ. No names are released until charges are filed, and every update is time-stamped and attributed. The number of public complaints drops by two-thirds. When a national network tries to sensationalize a later case, the lack of drama makes it a ratings dead zone.

What these approaches have in common:

- They treat the public as a stakeholder, not an adversary.

- They make the limits of the process explicit.

- They create time for evidence to be gathered, checked, and re-checked.

- They reduce the space for rumor, and thereby for error.

A final study, two years into the new model, finds that departments implementing these protocols have 18% higher clearance rates, 28% fewer reversed convictions, and a measurable rise in public trust—even in cities where the media pressure never lets up.

The best practices are not magic, but they are repeatable:

- Assign a dedicated public information officer for all major investigations.

- Establish a schedule of regular, fact-based press briefings.

- Publish educational materials on the limits, steps, and expected timeframes of investigation.

- Require peer review of all major investigative decisions, especially arrests.

- Use evidence-processing timelines to pace the investigation, not public demand.

- Implement a mandatory cooling-off period before filing charges in high-profile cases.

- Document every step of the process, and make the documentation accessible, redacting only for privacy or legal reasons.

- Measure, review, and publish the department's own error and clearance rates. Own the numbers, good or bad.

The result, over time, is a culture shift. The clock, once a weapon aimed at the heart of every case, becomes just another data point—a measure of progress, but no longer the only one. The story is told not in hours to closure, but in the weight and sequence of the evidence, the strength of the process, and the capacity to resist the panic.

There will always be pressure. But now, at least, there is a chain of defense.

And the truth, a little less fragile, has a chance to be heard above the din.

CHAPTER 12

Lives In The Balance: The Real-World Impact Of Flawed Investigations

The envelope arrives on a Wednesday, slotted between coupons and a late notice for a gas bill Anthony Miller hasn't managed to pay. He knows the feel of official paper before he sees the seal, knows by weight and stiffness that it will be bad news, or worse—news that expects him to feel grateful. He carries it inside, drops the rest on the counter, and takes the envelope to the kitchen table, hands braced against the scarred Formica like he's about to face a judge, not the ghost of a judge rendered as toner on legal stationary.

The kitchen light is blue-tinted, a cheap bulb from the corner store. In this light, Anthony's knuckles seem paler, almost translucent where the skin pulls tight. Twelve years, he thinks. Twelve years and this is the thing that shakes him, not the cell block at dawn, not the shriek of alarms or the Sunday emptiness when no one comes to visit. He flips the envelope, thumb hesitating on the glued seam. The letterhead is crisp, the signature line empty, like no one wanted to take ownership of what it says.

He tears it open, reads in silence.

The letter is three paragraphs, four if you count the "Sincerely" and the stamped title underneath. It begins with the customary regret:

"We have completed our review of your case, and in light of new exculpatory evidence and corroborative DNA results, the State of Illinois formally vacates your conviction in People v. Miller, 09-CR-1912. We acknowledge the years lost to incarceration for a crime you did not commit, and offer our deepest apologies for the miscarriage of justice."

He reads this twice, the words "acknowledge" and "apologies" floating unmoored in the sterile prose.

The second paragraph is the one that burns:

"It has been determined that the confession obtained on April 17, 2009, was made under conditions now recognized as inherently coercive and unreliable. The review committee cites recent research and updates to Interrogation Protocol, as detailed in the revised Neutral Question Guidelines (2017), which were not in effect at the time of your interview."

Anthony's hands begin to tremble at "coercive and unreliable." The paper shudders, tiny waves radiating from his fingertips, but he keeps reading.

The final paragraph is a formality, a recitation of statutes and remedies:

"Pursuant to statute 805 ILCS 23/10, you are entitled to compensation commensurate with the duration of wrongful incarceration. The board has approved a payment of $3.2 million, to be disbursed in four installments over the next eight years. Please contact the Office of Exoneration Services to arrange counseling, job training, and transition support. You remain eligible for all reentry programs available to returning citizens."

Sincerely,

Office of the Attorney General

No signature. Just a machine-printed name and a number to call for more information.

Anthony sets the letter down and closes his eyes. For a minute, he listens to the buzz of the refrigerator, the slap of his own heart in his ears. He tries, and fails, to summon anger. Mostly, it is fatigue.

Twelve years, he thinks again.

He had been nineteen when they took him in. The murder was a robbery gone sideways, a liquor store clerk dead in the space of a struggle, the register missing $187.82. He had been at his cousin's place, eating nachos and watching the Bulls lose. No one cared. No one wanted his alibi, not really. The detective—Sergeant Walsh, the name still sharp—brought him into the interview room, offered him a Coke, then spent the next eight hours building a world in which

Anthony was guilty. He remembers the rhythm of the questions, the way Walsh would repeat a detail until Anthony couldn't remember if he'd thought it, or said it, or if maybe he'd been there after all.

"You said you were wearing a gray hoodie. The witness says it was gray. Are you sure it wasn't you?"

"I don't wear hoodies," Anthony had said, the first time.

"Let's just say it was a hoodie. Maybe you forgot."

The tape is long lost, but the transcript still exists. Every word of it parsed, picked over, and now, according to the letter, officially deemed "inherently coercive." The confession—his own words, but not his memory—had been the only thing holding up the case by the end. Even then, he believed that if he just kept telling the truth, the world would right itself. He believed it right up until they read the verdict.

The letter says "new exculpatory evidence," but the evidence was always there. It's just that, for twelve years, no one wanted to see it.

Anthony lifts the letter, folds it along the existing crease, then a second time, and again, until it's small enough to vanish in his fist. He thinks about the math: $45,000 a year to keep him in Stateville

Correctional, times twelve. Five hundred forty thousand dollars, just to feed and clothe and monitor him for a crime he didn't commit. Then the $3.2 million, meant to make him whole, as if money can solder the cracks that run from his hairline to his heel. He wonders who adds these numbers, what they make per hour to decide the value of a ruined life.

In the living room, the clock reads 11:53. In six minutes, he is supposed to log on for the mandatory reentry check-in, a Zoom meeting with a counselor named Lisa who asks, every time, how he's coping with the transition.

The answer is always the same: "I'm trying."

The truth is, the outside world is a harder cell. He has a phone, but it feels like a tracker more than a tool. Every job interview is a story about the gap in his resume, the "incarceration period," and even when the application says "No Felonies" he knows the background check will tell a different story. He has been to three interviews in the last month: one for a warehouse gig, one for a janitor job, and one for the grocery store where his neighbor works the register. Each time, the conversation circles back to "So, you were in for a while?" Each time, he watches the interviewer's eyes go from hopeful to skeptical, then to tired resignation. No one hires a murderer, even a legally exonerated one.

The exoneration made the news. He watched the clip once, in a waiting room with two other men whose stories were a mirror of his own. The anchor used words like "vindicated" and "overturned," but Anthony knew that every person watching saw only the mugshot, saw only the label that would never peel clean.

He stands, refills his glass at the sink, and stares through the window at the street. Cars pass, indifferent. The sun is too bright, the air still too sharp for spring. He wonders how many of his neighbors know, or care, that the man next door is innocent now.

Down the block, a cluster of kids play basketball in the rec center's cracked lot. He used to play there, before. Now, he walks the other direction, keeps his eyes down. Once, he tried to join, but the game stopped when he stepped onto the court, the ball rolling to a standstill until he left again.

He wonders if the boys know what a false confession is, or if they would believe him if he tried to explain.

A stat he once read, in a yellowing magazine in the prison library, floats up: one in four exonerations involves a false confession. Twenty-five percent. He wonders what the other seventy-five percent are like, if they get letters, if they ever get to start over, or if they even want to.

He sits back at the table, the Zoom link waiting in his email. He clicks it, waits for the connection. Lisa's face appears, backlit by a lamp and a row of tidy books. She smiles, but her eyes are always tired, like she's been seeing through walls for too long.

"Hi Anthony," she says. "How are you holding up?"

He shrugs, lifts the letter so she can see it. "Got the official word," he says. "It's over now, I guess."

Lisa nods, the silence settling for a beat before she speaks. "How do you feel about that?"

He doesn't answer at first. The real answer is not for a screen.

"Like I lost twelve years," he says. "Like maybe it's not over, just different."

She nods again. She always does. "Have you talked to anyone else about it?"

"No," he says. He wants to say, No one wants to hear it, but that would sound like self-pity, and he's not interested in pity.

Lisa writes something down. He can't see what.

"Are you still having the nightmares?" she asks.

He hesitates, then nods. "Yeah. Same one."

She waits, not pressing.

He tries to explain. "I'm back in the cell, but it's my house. My mom's there, but she's younger, and she's cleaning the floor like she used to. I'm watching, but I can't talk. I want to ask her to open the window, but I can't move. Then there's someone outside, watching through the glass, and I know they're coming in for me. Every time, I wake up before it happens."

Lisa listens, her pen unmoving. "Do you want to talk more about your mom?" she asks.

He doesn't, but he nods anyway. "She died while I was in," he says, flat. "Cancer. Stage four."

Lisa is silent, the line humming in the background.

He tries to smile, but it's a memory, not a feeling.

She asks, "Have you thought about using any of the compensation to help you with housing, or maybe some training? We have resources—"

He cuts her off. "I don't need money. I need a way to go back."

She doesn't reply, just makes another note.

They talk for another twelve minutes, mostly logistics. He signs off, closes the laptop, and sits for a long time in the hush that follows.

On the wall, the clock ticks forward. It is 12:34. In the yard, the basketball game is over, the lot empty except for the echo of a lost shot.

He unfolds the letter, smooths it flat, and reads it one last time.

Then he gets up, puts on a jacket, and steps out into the world. The sun is still too bright. The air is the same as before. He walks the block once, then twice, as if waiting for the ground to shift, for something to announce that the story is different now.

But the world, as always, is indifferent. He is a blank page with too many erasures, and nothing to fill the space except the words someone else put there.

He walks home. He puts the letter in a drawer, next to the rest.

The fridge hums. The clock ticks.

Tomorrow, he will try again.

There are four witnesses to the robbery, but by the end of the second week, only one story survives. The story belongs to the woman in the red scarf, seated by the window at the Lucky Lantern, whose voice carries over the others by force of certainty. Her name is Louise Cantwell, but in the case file she is always "Witness A." On the morning of the crime, Louise orders her coffee black, her eggs over hard, and when the shots sound from the 24/7 Mart next door, she is the first to her feet, first to the glass, first to call out to the waitress—"I saw the man, I saw his face."

Next to her, three others: an elderly veteran with a tremor, a nursing student pulling double shifts, and a line cook on his break, all with names and addresses and, for the moment, memories distinct from Louise's.

But the difference does not survive the retelling.

The detectives arrive fast—too fast for the wait staff to clear the broken mugs—and conduct the first round of interviews at the window-side table. The interviews, meant to be separate, take place in rapid succession, with just a curtain and a thin sheet of plywood separating each "interview bay." The dominant witness goes first.

Louise's description is detailed: "Male, Black, late twenties, green jacket with orange stripe, jeans, high-tops, sunglasses—Ray-Bans, maybe knockoff." She adds, "He had a mole here," tapping her own left cheek with a painted fingernail.

She says it twice, then again for the officer, and by the time the nursing student sits for her turn, the details have migrated. She recalls the mole, remembers the sunglasses, even though her original statement said only "dark figure, hood up, could not see face."

In the police transcript, the change is immediate and permanent.

By day three, the suspect has a composite: oval face, mole on the cheek, Ray-Bans, orange-stripe jacket. The artist does not question the mole, simply renders it with a dot of pencil. The detective, unconsciously or not, references the mole in every witness interview after that.

When they bring in the photo array, the officer—well-meaning, overworked—fans the cards with the dominant face second from the left, just off center, where the eye goes first.

Darnell Washington is the only one in the lineup with a visible birthmark on his cheek. He has never owned a green jacket, but at the time of his arrest, he is wearing an orange hoodie, which the detectives note in the margin as "consistent with witness description."

The moment is frozen in court security footage, later played in slow motion: the lineup, the pause, the point.

"Number two," Louise says. "That's him. I'll never forget that face."

The others, one by one, echo.

In the courtroom, Darnell is seated next to a public defender whose tie has not been updated since the Clinton administration. The lawyer objects to nothing, except to the pacing, which is brisk, the judge impatient, the DA running on a full head of steam and several years of minor-league victories.

When Louise testifies, she stands, voice unwavering. "I saw the man. I saw his face." Her eyes meet Darnell's, then flick away, not in fear, but in practiced resolve.

The line cook testifies next. He had said, in his first interview, "I was on my phone. I didn't see much." On the stand, he says, "I saw the sunglasses. The Ray-Bans. And the orange jacket." He does not mention the phone. No one asks.

The defense calls a single witness: Darnell's mother, who swears he was home, watching TV with her and the twins. The prosecutor asks, "Was he ever out of your sight, even for a minute?" She hesitates, and it is enough.

The trial lasts two days. The jury deliberates less than three hours.

Guilty, armed robbery, eight to ten.

In prison, the days unspool like old tape, with Darnell marking time by the odd quiet of the yard, the squeak of sneakers on cinder, the date-stamped letters from home. His wife, Latisha, writes every week, her penmanship steadier than her voice when she visits. She brings the twins, then in kindergarten, both clinging to her legs until the guards wave them through the checkpoint.

The first visit, the twins won't look at him. By the third, they sit with him at the plastic table, draw pictures on napkins, and ask, "Daddy, when are you coming home?"

Latisha works two jobs—night shift at the nursing home, weekends at the bakery. She tracks every minute, every mile, every dollar, so that when the twins ask, she can say, "We're saving for a house," or "Daddy is coming home, just a little while longer." She tapes the report cards to the fridge, even though the fridge is old and hums like a broken generator.

On the outside, she faces the world as if daring it to judge her.

"You know he did it, right?" says a neighbor, more than once.

"No, he didn't," Latisha says. "And even if he did, he's still their daddy."

Some days, the strain is too much, and she sits in the car after work, hands shaking, waiting for the feeling to pass.

The twins grow. They lose baby teeth, outgrow their shoes, win third place in the school science fair for a baking soda volcano that floods the gymnasium. Darnell is not there. He calls, writes, but the calls are monitored and the letters censored for "inappropriate content," which in this context means anything resembling hope or frustration.

Eight years pass.

In those years, Darnell's mother dies, the twins enter middle school, and Latisha finally saves enough for a down payment on a two-bedroom in the old neighborhood. The first night in the new house, she pours herself a glass of wine and sits on the porch, watching the streetlights flicker.

She is thirty-two, and already feels a thousand years old.

It is a law student—third-year, unpaid internship—who uncovers the flaw.

He is working on a review for the Innocence Project, tasked with re-reading cold trial transcripts. He notices the drift in the witness statements, the perfect overlap in language, the repetition of "mole on the cheek" and "Ray-Bans." He runs a search and finds that only one witness mentioned the mole at first, and that in a later interview, the detail appears everywhere, even in statements from witnesses who had previously described the suspect as "too far to see, maybe just a blur."

The student writes a memo. The supervising attorney reads it, frowns, and pulls the raw interviews from storage. They are on DVD, poorly labeled, but the metadata shows time and date. She watches them, then the follow-ups, then the trial tapes.

It is clear: the dominant witness effect, textbook version, complete with drift, convergence, and the pressure of repeated group retellings. By now, the field literature says this happens in up to 69% of wrongful convictions involving eyewitnesses. The stat sticks in the mind, even after the other numbers fade.

A motion is filed. The DA's office resists at first, then relents when a new round of DNA testing—using methods unavailable at the time of trial—excludes Darnell and points to another man, serving time in a different county.

After eight years, Darnell is released.

He walks out wearing the same shoes he wore to court, soles patched with duct tape.

The return is not simple, not clean.

The twins, now in high school, are taller than Latisha. The first time Darnell tries to hug them, they stiffen, then relax, then pull away. The house is smaller than he imagined, but the air is his own.

For months, he wakes at 4:00 a.m., convinced that if he is not up by count, someone will come to take him back. He walks the neighborhood, hands in pockets, eyes down. Some people recognize him, but most just see a man lost in thought, or in time.

He applies for jobs. The gap in his resume is a chasm, but he lies, says he was "helping family downstate." He washes dishes, then moves to the night cleaning crew at the hospital, where Latisha sometimes brings him a sandwich at midnight, and they eat together in the break room, sharing silence.

The first birthday home, the twins buy him a cake. It is store-bought, vanilla with chocolate icing. He eats it in small bites, careful to leave none.

The dominant witness is never told of the reversal. In her mind, the case is closed, her role minor but decisive. She does not know how many others followed her words, or how the memory of one day became the memory of all.

In another part of the city, another trial waits, another composite drawn, another witness asked to recall what they saw, or what they think they saw, or what they remember someone else remembering.

The old stories never fade, just repeat.

Darnell sits on the porch, the sun warming the boards, the street full of distant traffic.

He is home, but the world is not the same as when he left it.

He looks at the twins, now arguing over whose turn it is to take out the trash. He watches Latisha, barefoot in the yard, waving to a neighbor.

He listens to the silence, and the memory of voices, and the echo of a life that will never fit back together as before.

But he is here, and that is enough.

For now.

The moment the detective zeros in on Elena Vasquez, the rest of the case becomes a matter of subtraction. The murder itself is a statistical blip: one realtor, late forties, killed after a home showing on the edge of town, no witnesses, no camera footage, and a weapon—a chunk of masonry—left behind in the dead leaves. The scene is cordoned, the lab work dutifully logged, but within six hours the file is stamped with Elena's name.

She is the last person to see the victim alive, a rival in the cutthroat world of suburban house-flipping, and, according to the initial interview, "evasive" in her answers. The fact that she has an airtight alibi for the hour of death is less important than the fact that, in the detective's phrase, "She fits the narrative." When the narrative fits, the evidence is made to fit as well.

The real work of building the case is in the meetings, not the field.

The meetings are held in a windowless conference room, the air thick with coffee and the residue of old dry-erase markers. The team leader outlines the timeline on the board, boxes and arrows, every step a linear progression toward guilt. When a junior investigator, new to the squad, raises a hand and says, "But what about the anonymous tip from the gas station clerk? She said she saw a different woman, red hair, leaving the scene," the room goes quiet. The leader, a veteran with twenty years and a wall of plaques, dismisses it: "Witness must be confused. Our suspect has dark hair."

The tip is logged, but not followed.

In the stack of evidence, there are fingerprints on the masonry—partial, but not a match to Elena. The forensics tech flags it in the report, circles it in yellow highlighter, but in the briefing the next day, it is omitted from the summary slide. When the prosecutor asks about the prints, the detective says, "Probably contaminated, or from before." The prosecutor nods. The logic is recursive: If Elena is guilty, then anything inconsistent must be noise.

The file grows, but not in the direction of the facts.

The trial is a formality, played out for the benefit of the local media and a jury pre-selected for their ability to stay awake through three weeks of circumstantial evidence. Elena's public defender, overworked and underfunded, tries to point out the gaps: the lack of motive, the alternate suspects, the ex-boyfriend of the victim who had a violent history and was in town that week. The judge sustains every objection from the prosecution, and in the end, the defense can only put Elena on the stand to say, again, that she did not do it.

She is convicted on the sixth day of deliberations, sentenced to life.

The appeals process is long, expensive, and without hope.

Sidebar: In the fifteen years Elena is incarcerated, the state spends $2.1 million in legal fees defending the conviction. When, finally, the case is overturned after a new DNA analysis excludes Elena and matches the ex-boyfriend, the state settles for $4.5 million. The reentry services—a suite of job training, housing, and therapy—are costed at $750,000, though the actual benefit to Elena is hard to measure.

The impact is not just personal.

In the years after Elena's conviction, her neighborhood stops calling the police. A city survey, conducted by the mayor's office, finds a 34% drop in crime reporting in the area. Residents cite "distrust of process" as the primary reason. When a car is broken into, or a fight breaks out in the parking lot, no one bothers to call the non-emergency line. The police data analysts notice, but attribute it to "improved community resilience" in their reports.

In a focus group at the community center, a social worker asks, "Why don't you call the police?"

A woman in a floral dress says, "Why would I? They're not here to help us."

A man in a mechanic's shirt adds, "They already made up their minds. You don't get to argue with them."

When asked about the Vasquez case, everyone in the room knows the name. Most have a cousin, or an aunt, or a neighbor who was questioned, some even suspect at one point. The feeling is not anger, but resignation.

"We're just a box to check," someone says.

Within the department, the detectives are aware of the problem, though no one names it out loud.

In an after-hours interview for a university research project, a detective says, "It's not that we want to railroad anyone. But once you have a theory, everything else looks like a distraction. You have to keep the case moving, otherwise it dies in review."

Another detective, new to homicide, says, "If you challenge the narrative, you better have iron proof, or you're going to get flattened by your own team."

The culture is not hostile, just efficient. There is no time, and even less patience, for uncertainty.

Elena is released at forty-eight, hair streaked gray, gait stiff from years of concrete floors and bad shoes. Her first weeks out are spent in a halfway house, where the schedule is strict but the air at least has a taste of weather and street noise.

Her legal team arranges for counseling, but the first psychologist quits after two sessions, writing in her file: "Subject exhibits extreme distrust of authority; unable to build rapport." The second psychologist lasts longer, but their sessions are mostly silent, Elena staring at the wall, the psychologist scribbling notes and trying different prompts.

After three months, Elena agrees to a full evaluation.

The report is clinical but damning:

"Subject exhibits symptoms of severe depression and complex PTSD, with persistent anxiety, sleep disturbance, and deep-seated mistrust of institutional processes. Interpersonal relationships are minimal; affect is blunted. Subject reports daily feelings of disassociation and hopelessness, occasionally punctuated by brief periods of anger."

In the interview, the psychologist asks, "What do you want, now that you're out?"

Elena stares at her, eyes unblinking. "I want them to say they were wrong. I want to live in a world where that can happen."

The psychologist, unsure if this is progress or not, writes it down anyway.

In the neighborhood, a new generation grows up in the shadow of the case.

The children of Elena's former friends cross the street when they see a patrol car. At the high school, a teacher asks her class to write an essay on "Civic Duty," and half the essays are about the police, but not in the way the curriculum intended.

In a corner store, the clerk tells a customer, "If you ever get picked up, don't say a word. Don't even tell them your name."

The customer laughs, but not really.

There is a theory, proposed in a recent seminar at the state university, that trauma is not just personal but procedural. That a single bad case, left uncorrected, can create a kind of psychological infection in a whole community. The theory is not yet published, but the presenter—an ex-prosecutor, now an academic—makes a convincing case:

"If you want to destroy trust, you only have to make one mistake, and refuse to admit it. The system will do the rest."

The audience, mostly grad students and a handful of local journalists, nods.

Elena moves to a new city, tries to start over.

She takes a job cleaning offices at night. The work is lonely, but she prefers it that way. She is saving for a car, though she does not drive, and may never feel safe enough to own one.

Sometimes, she receives letters from old neighbors, written in a looping script, telling her that things are better now, that they never doubted her, that they wish her peace.

She reads them, but does not write back.

In therapy, she is asked, "What do you feel, when you think about what happened?"

She answers, "Like I was never real to them. Just a name on a line, a space to fill."

The therapist asks, "What do you want to feel?"

Elena thinks, and says, "I want to feel like I exist. Like I matter."

The therapist writes it down, and the file grows, page by page.

The story circulates, not as a headline, but as a caution.

In the department, new detectives are warned: "Don't get tunnel vision. It'll ruin you." The warning is perfunctory, but sometimes it sticks.

In the community, the case becomes a legend, told in pieces: the woman who was railroaded, the prints they ignored, the witness who saw a redhead but was never called to testify. The story is not polished, or even accurate, but it is real in the way that only repeated pain can be.

Elena walks to work in the half-dark, her shoes new but stiff, her breath pluming in the cold. She is alone, but not invisible.

The world, she knows, will never see her the way she sees herself.

But she walks anyway, one step at a time.

The town hall is packed past fire code, every folding chair claimed, the aisles crowded with late arrivals clutching coffee, clipboards, or simply crossed arms. The meeting is called for seven, but the first wave of voices—urgent, angry, plaintive—begins fifteen minutes before the gavel hits the lectern. The room smells of floor wax and damp wool, the low ceiling capturing the heat of a hundred bodies and the edge of a February storm.

Tonight's agenda is posted on a yellow sheet at every entrance:

- Community Impact of Wrongful Convictions: Budget and Beyond

- Speaker: City Comptroller

- Q&A Session: Open Floor

At 7:04, the chair calls the meeting to order.

The comptroller, a pale man in an ill-fitting blazer, clears his throat and begins.

"First, I want to acknowledge the pain and disruption caused by the recent settlements. We are doing everything we can to mitigate the impact. But there is no getting around the numbers. This year, the city must pay $5.8 million in damages for two wrongful conviction cases. This amount exceeds our reserve fund, and as a result, we are forced to freeze certain non-essential services and defer scheduled capital improvements until further notice."

A hand shoots up. The chair ignores it.

"To be specific," the comptroller continues, voice wobbling on the hard parts, "we will be reducing funding for after-school programs, delaying the resurfacing of Lincoln and Park, and suspending the public library's Sunday hours."

A low groan moves through the crowd.

A woman near the back, holding a toddler, stands. "My son's program is the only safe place he has after 3:00. How is this justice?"

The chair asks for order, but the question is already alive in the room.

The budget director, seated next to the comptroller, reads from a spreadsheet: "We are required by law to honor settlements immediately. This means $2.4 million will be paid within sixty days, the remainder on a five-year schedule. Without additional state or federal aid, our options are limited."

A retired teacher, gray hair in a braid, says, "So the system screws up, and we all pay for it. Not just with money—look around. People don't trust anything anymore."

The chair tries to reset, but another hand goes up—this time, a man with a stack of court transcripts in a battered folder.

"I was on the jury for the Miller case," he says. "We were told the confession was ironclad. No one said anything about coercion, or about how the confession was taken. I can't sleep some nights, knowing we ruined a man's life."

A beat, then:

"And now we're ruining the whole town."

After the meeting, the chairs are stacked and the coffee emptied, but the tension remains.

In the hallway, a social worker explains to a reporter: "You can measure the impact in dollars, sure. But every time this happens, the trauma ripples out. Victims, families, kids. It never ends with the check. It gets into the air."

The reporter asks about the recent research, the numbers.

The social worker nods, recites from memory: "Every wrongful conviction case affects about three hundred people, minimum. Family, friends, neighbors, witnesses, the cops and the jurors, even the people who process the paperwork. Sometimes whole neighborhoods go silent—no one calls the cops, no one trusts the courts. The cost isn't just money. It's what you lose when you lose trust."

In a bungalow three blocks from city hall, the Miller family eats dinner in silence. Anthony, released and officially exonerated, sits at the head of the table. His sister cooks—her hands quick, eyes distant. His niece sets the table, careful with the silverware.

They do not talk about what happened. The court order says it's over, the settlement says it's closed, but Anthony knows, and the family knows, that the wound is not closing. It is hardening into something else.

A phone rings, ignored.

On TV, the news mentions the service cuts, the closed library, the deferred roadwork. No one says anything.

After dinner, Anthony stands on the porch, looks up at the gray sky, the buzz of streetlights, the cold coming off the river. He does not feel free. He feels, at best, unnecessary.

In another part of town, Latisha—Darnell's wife—sits at her kitchen table, a calculator and a stack of bills in front of her. The twins, now teenagers, are in their rooms, headphones on, windows open to the winter air.

She punches numbers, re-punches them, looks for a way through. The payout from Darnell's case went first to the lawyers, then to back rent, then to the schools and the debts that accumulated in eight years of survival. She is grateful, but the relief is measured in days, not years.

She reads an article online, quoting a study from the state university: "Exonerees are 6.5 times more likely to attempt suicide than the general population. Their families are three times as likely to report symptoms of PTSD or major depression."

She closes the browser, stares at the ceiling.

In the other room, Darnell calls out, "What's for dinner?"

She answers, but her voice does not carry.

The impact is not always visible, but it is everywhere.

A local business owner—once robbed, once a trial witness—testifies at a council meeting: "Since the Vasquez case, no one talks to the cops. My employees won't even call if someone smashes a window. Why would they?"

At the high school, a counselor says, "The kids are more cynical now. They don't believe in due process, or fairness. They think everything is rigged, so what's the point?"

In a focus group, an elderly woman says, "The library was my only reason to leave the house. Now they're closing Sundays. I can't afford the bus to the next town."

There is a ledger, maintained by the city clerk, that shows the balances: dollars paid, hours lost, trust depleted. But the real balance is off the page, in the spaces between neighbors, in the pauses before someone calls 911, in the silences after a meeting adjourns.

A week after the town hall, the chair of the meeting—alone in the office, filing minutes—pauses to look out at the empty council chamber.

She remembers, as a child, watching her father take the oath as a police officer. She remembers the pride, the sense that the badge meant something unbreakable.

Now, she wonders if that pride will survive another year, another payout, another apology that comes too late.

She closes her laptop, shuts off the lights, and walks home through the dark.

Outside, the world is unchanged, the damage invisible except to those who know where to look.

But the next morning, someone will still sweep the floors, open the doors, and wait for the people to come back. The cycle will repeat, and maybe, with time, the balance will shift.

But for now, the loss is measured in the quiet.

And in the hope—fragile, but persistent—that tomorrow will be less broken than today.

CHAPTER 13

Building Better Investigators: Training And Methodological Reform

Statistically, the single most reliable indicator of a wrongful conviction is not bad forensics or witness error or the malice of a single rogue cop. It is the compounding effect of cognitive bias—specifically, the species of bias that takes root in the first 48 hours of an investigation and, left unchecked, branches through every decision, interview, and report that follows. The 2022 National Registry of Exonerations study finds that, of all post-conviction exonerations since 2000, nearly 74% feature at least one cognitive bias error traceable to the investigative team. In the subset of homicide cases, the percentage climbs to 81.

It is not a matter of bad apples, but of unexamined mental habit.

To understand how the problem is attacked, begin at the epicenter: the Westside Metropolitan Training Facility, a campus of poured-concrete rectangles stenciled with motivational slogans and ringed, on three sides, by cyclone fencing. The fourth side faces the river and, in winter, the smell of algae and silt sifts in through the ventilation system. Here, every six weeks, a cohort of thirty to forty investigators—some rookies, some veterans with hairlines mapped by stress—cycles through a two-week course in Bias-Aware Investigation, a program designed to rewire habits so old they predate the badge.

The first day is the hardest. The course director, a retired homicide lieutenant with a degree in behavioral psych, opens with what she calls the "Cognitive Autopsy." A PowerPoint parade of cases: each begins with a headline ("Teen Cleared After Six Years in Prison") and ends with an annotated timeline in which every critical mistake is color-coded to a type of bias. The lead suspect is never the most likely, only the first one that feels right. The timeline of events is never as remembered, only as retold. In one slide, the photo of a man arrested for a string of robberies—his face grainy from a surveillance still—is paired with a transcript of the initial witness statement, which, in its first draft, makes no mention of skin color or beard, only "a man in a blue hoodie." By the second interview, after viewing the grainy footage and listening to other witness versions, the suspect is "definitely Black, with a beard, maybe six foot."

It is not malice, the director says. It is narrative gravity.

In the training room, twenty-eight officers and detectives squirm in their mesh-backed chairs. Some take notes, some stare at the faded carpeting, a few exchange small glances—half skeptical, half sullen. The bias talk, they've heard before, but always in the negative: Don't let it trip you up, watch out for tunnel vision. Never with the surgical dissection of their own profession.

By hour two, the director introduces the "Bias Typology Wheel"—a pie chart of the major cognitive pitfalls:

- Anchoring: the tendency to seize on the first available fact, regardless of quality.

- Availability heuristic: overvaluing the most recent or vivid detail, usually at the expense of the statistically relevant.

- Confirmation bias: collecting only the data that supports your initial theory, then blurring or discarding the rest.

- Groupthink: defaulting to the consensus of the team, even when your gut says otherwise.

- Outcome bias: retroactively justifying your process based on the result, not the evidence.

The room is then split into "scenario pods." Each pod receives a color-coded manila folder, each containing the file for a fictional—but not entirely fictional—case: theft, assault, sometimes a homicide. The instructions are simple: Read the file, list every possible theory of the case, then decide, by group vote, which suspect or explanation is most likely.

The first scenario is designed for failure. The case file is stuffed with deliberately misleading detail: a witness who seems certain but is actually coached, a timeline that features an unexplained half-hour gap, and a single piece of physical evidence (a button, a partial fingerprint) that seems to clinch the answer—until the final page, which, if read carefully, reveals a contradiction.

In Pod A, the officers run through the file, nominate a suspect, and build a timeline in thirty minutes flat. When asked to explain their reasoning, the group leader says, "The witness placed the suspect at the scene, and the fingerprint lines up. The timeline fits, assuming the suspect lied about his alibi."

The director then cues up the AV system. On the screen: a video of the actual scenario, as played out by actors. The group's suspect is present at the scene, but only as a bystander. The real culprit is a woman never mentioned by name in the witness's version, but whose car is visible in the background—her alibi, once cross-checked, fails.

The officers watch, grim, as their theory collapses on playback. The director pauses the footage.

"Who noticed the car?" she asks.

Only one hand, halfway up.

"Who questioned the witness's confidence?"

A glance around the table. None.

The director says, "Anchoring bias is not a rookie error. It is a feature of the system, unless you learn to see it."

She passes out a quote from the training manual: "If your first theory is not tested by a search for disconfirming evidence, it is not an investigation. It is a story you are telling yourself."

Some groan, others scribble it down.

By the end of the first week, the class is run through six scenarios, each more tangled than the last. The cases are sourced from real-world events, scrubbed of identifying detail, but the twist is always the same: the most obvious answer is, by design, wrong. The best groups learn to challenge their own conclusions, to treat every "gut instinct" as a potential booby trap. In the final exercise, the class is pitted against a set of real homicide files from the 1990s. The bias errors are mapped in advance, but it is up to the trainees to spot them.

On Thursday, the director walks the class through the difference between "deductive" and "inductive" logic. She writes on the whiteboard:

DED: Start with theory, test against evidence.

IND: Start with evidence, let the theory emerge.

She reads from the revised Neutral Question Guidelines, version 3.2: "Never trust a theory you could have written before seeing the evidence."

One detective, veteran of two decades, raises his hand. "So you're telling me to forget everything I know?"

"No," the director says, "just question why you know it."

The tension in the room is less now, replaced by something like curiosity.

In the afternoons, the class is taken to the Simulation Wing—a hallway of windowless rooms, each staged as an interview suite, a living room, or a crime scene. The rooms are wired with cameras and mics, every movement captured for review.

In one exercise, an officer must interview a "witness" (an actor, briefed with a complex backstory) about a burglary. The witness is nervous, contradicts herself, and at one point says, "I think it was my neighbor, she always watches my house." The officer latches onto the detail, drills into the neighbor, and never circles back to the witness's own timeline, which, if pressed, would have revealed she was home at the time.

After the session, the footage is played back for the class. The officer's face flushes as the gaps in his questioning are highlighted, one by one. The director stops the video.

"You assumed her suspicion was worth more than her own memory," she says. "Why?"

He shrugs. "She seemed sure. And nervous."

The director: "Availability and affect bias. You let her mood drive the direction. What did you miss?"

He reviews the notes, sighs. "I missed the timeline."

Others nod, some with relief, some with the grim recognition of a lesson they've learned before.

Midway through the course, the director brings in the outside expert: a cognitive psychologist, who runs the class through a battery of "blind spot" tests. One, called the Wason Selection Task, is designed to show how most people test for confirmation, not contradiction. Another, a short video involving a staged basketball game, asks the officers to count passes; almost none notice the person in a gorilla suit who walks through the frame. The psychologist, dryly, says, "What you look for is what you see. But what matters is what you missed."

By the end of week two, resistance gives way to a new kind of tension: uncertainty. The officers begin to second-guess their first reads, to interrogate each other's assumptions. In one session, two detectives debate the meaning of a single interview discrepancy for twenty minutes, each proposing three alternate explanations before settling on "more data needed." It is, the director says, progress.

At the close of the course, the class is given a final scenario: a fictional, high-profile murder, with three plausible suspects and a mountain of conflicting evidence. They are told only this: "The answer is in the file. Your job is not to find the quickest answer, but the right one."

The groups spend six hours on it. At the end, the majority lands on the correct theory, not because it is the most likely, but because it is the only one that survives every attempt to disprove it.

The director reviews the group's reasoning, and, for the first time, the whiteboard is left uncorrected.

On graduation day, the officers are issued a certificate and a pocket card listing the "Seven Deadly Sins of Bias." It is half joke, half reference guide.

But a month later, in the field, a detective from the course catches himself mid-interview: "That's anchoring," he mutters, and revisits his timeline. It slows the case by a day, but, in the end, the right suspect is found.

The program is not perfect. The director knows this. But the measurable outcome—a 28% reduction in documented bias errors, a doubling of successful appeals against wrongful initial theories—suggests the method is sound.

In the next funding cycle, the city triples the program budget.

In year two, the National Institute of Justice recommends the curriculum as a model for all departments over 100,000 population.

In the updated manual, the first rule is in bold:

EVIDENCE BEFORE THEORY, EVERY TIME.

And the faces of the cohort, by the end of the two weeks, are less set, more alert—watching, at last, for the things they might otherwise miss.

The difference between an old interrogation suite and a modern interview room is not just cosmetic. It is architectural, technological, and, above all, epistemological—the new space built not to extract confession, but to record, with clinical fidelity, the performance of memory, truth, and error.

The old rooms still exist in some precincts: windowless, fluorescent-lit, with a battered table, two chairs, and, if lucky, a ceiling-mounted camera that clicks on only when the officer remembers to flip the switch. The tapes are often erased, sometimes misplaced, always suspect. In these rooms, the story is whatever survives to the case file.

The new rooms—like the ones in the Westside Training Annex and, increasingly, in urban departments nationwide—are designed from floor to ceiling for transparency and auditability. The walls are painted in matte gray, a color tested for minimal reflectivity and psychological neutrality. The lighting is soft, indirect, shadowless. There are three cameras, not one, positioned to capture every angle: two fixed in opposing corners, one concealed in the wall behind a one-way mirror. All are 4K, time-synced, with redundant feeds to on-site and cloud storage. The microphones are parabolic, sensitive enough to pick up a whisper under a breath, but tuned to filter out HVAC and hallway noise. There is no "off" switch accessible from inside the room.

At the door, a placard in five languages: "All interviews are recorded for your protection."

The protocol for the AV system is itself a minor treatise in the philosophy of evidence. Each recording is tagged with a digital signature—time, date, room, badge numbers for all present. The file is encrypted at point of capture, then hashed and uploaded to a secure server. The chain of custody is automated: every access, copy, or playback is logged and, in most jurisdictions, reportable to both defense and prosecution.

Supervisors are required to review a random sample of every week's interviews, using a checklist developed in partnership with the Innocence Project and the state bar. The checklist is exacting:

- Were all Miranda warnings delivered clearly and on camera?

- Were all breaks, pauses, or off-camera conversations documented in real time?

- Was the suspect (or witness) given opportunity to clarify, correct, or decline?

- Did the interviewer ever use leading, coercive, or suggestive language?

- Is the time sequence unbroken and continuous?

The system is designed to protect everyone in the room.

Research backs the investment. In a 2021 study by the National Center for Policing Innovation, implementation of mandatory AV recording in twelve test cities led to a 56% reduction in the use of high-pressure tactics during suspect interviews. Complaints of coercion dropped by two-thirds. More surprising: the conviction rate for truly guilty parties increased by 19%, owing to the strength and credibility of untainted confessions. Conversely, the number of wrongful conviction reversals in these cities fell by 41% over five years, compared to matched controls.

One case—cited in every reform seminar—features a suspect in a triple homicide. The initial confession, taken before the AV system was live, is detailed but riddled with inconsistencies. On playback, the suspect's statements drift and contradict, but, with only the written summary surviving, the errors are missed. On re-interview, this time with full AV, the contradictions are exposed in real time: the suspect is clearly uncertain, sometimes echoing the interviewer's language verbatim. The AV recording is reviewed by the DA's office; charges are dropped within a week. Three months later, a DNA hit on another suspect closes the case. The AV footage not only protects the innocent, but redirects the investigation toward the real perpetrator.

The technical specs for admissibility are now the subject of entire conference tracks at the state and federal level:

- Video must be at minimum 1080p, with audio at 24-bit, 48kHz sampling.

- File signatures must be verified by hash at each transfer point.

- All edits (even redactions for privacy) must be noted, time-stamped, and available to both parties.

- Storage retention is ten years for felonies, five for misdemeanors, and until minor age for juvenile interviews.

- Any failure in the chain—missing segment, unlogged access, corrupted file—must be reported within 72 hours, with a formal hearing if admissibility is challenged.

Departments adopt internal audits to pre-empt claims of tampering or technical malfunction. In one midwestern city, the policy is to print a chain-of-custody summary for every case involving a recorded interview, then include it in the case file. The log is reviewed not just by investigators, but by prosecutors and, if requested, defense attorneys. Tampering is now as detectable as it is punishable.

The new system has other, less quantifiable effects. Officers, knowing every word is on record, become more careful—sometimes stilted—in their approach. The "old hands" at interrogation, some with decades of experience, struggle at first to adapt. One describes the change as "doing surgery with an audience." But as the months pass, the interviews become more methodical, less adversarial. Suspects, aware they are being recorded, are less likely to allege later that they were threatened or coerced. The complaints that do arise are quickly resolved by playback.

There is, in some precincts, grumbling about "the death of the art" of interrogation. But the new generation of investigators is trained from the start to treat the AV system as a tool, not a constraint. In the Westside Training Facility, trainees are drilled on the protocol until it is automatic: check the camera lights, verify the digital signature, announce the start of the session on tape, run through the rights, then begin.

In the weekly debriefs, the training director reviews the "capture logs" for errors. Any instance of a missed warning, or an off-camera consult, is flagged. The trainees must watch their own interviews and critique, not just for content, but for process. The effect is immediate: error rates fall, and the narrative drift that once infected so many cases now struggles to find a foothold.

In the rare event that a suspect tries to manipulate the system—deliberately giving conflicting statements to see if one is used over another—the AV record is the arbiter. Prosecutors and defense alike rely on the raw footage. Judges, once forced to weigh competing versions of what happened in a closed room, now play the clip in chambers and rule on the facts as captured.

A sample protocol, excerpted from the updated Interview Recording Manual:

- "Upon entering the interview room, all parties must state name, badge or ID number, and reason for presence. No interview may begin unless the status light on all three cameras is solid green."

- "If an interview is paused for any reason, the camera must continue to run. Any discussion during the break must be documented and, if possible, remain in the room."

- "Chain of custody must be verified by file hash and digital signature at every transfer: from capture device to server, server to backup, and, if burned to disc, from disc to physical storage."

- "Access logs will be reviewed weekly by unit supervisor. Any unreported access or deletion is a disciplinary offense, reportable to Internal Affairs."

There are growing pains, but also growing confidence. Civil suits for wrongful conviction begin to cite the absence of AV documentation as a primary cause; in jurisdictions with the system in place, settlements drop, and public trust—measured in regular community polling—edges upward.

In time, the old interview rooms are gutted, their tables and two-way mirrors auctioned or left to dust.

The new rooms are brighter, quieter, and, more than anything, watched—by supervisors, by the public, by history itself.

The story, once told in the shadows, is now played in full light.

And the truth, sometimes messy, sometimes raw, but always whole, is at last allowed to speak for itself.

In practice, the transition from legacy policing to a system inoculated against error is neither linear nor painless. The success stories are not a matter of memo or mandate, but of incremental battles: against habit, budget, bureaucracy, and sometimes the inertia of defeat.

The Minneapolis Model

When the Minneapolis Police Department first piloted the Bias-Aware Investigation Training, internal reaction was, in the words of a sergeant quoted in a local paper, "mixed to hostile." Many officers saw it as a box to tick, another three-ring binder to skim before reverting to business as usual. The program's architect—a former detective named Erica Madsen—anticipated as much. Instead of launching department-wide, she targeted three precincts with the highest wrongful conviction rates, embedding training liaisons directly into each unit.

The first year was rocky. Officers resented the time lost to workshops, and many dismissed the exercises as "psychobabble." But Madsen insisted on full cycles: every scenario completed, every debrief attended. The breakthrough came, not with the early adopters, but the department's "problem unit," North Precinct. There, a pair of detectives—tough, old-school, famous for their clearance rates—were exposed during simulation. Over and over, they anchored to the first suspect, ignored alternate theories, and failed to catch the plants in each mock file. The recordings were humiliating, but the program required them to review and annotate their own mistakes.

Within six months, their solve rates dipped, as they started second-guessing their instincts. But by the end of year one, the error rate (measured by "false suspect" flags in controlled scenarios) dropped by more than half. By year two, it had dropped 83%. The North Precinct posted its highest closure rate on major crimes in a decade, while use-of-force and citizen complaints fell citywide.

A patrolman who started as a vocal skeptic was quoted after his fourth scenario cycle:

“I thought it was nonsense, that you can’t teach instinct. But I caught myself anchoring on a suspect last month, and I stopped. We found the real guy three days later. I guess I’d rather be embarrassed in class than on TV.”

Internal data published after the third year of reform shows:

- Wrongful conviction reversals in Hennepin County: down 56% versus state average.

- Average time to closure, major crimes: up 12% (expected, due to more thorough review), but the clearance rate improved from 72% to 84%.

- Public trust metric, as measured by annual city survey: from 39% “good or excellent” to 61% in three years.

The Houston Approach

Houston's department was famous for both its size and its adversarial culture, the kind of place where "evidence before theory" was seen as a luxury afforded by departments that didn't have to clear a thousand cases a month. In 2018, a civil suit over a high-profile wrongful conviction (a teenager sentenced to life on a confession later found to be coerced) forced the city's hand. The settlement required the department to implement not just AV recording, but an independent Case Review Unit with full subpoena power.

The AV system was installed in all major precincts within a year—more than 200 rooms, networked, with access controlled by an external audit team. The early months were a parade of technical glitches, user errors, and some old-guard officers who "forgot" to start the cameras. But the oversight unit flagged every error and issued weekly compliance reports, not only to department heads but also to the public.

Initially, officers gamed the system, running "off the record" interviews in cars or hallways. But every time a non-recorded statement was offered as evidence, the oversight team flagged it, and, if appropriate, recommended discipline. It took less than two quarters for compliance to reach 98%.

The results were dramatic. Complaints of coercion during interviews dropped from an annual average of 40 to just six in the first year. Of those, every one was resolved by reviewing the footage: four exonerated the officer, two resulted in retraining.

The biggest impact, though, was on the court side. Prosecutors found that juries were more likely to convict when presented with full, unedited AV records—especially when suspects were treated with respect, and the process was transparent. Conversely, cases built on "off the record" confessions were thrown out or settled. The DA's conviction rate climbed, and, within two years, civil litigation for wrongful arrest or coercion dropped to single digits.

From the first annual review, a quote from a detective with two decades in homicide:

"I used to think the camera would make us look weak, or second-guess every move. But it's actually a shield. I can point to the tape and say, 'Here's what really happened.' Takes the guesswork out of it."

Data from the City Auditor, 2019–2022:

- Average annual lawsuits for wrongful conviction: down 74%.

- Confession retractions (suspect recants after AV review): up 27%, but in almost all cases, the original interview was found valid.

- Officer disciplinary actions for interview violations: high in first year, then near-zero.

- Cost of AV system: $3.7M over three years.

- Estimated savings in litigation and settlement: $11.4M over same period.

The Portland Paradigm

Portland's experiment with reform focused not only on internal process but also on external engagement. Following a series of high-profile protest actions and several years of mutual distrust between police and community, the city piloted a public oversight board, with access to both AV records and scenario-training modules.

The board—composed of citizens, attorneys, and academics—reviewed a set of randomly selected interviews each month and published a digestible report, including trends, errors, and successes. Their reviews were sometimes critical, but more often focused on how officers adapted to the new "full-light" environment.

A former public defender who joined the board said:

"At first, I thought the police would find a way to keep doing what they always did. But the more we watched, the more we saw real changes. Not perfect, but progress. And the fact that we could see the data for ourselves made it a hundred times more credible."

By design, Portland phased in its reforms—first in the training division, then in major crimes, then across all units. Every six months, metrics were published:

- Clearance rates by unit

- Citizen complaint data

- AV system compliance

- Surveyed perceptions of police fairness (run by an independent polling firm)

By year two, complaints about "biased investigation" or "unfair interviews" dropped by more than 60%. Public confidence, measured quarterly, rose 41%. Even the department's union, initially a vocal opponent, issued a statement of qualified support, citing reduced stress on officers and fewer disciplinary proceedings.

One officer, quoted in an internal newsletter, captures the culture shift:

"It's weird being watched all the time, but now I can say, with proof, that I followed the rules. And when I screw up, it's a learning thing, not a career-killer. We actually get better."

The department also created a "Peer Feedback Team"—veteran detectives tasked with randomly reviewing interviews and offering constructive feedback. Not only did this accelerate error correction, but it created a culture where critique was seen as professional development, not an attack.

Cost-benefit analysis from the City Council report:

- Upfront investment: $2.1M for training, $1.4M for tech.

- Reduction in civil payouts and court settlements: from $4.2M per year (2016–2018 average) to $1.3M (2020–2022).

- Increase in clearance rate: from 66% to 78%.

- Public trust ("good/excellent" rating in city survey): 42% to 59%.

Synthesis and Summation

The case studies converge on three principles:

- Reform is sustainable only when measured, not mandated.

- Initial resistance is real, but adaptive cultures convert skepticism into performance.

- The transparency created by technology and process protects everyone—officers, suspects, community, and, crucially, the legitimacy of the justice system.

National surveys, run by the Institute for Justice Reform, suggest that departments implementing a comprehensive reform package—training plus AV plus external audit—see a 29% lower rate of post-conviction challenge, a 31% drop in major case litigation, and, over five years, a net positive return of $3.72 for every dollar spent.

But the numbers tell only part of the story. In Minneapolis, a detective attends his daughter's high school graduation and is thanked, by name, from the podium—for "helping make our city safer, and more fair." In Houston, a sergeant who once called the AV system a "waste of tape" is promoted to head of the Peer Review Team. In Portland, a community activist and the chief of detectives sit side by side on a radio call-in show, arguing, not about whether reform is real, but how to make it go faster.

The cases that once haunted the system—names and faces locked in the memory of error—are now counterweighted by a new generation of stories. Not perfect. But, by every metric that matters, better.

And, on the balance sheet of justice, the savings are more than dollars: they are measured in lives, trust, and, at last, the slow restoration of faith that the system can, in fact, correct itself.

Every reform, no matter how logical or evidence-backed, faces a wall of resistance: some of it bureaucratic, some political, but most of it the ambient drag of tradition and the fear of unknown risk. Departments that fail at implementation often trip not on the novelty of the reform, but on the shoals of "we've always done it this way" and "there's no room in the budget." Successful programs, by contrast, treat resistance not as a monolith, but as a series of discrete problems to be mapped, modeled, and managed.

The Four Domains of Resistance

1. Budget and Resource Constraints

The most immediate argument against system-wide reform is fiscal: no city, county, or agency claims a surplus of dollars or time. The investment needed for AV upgrades, new training programs, and additional oversight staff can run to millions in upfront costs. Grants and pilot funds are available, but often earmarked or hedged by matching requirements.

A city in the Southeast, population 200,000, faced a $2.3M price tag for AV system installation, plus $700,000 annually for maintenance and storage. The first three city council meetings were deadlocked, with public comments alternating between "the system is broken" and "taxes are already too high."

The breakthrough came when the department's financial officer presented a three-year projection: estimated cost of wrongful conviction litigation (past decade average) was $5.6M per year. Civil settlements, some running to seven figures, could be cut by 70% if the AV and audit systems were in place. A grant from the Department of Justice covered the first year of implementation, with local dollars phased in as the savings appeared.

A budget director, quoted in the city's white paper: "The money is either spent upfront, or lost on the back end. It's just a question of whose spreadsheet you want to read."

2. Labor Relations and Union Concerns

Any change to interview protocols, especially the advent of always-on AV, is met by union scrutiny: are officers being surveilled? Will honest mistakes become grounds for discipline or career ruin? Is privacy protected, and who gets to watch the tapes?

In Houston, initial negotiations between the police union and the reform team were tense. Officers wanted assurance that AV footage wouldn't be used for petty disciplinary actions, or weaponized by adversaries in labor disputes. The union demanded a seat on the oversight board, and a formal "grace period" for adaptation.

The solution, hammered out in six months of negotiation, included:

- A first-year window during which AV errors led only to retraining, not punishment (except in cases of deliberate tampering).

- Access protocols: only supervisors and oversight staff could review footage, and only for flagged cases.

- A peer-review mechanism: officers could appeal any critique or adverse report to a board with union representation.

After the initial spike in "technical errors," most officers acclimated to the new norm. By the end of year two, union complaints dropped to near zero. In fact, the union president later said:

"We were against it, then we saw it made our guys safer and kept frivolous complaints down. Now we want it everywhere."

3. Legal and Regulatory Barriers

Recording interviews, especially with minors or in private settings, is governed by a web of state and federal rules. Some states require explicit consent, others permit "one-party" notification, and still others have statutes limiting what evidence is admissible. Defense attorneys sometimes object to the "burden" of reviewing hours of raw footage; prosecutors worry about the risk of accidental leaks or privacy violations.

Departments that succeed at reform make legal teams partners from the outset. In Portland, the city attorney's office was tasked with auditing every step of the AV and chain-of-custody protocols, making sure that all documentation, redactions, and access rules met or exceeded state law. When a defense attorney raised a novel objection—claiming that AV review "tilted the field" in favor of police—the city preempted the issue by providing defense teams with equal access and training on how to analyze the footage.

A judge, at a panel on evidentiary reform: "The transparency is not a weapon. It's a safeguard. Both sides see the same thing. The truth is in the tape, not the transcript."

4. Culture and Organizational Inertia

Most insidious is the fourth domain: the belief, held in every system, that the new idea will never work here. Officers cite the uniqueness of their city, the criminal element, or the "reality" of the streets. Supervisors worry that extra layers of process will slow them down or erode the trust within the ranks.

This is the slowest challenge to overcome, but not impossible. In Minneapolis, reformers seeded the training teams with "converted skeptics"—officers who had publicly resisted the program, but, after multiple cycles, had become its strongest advocates. These officers taught the courses, ran the simulations, and shared candid stories of error and correction. Their presence made it harder for the next wave to dismiss the curriculum as "ivory tower" or "out of touch."

In Houston, senior detectives were incentivized to join the Peer Review Team, with pay bumps and public recognition. In Portland, the external oversight board included retired officers alongside academics and community members, lending credibility to its findings.

The cultural drag never goes to zero, but with every measured cycle, skepticism becomes grudging respect, and sometimes—often enough to matter—pride.

The Anatomy of a Pilot Program

The most reliable way to break through resistance is to show, not tell. This means running a small, tightly monitored pilot, collecting every possible data point, and using the results to scale up.

Typical timeline:

Month 1: Planning and Stakeholder Alignment

- Assemble core team: training, IT, legal, labor rep, community liaison.

- Inventory existing technology, policies, and personnel.

- Conduct baseline survey: officer attitudes, public trust, current error rates.

Months 2–4: Training and Infrastructure

- Retrofit one precinct with AV, chain-of-custody, and compliance tools.

- Run "train the trainer" cycles with scenario pods.

- Set up feedback loops: anonymous reporting, peer review, union input.

Months 5–6: Soft Launch

- Conduct all interviews in pilot precinct using new protocols.

- Review every interview, document every error (even minor).

- Hold weekly debriefs with pilot staff, plus monthly public briefings.

Months 7–9: Evaluation

- Survey officers, supervisors, defense, prosecutors, and community.

- Analyze data: error rates, complaint volume, clearance rate, court outcomes.

- Identify pain points, unintended consequences, or technical bugs.

Months 10–12: Adjustment and Preparation for Scale

- Revise training and policy based on pilot results.

- Build or expand oversight capacity.

- Present findings to leadership and city officials, emphasizing cost/benefit.

- Draft timeline for citywide or department-wide adoption.

A data point from a major pilot: after one year, not only did the pilot precinct cut error rates in half, but its clearance rate outperformed all others in the city, and public survey confidence in police rose 27%. Officers who had started the year in opposition voted 7 to 1 to retain the program.

Metrics That Matter

Key metrics for monitoring, as identified by a cross-jurisdictional review:

- AV Compliance Rate: percent of interviews with unbroken, verified footage.

- Error Correction Interval: average time between error detection and retraining or fix.

- Complaint Resolution Rate: percent of citizen or legal complaints resolved by AV or oversight audit.

- Case Clearance Rate: percentage of major crimes closed within standard window.

- Training Penetration: percent of officers who have completed all bias and AV modules.

- Stakeholder Confidence: regular surveys of officers, prosecutors, defense, public.

Sustaining the Momentum

The best programs avoid "set it and forget it." Instead, they:

- Publish all metrics, good and bad, in quarterly reports.

- Invite external audits (state agencies, nonprofits, university partners).

- Update policies yearly to reflect new case law, technology, or stakeholder needs.

- Incentivize continual improvement—recognition, advancement, peer-to-peer teaching.

- Listen to the field: incorporate anonymous officer and community feedback into each cycle.

A Template for Action

For agencies or cities looking to replicate, the following action plan offers a stepwise, adaptable guide:

1. Secure top-level buy-in: mayor, chief, union, city attorney.

2. Identify pilot precinct or unit, ideally one with mixed outcomes and a range of veteran and new staff.

3. Map the current process: where are the bias and AV failures happening? Who owns each step?

4. Establish stakeholder working group, including at least one skeptic from each major constituency.

5. Select or design scenario-based training and AV systems tailored to department needs.

6. Launch with a clear, time-bound pilot; over-communicate goals and expectations.

7. Measure everything: compliance, errors, complaints, clearances, cost.

8. Debrief regularly, and make course corrections in real time.

9. Scale up only after three consecutive positive cycles.

10. Publish outcomes for all, and adapt for next iteration.

The Plan in Practice

Three years after implementation in the earliest adopter cities, the composite results are unmistakable: fewer wrongful convictions, more effective investigations, and a measurable, if sometimes fragile, improvement in the relationship between law enforcement and the communities they serve.

The reforms are not a panacea. No protocol can erase error, or malice, or the entropy that attends every human system. But with the right tools, the errors are caught earlier, the damage contained, and the stories of success begin to outnumber the stories of failure.

Every system wants to drift toward the easy, the familiar. The art of reform is in the scaffolding: the structures and processes that hold the new reality in place until it becomes, at last, just the way things are done.

And in the final accounting, it is not the tape, the camera, or the manual that reforms the system.

It is the willingness to see error as a call to action, not a cause for denial.

To believe, even after all the failures, that the process can work.

And to keep building, one step at a time, until the old stories are finally replaced by new ones.

CHAPTER 14

The Ethical Investigator: Moral And Legal Responsibilities

The conference room, ringed with glass and off-white acoustic panels, is arranged for confrontation: three long tables in a flattened U, all chairs facing the center, where a whiteboard proclaims in dry-erase blue, "ETHICAL FRAMEWORK FOR INVESTIGATIONS." On the tables, rows of spiral-bound handbooks, soft copies of the same in mismatched tablets, and a scatter of case files like placemats. The badge numbers on the nameplates suggest every precinct in the city is represented, plus a handful of county and state patches. The median age hovers in the forties, but the faces and uniforms are all generations, all skin shades, all hairlines from army-issue to modern fade.

At precisely 09:00, the facilitator enters—mid-fifties, close-cropped, wearing a suit with the kind of lapel pin that signals ten years of commendations without a word. They nod to the crowd, then to the training coordinator, and stride to the board. The room falls quiet except for the rasp of a cop in the last row opening a fresh can of energy drink.

"Let's get started," the facilitator says, voice pitched for command but softened by habit. "Some of you know me, most don't. My job today is to push your thinking, not to tell you how to do your job." A brief scan, weighing who is ready to resist.

"We're here to talk about ethics in investigations. Not policies, not codes—those are the floor. The question is, what's above the floor?"

Someone up front, a detective with sergeant's stripes and the posture of a doorjamb, raises an eyebrow.

The facilitator clicks to the first slide, a bullet list. The font is too small, but the header is readable: "Beyond Compliance: The New Standard."

"Let's be honest. A lot of us grew up in a culture where following the law was considered enough. Do the minimum, and you're clean. What's missing from that picture?"

A silence, the practiced kind.

From the right, a hand: "If you're only doing the minimum, you're probably not looking for the whole truth." The speaker is a woman, mid-thirties, hair tight in a bun, her badge reading "Criminalist II."

"Good," says the facilitator. "The law is a floor, not a ceiling. Ethics is what happens above the minimum."

They step to the whiteboard, wipe an old diagram, and draw two lines—one low, one high.

"Here's the law." Tap. "Here's the ethical ceiling. Our goal is to get as close to the ceiling as we can, even when no one's watching."

A beat, then the facilitator uncaps a red marker and writes: "TRUTH."

"The only thing that should matter is this."

A few heads nod. Others fixate on the table, checking phones, fiddling with pens. The facilitator waits, then cues the real discussion.

"Let's ground this with a story. Four years ago, a case in another city: homicide, high school kid shot in a park. Two witnesses, both say the same thing—suspect is a tall male, blue windbreaker, scar above the eye. Detectives bring in a guy who fits, run him through the usual. He breaks, confesses. The city goes wild, case closed."

A pause. The facilitator lets the ending hang, then adds: "Eighteen months later, DNA on the weapon—abandoned in the park, never tested until post-conviction—excludes the suspect. Turns out the real shooter was two inches shorter, no scar, different ethnicity. The confession came from a twelve-hour session, off camera, no lawyer."

Around the room, a shift—some eyes narrow, some jaws clench.

"All legal," the facilitator says. "No laws were broken. The investigators did everything by the book. So why did a kid lose a year of his life for a crime he didn't commit?"

A long silence, then someone—older, male, silver mustache—speaks up. "They wanted a closure, not the truth."

"Yes," says the facilitator. "Closure is not the same as justice. That's the conflict at the heart of this job."

The facilitator circles "TRUTH" in red, then underlines "CLOSURE" in blue beneath it.

"We are all trained to close cases. The public expects it. The chief expects it. But what's more important: closing the file, or knowing we actually got it right?"

The rhetorical question sits, heavy. It's clear no one wants to answer first. Finally, a man in the back–his blazer patched at the elbow, more public defender than cop—shrugs and says, "I'd rather take the heat for a slow case than put the wrong guy away. But I know I'm the minority."

Laughter, a little too loud.

The facilitator holds up a case file, flips it open. "Here's another one. Burglaries, lower east. Pattern of break-ins, two witnesses see the same thing—suspect is a teenager, tall, walks with a limp. The officers canvass, find a kid who limps, pick him up, get a confession in less than two hours."

"Three months later," the facilitator says, "the burglaries start again—same MO, same area, same description. Turns out the confession was garbage. The real suspect is caught by accident, shoplifting, a block from the last scene. He's older, and the limp is a fake he uses to throw off witnesses."

The facilitator closes the file. "Why did the system fail? Because the shortcut was easier than the hard road. It's always easier to believe the first thing that makes sense. It's harder to dig for what's real."

At the front, the sergeant speaks up. "That's not just laziness. It's pressure. We get the case log every week—if the numbers are bad, someone's getting transferred."

The facilitator nods, not disagreeing. "Pressure is real. But the consequences are real too."

They turn to the group. "Show of hands—who has ever felt pressure to close a case fast, even when you didn't have every fact?"

Every hand goes up, some quick, some after a glance around the room.

"Who's ever felt the urge to skip a step, just to get it off your desk?"

Fewer hands, but still half.

The facilitator smiles, then looks at the training coordinator, who is taking notes on a tablet. "You can put the numbers away—we all know this is universal."

They circle back to the point: "But here's the problem. Every time we take the shortcut, we raise the risk of error. And every time the public sees an error, their trust in us drops. That's why ethics matters—not just for the people in the case, but for everyone who relies on us to be more than just efficient."

From the right, another comment: "But there's always a trade-off. If you spend forever on every detail, you never close a case. There's a backlog for a reason."

"True," says the facilitator. "So we need a system that balances urgency with accuracy. That's what we're here to build."

They draw a new word on the board: "PROCESS."

"Process is what keeps us honest when the pressure's on. If we build an ethical process and stick to it, the results will follow—even if it's slower than we like."

A voice, young, barely out of academy: "What if the process gets in the way? Sometimes the red tape is worse than the shortcut."

"Good point," says the facilitator. "But the tape is there for a reason. Most of the time, it's to protect you—from mistakes, from liability, from yourself."

A murmur: a mix of assent and resignation.

At the end of the row, a woman with captain's bars leans forward. "What's the alternative? We run every case past a philosopher before making an arrest?"

More laughter, this time with less edge.

The facilitator puts the marker down and folds arms, stepping away from the board. "The alternative is to ask better questions, and to check our own work. The ethical ceiling is about asking: What if I'm wrong? What will happen if I move too fast? Who pays the price for my error?"

A pause. "It's not about being perfect. It's about being honest, and transparent, and willing to admit when we need to look again."

The room settles, the tension shifting from pushback to consideration.

The facilitator picks up a case file from the table, holds it up. "Let's try this. Split into groups. I want each table to work through the case, but every ten minutes, stop and ask: Where could we be wrong? Where are we skipping steps? Who's being left out?"

The assignment is met with a mix of groans and competitive grins. The groups re-form, pushing the handbooks aside, flipping open the files.

The training coordinator sets a timer.

Around the room, the sound of paper flipping, voices lowering, ideas colliding. Occasionally, a shout: "You're missing the timeline!" or "No way that witness saw the whole thing." The facilitator walks the perimeter, stopping to listen, sometimes prodding with a "What's the ethical risk here?" or "Are you taking anything for granted?"

One group debates for nearly the whole period whether a suspect's prior record should color their theory, or if that's bias by another name. Another group gets lost in a forensic detail, arguing if a partial shoeprint is enough for probable cause. At every table, the tension is the same: the urge to solve clashing with the demand to be sure.

At the ten-minute mark, the facilitator calls time. "Now," they say, "switch cases with the group to your left. Start over, but this time, look for the mistakes the first group made."

More groans, but also a flicker of competition.

The new groups dig in, immediately flagging overlooked leads, untested evidence, or holes in the timeline. Occasionally, someone looks up and says, "I never would have caught that on my own."

After another round, the facilitator gathers the room's attention.

"What did we learn?" they ask.

From the back, someone says, "Everyone misses something."

Another voice: "You need fresh eyes, or you get tunnel vision."

The facilitator nods, writing "TEAM CHECK" in large letters on the board. "The ethical process isn't just about doing it alone—it's about building in review, critique, and the humility to accept when you're wrong."

They set down the marker, step to the front of the room.

"Here's my last question," they say. "If you could guarantee you'd close cases 10% slower, but with half the errors, would you take the deal?"

A rumble of discussion, some hands shooting up, others shaking their heads.

The room divides instantly. Some say yes—"Fewer errors, more justice, worth it." Others argue, "Slower means more victims, more crime unsolved."

The debate spills into the aisles, voices rising, competing, but no one is checked out anymore. The tension is exactly as the facilitator wanted: the hard questions are on the table, and the room is awake, not just to the minimum but to the possibility of more.

As the timer winds down for break, the facilitator catches the captain on her way out.

"Still think we need a philosopher?" they ask, half-joking.

She smiles, dry. "Maybe not a philosopher. But I see your point."

The facilitator glances at the board, where "TRUTH" and "PROCESS" are circled, equal and unresolved.

"That's all I'm asking for," they say. "Start with the ceiling. The floor will take care of itself."

The captain nods, then slips into the hallway, already on the phone.

Inside, the next round of training materials waits on the table, and the room, once skeptical, is now primed for the second act.

After the break, the energy in the conference room is sharper—caffeine absorbed, defenses recalibrated. The facilitator, refreshed and now in shirtsleeves, flips to a new sheet on the whiteboard: a crisp outline with five numbered points. The heading reads "Ethical Decision-Making Model (Law Enforcement Edition)," the parentheses underlined twice.

"Let's move from theory to practice," the facilitator says. "We'll walk through a stepwise model. Not a check-the-box system—a way to keep your bearings when the heat's on." They gesture for everyone to open their training packets, where the same five steps are printed in bold, with shaded boxes for notes.

"Step one: Identify the ethical values at stake."

The room tracks the words, some copying, most reading ahead.

"This isn't just 'what's legal,'" the facilitator continues. "It's justice, truth, public safety, and individual rights—sometimes in conflict, sometimes aligned. If you don't name the values, you'll never see the trade-offs coming."

To illustrate, the facilitator pulls up a case summary on the projector: a robbery, two suspects, a victim with memory gaps, and a city on edge after a string of unsolved crimes.

"In this case, there was huge pressure to keep the public safe. But also a responsibility to get the truth, and not railroad the suspects."

They underline "public safety" and "truth."

"At intake, the team focused on the string of crimes, not the evidence for this one. The ethical value of truth was crowded out by the value of safety—resulting in a quick arrest, but also an error."

The facilitator scans the room. "In your own work, when have you felt a tension between values?"

The woman from earlier—the Criminalist II—speaks up. "We had a domestic where the victim was asking us to drop charges. It was clear she was scared, but the law says we have to push ahead. The ethical value of autonomy clashed with our duty to prevent harm."

Heads nod. A younger officer adds, "Same with juvenile suspects—sometimes the best thing for the kid isn't what the statute says. But you can't always explain that to the family."

"Good," says the facilitator. "If you start every case by asking, 'Which values are in play?', you're ahead of ninety percent of the field."

On the board, they write:

1. Identify values

2. Gather facts

3. Consider options

4. Choose ethically best action

5. Document reasoning

"Step two: Gather all relevant facts, no matter how inconvenient."

The facilitator cues up a second scenario: a burglary with a neighbor as sole witness. The witness is credible, but has a history of embellishing stories for attention.

"In the actual investigation, the detective trusted the witness out of habit—she'd helped on prior cases. But the fact she'd exaggerated before was left out of the report. That oversight didn't just risk the case; it created a blind spot."

From the second row, the mustached officer interjects. "Sometimes you just don't have time for the full deep-dive, especially when cases stack up."

Facilitator: "Fair. But even in a rush, you can log the missing pieces—'Did not have time to interview neighbor B, will return tomorrow.' That way, when someone reviews the file, the gap is flagged and not hidden."

The group is invited to reflect on current caseloads. Several admit to taking "shortcuts" but not always logging them.

A detective with a goatee and the face of a man who hasn't slept in weeks leans forward: "It's not just about catching bad guys, it's about building a case that doesn't collapse at the first pushback. If you leave out a fact, you're gifting the defense a weapon."

The facilitator smiles. "Exactly. Step two protects you as much as anyone else."

They write "Transparency = Insurance" next to the step.

"Step three: Consider all available options, and the consequences of each."

The facilitator turns to the board. "We're trained to think in binaries—arrest or release, charge or don't charge. But there are usually more options, especially early on. You can delay action, consult a supervisor, request more info, or even recuse yourself if there's a conflict."

To demonstrate, they read an anonymized summary: "A patrol officer had a conflict—suspect was her ex's brother. She debated whether to push the case up or let someone else handle it. She chose to move it to another unit. The suspect was, ultimately, exonerated—but if she'd pushed ahead, the whole case could have been tainted."

A voice from the back: "Isn't that just basic professionalism?"

"Yes," the facilitator says, "but it's only obvious when you stop to think about the options. Stress and habit can blind you to the alternatives."

They invite the group to consider: "What options do you have, that you don't always see?"

Several mention consults—running the facts by another detective, or holding for a second opinion. Others bring up the use of technology: "Sometimes a three-minute database search can change the entire direction, but we don't think of it because we're stuck in the old flow."

The facilitator nods, captures examples on the board.

"Step four: Choose the action that best upholds the ethical standards you named in step one."

"Sounds simple," the facilitator says, "but it's where the pressure comes back in. When you actually pick an action, you're balancing those values—justice, safety, truth, rights. If you make the choice consciously, you'll sleep better at night, even if someone second-guesses you later."

To underline the point, the facilitator sketches out a scenario: "Suppose you have enough for a search warrant, but a gut feeling the lead is shaky. Do you execute now and risk damaging an innocent family's reputation, or wait for more evidence and risk losing the suspect? The ethical process forces you to weigh both sides—and to own the decision, either way."

The room is silent for a moment, each person parsing their own recent history for analogs.

Then, from the left, a story: "I had a call where we could have arrested on a technicality—small-time drug charge, but the kid was maybe borderline special needs. I called the SRO and asked for a background. Turns out the kid was already on a restorative path with the school. We held off, referred him instead, and six months later, he was clean. If I'd gone with the first impulse, that kid would have been in the system for years."

The group murmurs assent, several writing down the story.

The facilitator grins. "That's the ceiling in action."

Finally, "Step five: Document the decision-making process."

The facilitator taps the last point. "If you didn't write it, it didn't happen. That's not just for the court or the supervisor—it's for you, in case someone comes back in a year and asks why you did what you did."

A hand: "Feels like a waste of time sometimes—no one reads those notes."

"Not true," says the facilitator. "Internal Affairs, external review, even you in five years—someone will read them. And if they show you worked the process, you're protected."

At this, a detective in the front raises a hand. "Can I share something?"

"Please," says the facilitator.

"I had a shooting last year. The facts were murky, and I was the first on scene. I logged every step—why I decided to secure the suspect, why I waited for backup before entering, every deviation from the usual. Six months later, the family filed a complaint. But when the IA team reviewed my file, the notes explained everything. No discipline, no drama. They even used it as a positive example in the training unit."

A ripple of relief around the room—proof that the process isn't just theory.

"Thanks for sharing," the facilitator says. "That's exactly what we mean. If you follow the process, and document it, you're less likely to get burned—even if the case is tough."

The facilitator caps the marker and turns to the group. "Here's the bottom line: You protect yourself, the department, and the investigation when you make ethical decisions visible. It's not just the right thing—it's the smart thing."

They glance at the clock, then the training coordinator. "Let's spend the last ten minutes workshopping real cases. In pairs, walk through a current or recent case, and run it through the five steps. Note where you faced a values clash, a missing fact, a tough decision. And, if you didn't document your reasoning, write a quick retroactive note for practice."

Pairs form, heads come together, and the room hums with low, urgent voices.

At one table, the Criminalist II and the mustached officer debate a cold case with a dead witness. At another, the sleep-deprived detective and a patrol rookie try to reconcile conflicting statements in a bar fight.

The facilitator and coordinator float, offering prompts:

"What value is at stake here?"

"Where did you feel uncertainty?"

"Did you consider alternatives?"

"Is the documentation clear enough for a stranger to understand?"

The pairs scribble, consult, sometimes disagree, but always return to the process. For the first time, the ethical model feels less like an abstraction and more like a tool.

At the end, the facilitator calls for a quick debrief.

"Who wants to share something they learned?"

From the right, a patrol officer says, "I realized I skipped steps sometimes—I just go with the supervisor's gut. But I can see how it backfires if the case goes sideways."

Another, the goateed detective: "I'm going to start logging my doubts, not just my decisions. That way, if I miss something, at least I was honest about the risk."

A few others offer similar confessions—small, but real.

The facilitator collects the examples, then sums up.

"Ethics is not about being perfect. It's about having a process, working it, and writing it down. When you do that, you serve justice and protect yourself."

The room, once skeptical, is now on board. The sense is that this model, unlike so many before it, could actually stick.

The facilitator thanks the group, then cues the coordinator to pass out a summary sheet: "Five Steps on One Page."

As the officers gather their materials, several linger, already discussing how they'll use the process in tomorrow's shift.

The facilitator packs up, watching as the room empties into the hallway.

On the board, the five steps gleam in dry-erase, waiting for the next class, or the next hard case.

After lunch, the seminar reconvenes in a new formation: three chairs up front, set for a panel. The facilitator stands briefly to introduce the guests—a trio meant to personify the spectrum of accountability.

On the left sits the Internal Affairs officer, suit immaculate, eyes cool behind wire frames. Center, the veteran detective—retired but unmistakably still a cop, body language both guarded and at ease. Rightmost, the civilian oversight board member, not a uniform but a nonprofit director with a reputation for directness. The room shifts in anticipation; panels are rarely dull.

The facilitator frames the session. "We've built the ethical ceiling, and we've walked through the five-step model. Now we focus on the question: How do we keep the process honest?"

A brief smile, then the floor is ceded to Internal Affairs.

"I'll be blunt," says the officer, clearing his throat. "We exist because error and misconduct exist. Not all error is malice, but even the best intentions can go sideways. The only way to correct the record is with a trail that can be followed, start to finish."

He looks around the room, scanning for resistance, then continues.

"Our main tool is the Internal Review Board. For every major investigation, we assemble a team that wasn't involved in the original work. They retrace the case from the first report to the last piece of evidence, using only what's documented in the file."

He holds up a thick binder. "If you wrote it down, it's real. If you didn't, it didn't happen. We teach our people that your case notes should tell a story anyone can follow—why you pursued certain leads, why you discarded others, how you reached your conclusions."

A hand goes up—one of the night-shift detectives, a practiced cynic. "What about the stuff that's just instinct? Not every decision gets a paragraph."

The Internal Affairs officer nods, as if anticipating the pushback. "Then note the intuition. If you can't justify it, at least own it. You'd be surprised how many cases blow up over an undocumented hunch. The courts—and the public—don't accept 'I just knew' as evidence."

He glances at the civilian oversight member, a prompt.

She picks up without missing a beat. "From the community side, the problem isn't that cops make mistakes—it's that the process is invisible. We see the aftermath, but not the logic. Our board reviews cases after the fact, and our mandate is to look not for guilt or innocence, but for whether the system worked as promised."

She shifts, voice warm but iron. "When we audit a case file, the first thing we look for is reasoning. Not just a checklist of actions, but the why behind each one. When the public can see the logic—what evidence was weighed, what options were considered—they're more likely to accept the outcome, even if it's not what they wanted."

She pauses, then adds: "Our board includes people with no law enforcement background. If they can follow your story, anyone can."

On cue, the veteran detective adds his perspective, voice low and dry.

"In the old days, we ran cases off the wall—pinboards and red string. Everyone in the squad room could see the theory and challenge it. When we started digital, that got lost. Now, we use peer audits—one detective from another shift, or even another unit, reviews the open file and has to write a short critique. Sometimes it's just 'all good,' but sometimes they spot something you missed."

He glances around. "Last year, I had a case where I was sure I had the guy. Everything lined up—M.O., witness, even the dumb luck of a matching car. But on peer review, the other detective noticed the timeline was off by half an hour. Turns out, I'd misread a cell tower dump. If we'd charged him, he'd have had a perfect alibi, and we'd have blown the whole thing."

He leans back, hands folded. "The peer review didn't just save the case—it saved me a year of pain."

The facilitator turns to the audience. "Let's open it up. What questions do you have for the panel?"

A uniformed officer raises a hand. "A lot of us are worried that every mistake becomes a disciplinary. How do you balance correction with not just hammering people for honest errors?"

Internal Affairs: “It’s about intent. If the error was honest, and you documented your uncertainty, you’ll get retraining, not a reprimand. But if it looks like you hid the ball, or doctored the notes, then yes, it becomes a disciplinary. The best defense is openness.”

Civilian oversight: “We’re not in the business of punishing, but of learning. Every error is an opportunity for process improvement. The worst thing is to cover up a small mistake, and let it fester into a big one.”

A detective from the middle row speaks up. “Sometimes it feels like we’re being second-guessed by people who’ve never worked a case. How do we get buy-in from the public when they don’t see what we see?”

Civilian oversight: “That’s on us, too. Our job is to communicate, not just to critique. That’s why we publish summary reports with plain-language explanations. If you give the public the real story, most will accept it. The key is to never assume ‘trust’—you have to earn it every time.”

A hand, hesitant: “How do you keep peer review from becoming personal? In a small department, everyone knows everyone.”

Veteran detective: "Keep it professional. Never say, 'You blew it.' Say, 'Did you consider this angle?' Over time, you get used to giving and getting feedback. It's a muscle—awkward at first, but essential."

The facilitator sums up. "We all want the same thing: a system that works, and a community that trusts it. Accountability isn't about catching each other out—it's about getting it right."

They give each panelist a minute for closing advice.

Internal Affairs: "Document everything. Your future self will thank you."

Civilian oversight: "Let the public see the work. It's the only way to close the trust gap."

Veteran detective: "Never run a case in a vacuum. If you're stuck, ask for another set of eyes."

The panel ends to a light round of applause, but more importantly, a line forms at the front for follow-up questions.

As the room empties, the facilitator wipes the board clean except for the phrase, "Ethics is accountability you can see."

On the table, the five-step model sits next to new handouts—templates for peer review, sample documentation pages, and a checklist for civilian audit.

The next session won't start for ten minutes, but already, small groups are trying out the tools, some testing the audit form on yesterday's case, others debating how best to log an intuition.

The change is incremental, not dramatic. But in the layered voices—internal, external, peer—there is a new tone: cautious, but genuinely collaborative.

The system, if not perfect, is at least now designed to notice its own errors, and to fix them before they ruin lives.

The panelists file out, leaving behind the scent of strong opinions and the faint promise of reform.

And in the room, the story is different than it was just a year ago.

The final session is not a lecture, but a briefing—one designed to prove that ethical theory is not just idealism, but the engine of better outcomes. At the front, the projector glows with a title slide: "Ethics and Effectiveness: The Data."

The facilitator, flanked now by a guest in chief's stars, invites the room to settle. There's less fidgeting, more pens poised to take notes. The facilitator opens with the numbers.

"Let's look at what happens when you implement strong ethical frameworks, real accountability, and documentation that tells the whole story."

First, a bar graph: Case Clearance Rates, Before and After Ethical Training Implementation.

"In five cities that piloted these models, the average clearance rate for major crimes rose from 64% to 79% in three years. That's not because cases got easier—it's because teams made fewer errors, wasted less time on the wrong theory, and built better, more reviewable files."

Next slide: Wrongful Conviction Rate.

"Overturned convictions dropped by half in the same departments. Most reversals in the old system were due to tunnel vision or missing documentation. With the new process, those gaps are filled, and fewer cases collapse on appeal."

Another: Public Trust, as measured by annual city surveys.

“In three years, approval of police as ‘fair and effective’ doubled—especially in neighborhoods that had previously been most skeptical.”

The chief steps up, voice steady and practiced.

“In our city, we were famous for high clearance, but also high reversal. The media shredded us when a case blew up, and every time, we’d hear the same thing: ‘How did you miss it?’ After we rolled out the five-step and accountability systems, we saw a 40% drop in wrongful arrests in eighteen months. Community tips went up by a third. And, maybe most important, officer job satisfaction scores rose for the first time in a decade.”

He pauses, scanning the faces in the room.

“I won’t pretend it was easy. Change never is. But we’ve stopped making the same mistakes, and we’re earning back the trust that was lost. I’d make the trade again, every time.”

The facilitator recaps. “The message is simple: ethical investigations aren’t just right—they’re more effective. You’ll solve more cases, get blindsided less, and, over time, rebuild the bond between law enforcement and community.”

Around the room, heads nod—not out of compliance, but recognition.

The facilitator shifts to the last exercise: "Before you go, I want each table to talk through one immediate change you'll make on your next shift. Not next week—tomorrow."

At the first table, the Criminalist II and the mustached officer agree to document their uncertainties as carefully as their certainties. "Even if it's just a sticky note in the file, at least we'll know where we left a gap."

Another pair, the sleep-deprived detective and his rookie partner, pledge to run every major theory past a peer before moving forward, even if it means five minutes at the end of shift.

The captain from the front, at her table, says, "I'm going to build peer review into the squad's routine, not just wait for annuals. Every time a big case lands, we'll have another team look it over."

Across the room, similar resolves: "Audit the timeline on every case." "Log every reason for dropping a lead." "Invite a civilian liaison to at least one review meeting per month."

The facilitator moves from table to table, writing down the action points. "These are simple, but they add up. In a year, you'll be amazed at the difference."

They thank the chief, who offers a final challenge: "The public expects us to be perfect, but what they really want is progress. If you can show the work, and show you're learning from every case, the public will meet you halfway."

As the session ends, the facilitator erases the board, leaving only two words:

ETHICS = EFFECTIVENESS

The officers file out—some to the street, others to evening shift—carrying packets, checklists, and, maybe, the beginnings of a different mindset.

In the corridor, a rookie stops to take a photo of the two words on the board.

In the parking lot, the veteran detective dials a colleague: "Hey, can you look at a file for me tomorrow? Just want a second set of eyes before I run with it."

In the admin office, the training coordinator logs the attendance and notes, "First time we didn't lose anyone after lunch."

Upstairs, the chief sends a summary to the city manager, CC'ing the oversight board: "Positive response. Recommend scaling up to all precincts by next quarter."

And in precincts across the city, the next morning, new case files begin with a sticky note: "Check the ceiling."

Because in this model, ethics is not a limit, but a method.

A tool for justice, and a path to better work.

The system is never perfect. But it's now, at last, worthy of the people who depend on it.

CHAPTER 15

Justice Reimagined: A Path Forward

The university auditorium is all tiered seats, molded plywood and muted blue, designed for acoustics and the unyielding forward attention of students. Above the stage, a crisp LCD banner reads: "SYSTEMS OF JUSTICE: FAILURE AND REFORM." Below, the panel waits—five faces, five name placards, five postures of readiness—while the crowd settles in. There are undergraduates in hoodies, criminal justice grad students in jackets they'll return after the semester, two dozen faculty from three departments, a wedge of working law enforcement, and in the back row, a familiar local journalist with a tripod and the poise of a hawk.

The moderator, a sharp-suited academic with a résumé in restorative justice and a voice built for conviction, brings the room to order with a practiced handclap. "We'll begin right on the hour," he says, as if this is not already a minute late. "Today's panel: 'Diagnostic Errors—The Roots of Wrongful Conviction.' Each speaker will present, then we'll open to questions."

At his left, a legal scholar in thick glasses and a smart blue dress. Beside her, a retired homicide detective, hair still regulation short, hands folded on a notepad like he's ready to take a confession from the room. Center stage is the exonerated: a man in his forties, suit borrowed from a cousin, eyes hard and clear, every bit of him arranged for the paradox of being both subject and object. Next is a data scientist from the State Innocence Registry, then a woman whose badge is replaced by a university lanyard and a history of investigating other investigators. The moderator reads off their names, but the audience already knows who they came to hear.

The slides are queued, the laptop light dimmed. The moderator cues the first: a headline, white on black—"Diagnostic Errors: Not an Exception." Below it, a quote from a recent review: "Cognitive bias is present in 74% of documented wrongful conviction cases." The moderator reads it aloud, then pivots.

"Let's start with the scholar. Doctor?"

The legal scholar stands—she insists on standing, always—and scans her notes, more for comfort than necessity.

"We've spent years blaming wrongful convictions on isolated bad actors or outdated forensic methods. The data, as we now know, tells a more uncomfortable story: most errors are systemic, not personal. In over 80% of overturned homicide cases, the initial misdiagnosis was traceable to bias—confirmation, groupthink, anchoring to early suspects. Only rarely is it malice. Mostly, it's process failure."

She clicks the slide: a pie chart explodes in color.

- Confirmation bias: 47%

- Groupthink: 19%

- Tunnel vision: 15%

- Evidence misinterpretation: 10%

- Other: 9%

"This is not just a policing problem," she says. "It happens in prosecution, in defense, in the forensic labs, in the press. Everyone wants a story that fits the first theory. That's the root."

She sits. The audience, primed for debate, is silent instead.

The moderator turns. "Detective Norris, as someone from the field—does this square with your experience?"

Norris shrugs, microphone pinched in his hand like a cigarette. "I can't argue with the numbers," he says. "But I'll say, from thirty years, it's not always clear where the bias starts. We get a case with three hundred leads, a city council breathing down our neck, a family screaming for answers. It's not that we ignore evidence. It's that you can only work one theory at a time, or you drown. Problem is, once you pick, it's damn hard to change course."

He glances at the exonerated, then back to the audience. "I've closed cases that still keep me up at night, not because I broke rules, but because the process rewarded speed over doubt. When the department expects a 'face in custody' by the press conference, you push the most promising theory. That's the game."

The moderator asks, "Is that a training issue, or a culture issue?"

"Both," Norris says. "But mostly culture. Training can warn you about bias all day, but if the boss cares more about clearance than accuracy, you do what gets you promoted."

The exonerated man, introduced as Anthony Miller (no nickname), shifts forward. The moderator nods to him.

"I want to thank Detective Norris for being straight," Miller says. His voice is measured, but there is a frequency beneath it, more vibration than volume. "When I was arrested, the detectives told me they 'already knew' it was me. They said it during the Miranda, they said it during every interview, even after my alibi checked out. They said, 'You match the profile. You match the story the community expects.' I confessed, because after twelve hours, I couldn't tell if I was remembering or just trying to survive. When you get out, they say you're the exception. But there's a room of us now."

He gestures, and the moderator advances the slide: a grid of headshots, hundreds of faces, each labeled "Exonerated." Below it, a figure: 2,184.

"The first week I was home, I had a nightmare every night that I was back in the interview room," Miller says. "You don't know how long it takes to trust your own memory again."

There is a moment of silence, thick and uneven. In the back row, a student coughs into his sleeve. The journalist looks up from her phone, makes a note.

The moderator asks the data scientist to speak.

She does, but only after a moment of collecting herself. "Our registry tracks every exoneration in the state, plus the cause. What's most striking isn't the volume—though that's bad enough—but the shape of the problem. False confession is a factor in 27% of cases. Eyewitness error, 61%. In homicide, tunnel vision is in play in 92% of the false confession cases. But here's the kicker: more than half of exonerated people were convicted even though the original forensic or witness evidence was questioned at trial. Meaning, the system had the chance to course-correct, but didn't."

She advances the slides:

- Slide 1: Bar chart, "Causes of Wrongful Conviction: State Registry, 2000–2022"

- Slide 2: Heat map, "Incidence by Population—BIPOC Individuals Overrepresented"

- Slide 3: Trend line, "Clearance Rate vs. Error Rate: 1990–2022"

"The public thinks these are rare events," she says. "But the error rate for serious felony conviction is about 3%, based on best estimates. In our state alone, that's hundreds of people, every year, serving time for things they did not do."

The moderator says, "Thank you," then opens to the next panelist.

The former internal affairs investigator leans into the mic. "I want to say, it's better now than twenty years ago," she says. "AV systems in interview rooms, better training, more accountability. But we still see the same basic failure: the need to resolve uncertainty too fast. In Internal Review, we'd get stacks of files where the team ignored alternative suspects, or discounted evidence that didn't fit. I've read confessions that were word-for-word what the interrogator wanted. Sometimes, the error is clear as day. Other times, it's so woven into the process that you need a team of auditors to see it."

She glances up. “The most honest officers are the ones who admit they could be wrong. That’s still the exception.”

The moderator sums up, clicking a slide labeled “Synthesis.” The text is concise:

- Coercive methods produce unreliable confessions.

- Deductive investigation breeds tunnel vision.

- Populations already at risk are hit hardest.

- Reforms exist, but are uneven and underfunded.

- The public sees error as anomaly, not system.

He asks for final thoughts from the panel.

The scholar says, “You can’t fix what you don’t see. The first step is transparency—admit the problem, audit the process.”

Norris: “Teach every new cop that doubt is a tool, not a weakness.”

Miller: "Treat every confession like it could be a mistake. Because sometimes it is."

The data scientist: "Publish the numbers. All of them. Don't let any agency bury the stats."

The investigator: "Make the public part of the process. Community oversight isn't a threat—it's a check."

The moderator opens the floor to questions. The first hand up is a grad student, hair buzzed, arms folded like a wrestler. "If the problem is so obvious, why isn't it fixed? Why aren't there laws about this?"

The scholar answers. "There are, in places. Some states mandate AV recording, some require corroboration for confession. But there is no national standard, and every agency is different. And inertia—'we've always done it this way'—is a hell of a force."

A working cop in the audience stands, voice steady: "Isn't some of this hindsight bias? It's easy to say what went wrong when you see the ending."

Norris: "That's fair. But you can build process that tests for error at every step, so you're not just guessing. The job isn't to be perfect. It's to be accountable."

The moderator notes, "We'll have a session later on best practices and reforms," and glances at the clock.

The last question is from the local journalist: "Does the panel believe the public actually wants uncertainty? Isn't there a demand for quick closure?"

Miller takes this one. "People want justice, not just answers. But they won't know the difference unless you show them. If the system is honest about its limits, the community will learn to accept doubt. Maybe even trust it."

The session ends with a round of applause, more solemn than raucous. The panel packs up, the moderator hands off to the next session, and the audience breaks in clusters—some heading for coffee, some for the hallway, some already debating the implications.

On the screen, the last slide lingers: "DIAGNOSIS: SYSTEMIC."

The air in the auditorium is thin but charged, ready for whatever comes next.

The lights dim again, and the crowd, caffeine-fueled and restless, settles into the churn of a second session. At the podium, the new presenter—a tall woman in a tailored gray blazer, hair in a blunt bob, demeanor brisk and uncompromising—taps her tablet and cues the next slide: "THE PATH TO ERROR-PROOF INVESTIGATION: THREE LEVELS OF REFORM."

She introduces herself as a former chief of a mid-sized city police department, now an adjunct professor and consultant for departments under federal consent decree. Her voice is taut with the memory of negotiating with both city council and union, and she wastes no time with preamble.

"I'm not here to talk about ideals," she says. "I'm here to talk about what works—and what will get you sued if you ignore it."

A ripple of nervous laughter. She gestures to the screen.

"First level: DEPARTMENTAL."

The slide animates, and three bullet points appear:

- Mandatory AV Recording of All Interviews/Interrogations

- Inductive-First Evidence Collection Protocol

- Ongoing Bias-Awareness Training

She speaks with the precision of a drill instructor.

"If you want to break the cycle of diagnostic error, you need to record every minute of every interview. No exceptions. No 'lost footage.' We made it policy, and in the first year, complaints about coercion dropped seventy percent. Reversals on confession fell to zero. It's a pain for IT, but the cost is nothing compared to a single wrongful conviction payout."

She paces, driving the point home. "The second piece is evidence collection. Most departments still teach the 'theory first, evidence later' model. It's efficient, but it makes you blind. Our new protocol: every major case starts with an evidence matrix—nothing gets ruled out until a supervisor signs off. You don't throw out the outliers. You chase every one, until it's dead."

The final point: "Bias training is not a box to check. It's a biweekly scenario, reviewed by peers and supervisors. You want to weed out error, you have to make it a reflex."

She clicks to the next slide: a dashboard, showing a line graph with a plummeting trend.

"In year one of implementation, our wrongful arrest rate went from one in two hundred to one in twelve hundred. The city's legal costs halved. Public trust, as measured by monthly community survey, jumped by eighteen percent."

A skeptical hand goes up. The presenter calls on it.

"How did you get buy-in from the rank and file?" asks a man in a sheriff's uniform, voice dry.

"We didn't," she says. "Not at first. But once the AV footage started clearing officers of false complaints—and once we built peer review into the promotion path—they realized it was a shield, not just a spotlight."

She moves to the next level.

"STATE REFORM," the slide reads, with new bullet points.

- Model Statute: Voluntariness and Recording of Confession

- State-Level Oversight Commission (Independent)

- Certification and Continuing Education Mandates for Investigators

She points at the first bullet. "Several states have passed laws requiring not just Miranda, but a full video record and independent review of all major crime confessions. If your state hasn't done it, it will. The data is unambiguous: those states have the lowest reversal rates and highest clearance rates."

Second bullet: "An oversight commission—staffed by legal, law enforcement, and community reps—reviews every wrongful conviction claim. Not just for the individual, but for process failure. If you're in a state without oversight, expect the feds to show up eventually."

She pauses, then leans on the lectern. "Most departments balk at certification. But in every other profession—medicine, law, teaching—you can't practice without it. We now have a model where investigators are licensed, and to renew, you need continuing ed in evidence, bias, and tech."

A slide flashes: a photo of a badge with a new seal—INVESTIGATOR CERTIFIED. Below it, a quote from a local mayor: "Restoring credibility, one officer at a time."

She nods at the quote, then gestures for questions.

A woman in the third row, city council pin on her lapel, asks: "How do you keep oversight from being just another bureaucracy?"

"We make the reports public," says the presenter. "Every quarter, the oversight board publishes an audit. Good, bad, or ugly. If there's a process failure, it's in the report. Nothing dies in committee."

She advances the presentation to the final level.

"FEDERAL," the slide blares, with three new points.

- National Investigative Standards and Accreditation

- DOJ Funding for Evidence-Based Reform

- Legal Protections for Vulnerable Suspects

"Right now, there are pilot projects for national standards," she says. "These include minimum tech specs for AV, a required chain-of-custody for all evidence, and a national registry for training and certification. Departments that comply get priority for federal grants."

Second: "If you want reform to stick, you need money. DOJ now offers funds for departments that can show reduced error, improved training, and active oversight. It's competitive, but the cities that win the grants see dramatic improvements within two years."

She lets the third point hang for a moment. "The most overlooked piece is legal protection. Every year, thousands of suspects with intellectual disability or language barrier are interrogated without proper safeguard. The new model mandates a legal advocate, or at minimum, an independent observer in every interview with a vulnerable suspect. Departments that ignore this get hammered in court."

She cues the next slide: a table, state by state, showing where each reform has been implemented.

Green means full compliance. Yellow is partial. Red is pending.

The room notes that the green states have the lowest reported reversal rates.

She flips again, showing two case studies.

The first: Minneapolis, post-reform. The line of reversals drops; public trust spikes.

The second: Houston, pre- and post-reform. Lawsuits plummet, AV compliance soars, and, to the surprise of many, officer satisfaction improves.

A student in the front asks, "What's the hardest part of implementing all this?"

The presenter answers instantly: "Culture. People want to believe their way is the best. The challenge is to prove, with data, that a new way is better. And to reward the people who lead, not just those who complain."

She wraps up, her slide showing three overlapping gears: DEPARTMENTAL, STATE, FEDERAL.

"Change is not optional," she says. "If you wait, you will end up as a case study for the next conference. If you lead, you get to define the narrative."

A beat, then: "We have the blueprint. Now it's time to build."

The audience responds—some with claps, some with note-taking, some with the long exhale of those recognizing what the next five years of work will be.

At the side of the room, the journalist packs up, already composing the headline.

In the hallway, students huddle, some energized, some overwhelmed. An assistant professor copies the slides onto a thumb drive, mumbling, "We can pilot this next semester."

The panel reconvenes for Q&A, but the real work is now in the air—tangible, frictional, as the first ripples of institutional change begin to move.

As the session adjourns, the last slide stays up for anyone still in the room:

"THE FUTURE OF JUSTICE IS TRANSPARENT, EVIDENCE-DRIVEN, AND ACCOUNTABLE."

A few linger to take photos.

For the rest, the next chapter starts now.

At the edge of the city, the academy rises from a rectangle of lawn and parking lot, its cinderblock walls painted the color of optimism. Inside, the air smells of disinfectant and the last vestiges of floor wax. The recruits—forty in this cohort, a field of haircuts and starch—sit in rows before a screen where, instead of a badge or flag, the words "INDUCTIVE INVESTIGATION PRACTICUM" are frozen in sans-serif.

The instructor, a woman in her fifties with a detective's carriage and an educator's smile, surveys the class. She flicks a switch and the screen advances: "DAY 2: HOW TO THINK WHEN YOU DON'T YET KNOW."

"All right, team," she says. "Yesterday, we talked about why old-school interrogation fails. Today, we build from scratch. Remember, the point is not to make an arrest. It's to make the error rate as close to zero as possible."

The first simulation starts. The recruits are split into scenario pods—each with an actor playing a witness, a partner to keep notes, and a supervisor with a checklist. The exercise: a theft in a hardware store, no obvious suspect. The only prompt: "Gather the facts. Do not form a theory until the evidence demands it."

At Pod 4, a recruit in new boots—Mendoza, per his nametag—sits across from the witness, who plays nervous, eyes flicking to the corner. Mendoza's first question is textbook: "Can you walk me through your day, step by step?"

The witness rambles. The note-taker scribbles.

At minute five, Mendoza slips: "Did you see the suspect take the item, or just after?" The supervisor raises a hand, pauses the exercise.

"Notice," she says, "how that frames the question? You've already assumed the person in the aisle is the suspect."

Mendoza flushes, nods. They rewind, start again, this time with the language cleaned up: "Who else was nearby? Did anything seem unusual before or after?"

Other pods hit similar snags. One recruit, eager, tries to pin down a timeline too quickly; another, stuck on the color of a jacket, ignores the witness's discomfort. Each time, the supervisor pauses, points to the checklist: "Did you let the evidence lead, or did you lead the evidence?"

By the third run, the pods have it down. No one says "suspect" until there is one; every contradiction is logged, not explained away. The note-takers are encouraged to write in the margins: "Unsure," "maybe not," "incomplete." At the end, the recruits are called to debrief as a group.

The instructor stands at the whiteboard, marker in hand. "What did you notice about your thinking?"

Mendoza raises his hand. "You want to solve it so badly, you start guessing ahead. But that makes you miss things."

Another voice, quiet but certain: "When I asked open questions, the witness actually remembered more."

"Yes!" says the instructor. She writes it in bold: "OPEN = MORE." Then, under it: "DOUBT = GOOD."

She cues up a new video. It's a recording from a real case—AV room, two officers, one suspect. The class watches as the officers, in old-school formation, cycle the suspect through the same questions until the answer conforms to their theory. The instructor freezes the frame.

"What went wrong?" she asks.

A recruit in the back calls out, "They never checked if the suspect could have even been there."

"Exactly," says the instructor. "Now, let's see how it should have gone."

The next clip is a controlled scenario, same facts, but the investigators are trained on the new protocol. Every fact is cross-checked, every timeline verified, every statement treated as provisional. When the scenario ends, the actual culprit is found not by confession, but by the logic of the evidence matrix.

The recruits murmur, some with relief, some with the beginnings of pride.

In the final hour, a senior officer—one of the new-era captains, gold badge and all—enters for the ethics talk. He stands at the lectern, hands folded, voice resonant.

"I know some of you came here to make a difference," he says. "That's good. But the truth is, our profession is measured less by what we do, and more by what we choose not to do. The measure of good policing isn't how many arrests you make. It's how accurately you serve justice."

He pauses, scanning the faces.

"If you think you're never going to make a mistake, you're in the wrong job. But if you build the habits here—challenge your instincts, check every fact, protect every person's rights—then you will leave this place worthy of the trust your badge represents."

A stillness, not the bored kind, but the kind that follows something real.

The instructor closes the day with a final slide:

- EVIDENCE BEFORE THEORY

- OPEN BEFORE CLOSED

- DOUBT BEFORE CERTAINTY

She looks out over the class.

"This is not about being soft," she says. "It's about being right."

As the recruits file out, the academy wall gleams with a new addition—etched in steel, just above the exit:

"Justice, like truth, cannot be forced. Only found."

The door clicks behind the last trainee, but in the empty room, the echo of the lesson remains.

The next generation, at least, will start from here.

And for the system, that's how change begins—one class, one habit, one choice at a time.

Don't miss out!

Visit the website below and you can sign up to receive emails whenever Brian Leslie publishes a new book. There's no charge and no obligation.

https://books2read.com/r/B-A-RFIV-OWQVI

BOOKS 2 READ

Connecting independent readers to independent writers.

About the Author

Brian Leslie is a coercive interrogation & interview techniques expert, with over 14 years of previous law enforcement experience which includes major case investigation and specialized training, as well as a term serving as Chief of Police. Mr. Leslie has testified and been qualified as an expert in Federal, State and Military Courts throughout the United States.

Read more at https://www.brianlesliemedia.com.

TRUE AMERICAN PUBLISHING

About the Publisher

As a boutique book publisher, we take on only a few new authors per year. We focus on building an author's brand, thereby directing more resources towards their overall success. Authors accepted by True American Publishing become creative partners, therefore, participating in their own success.

www.ingramcontent.com/pod-product-compliance
Lightning Source LLC
LaVergne TN
LVHW090256210926
848480LV00001B/45